COLOR[ADO]
MOUNTAI[N CLUB]
GUIDEB[OOK]

CLIMBING COLORADO'S SAN JUANS

A Comprehensive Guide to Hikes, Scrambles & Technical Climbs

BOB ROSEBROUGH
& MATT PAYNE

The Colorado Mountain Club Press
Golden, Colorado

WARNING: Although there has been an effort to make the trail and route descriptions in this book as accurate as possible, some discrepancies may exist between the text and the trails and routes in the field. Hiking and climbing in the mountains involves some risks. This guidebook is not a substitute for your experience and common sense. The users of this guidebook assume full responsibility for their own safety. Weather, terrain conditions, and individual technical abilities must be considered before undertaking any of the routes in this guide.

Climbing Colorado's San Juans: A Comprehensive Guide to Hikes, Scrambles, and Technical Climbs

Portions of this book first appeared in *The San Juan Mountains* by Bob Rosebrough, 1986, 1988.

Published by The Colorado Mountain Club Press
710 10th Street, Suite 200, Golden, CO 80401
303-996-2743 | cmcpress@cmc.org | cmcpress.org

Founded in 1912, The Colorado Mountain Club is the largest outdoor recreation, education, and conservation organization in the Rocky Mountains. Look for our books at your local bookstore or outdoor retailer, or online at cmcpress.org.

Corrections: We greatly appreciate when readers alert us to errors or outdated information by emailing cmcpress@cmc.org.

Matt Payne: photographer, unless otherwise noted
Tim and Carrie Cooney, climb13ers.com: South Lookout description, information for Off the Beaten Path segments
Vicki Hopewell: design and composition
Sarah Gorecki: publisher

Cover photo: Sunrise from the summit of Turret Peak, August 2016.

Distributed to the book trade by:
Mountaineers Books
1001 SW Klickitat Way, Suite 201, Seattle, WA 98134
800-553-4453 | mountaineersbooks.org

We gratefully acknowledge the financial support of the people of Colorado through the Scientific and Cultural Facilities District of greater metropolitan Denver for our publishing activities.

TOPOGRAPHIC MAPS created with Gaia GPS software, © Gaia GPS, © OpenStreetMap contributors

Printed in the United States of America

ISBN 978-1-937052-77-5

22 23 24 / 10 9 8 7 6 5 4 3 2 1

We dedicate this book to our fathers,
Haskell Rosebrough and Ray Payne,
who introduced us to the mountains.

CONTENTS

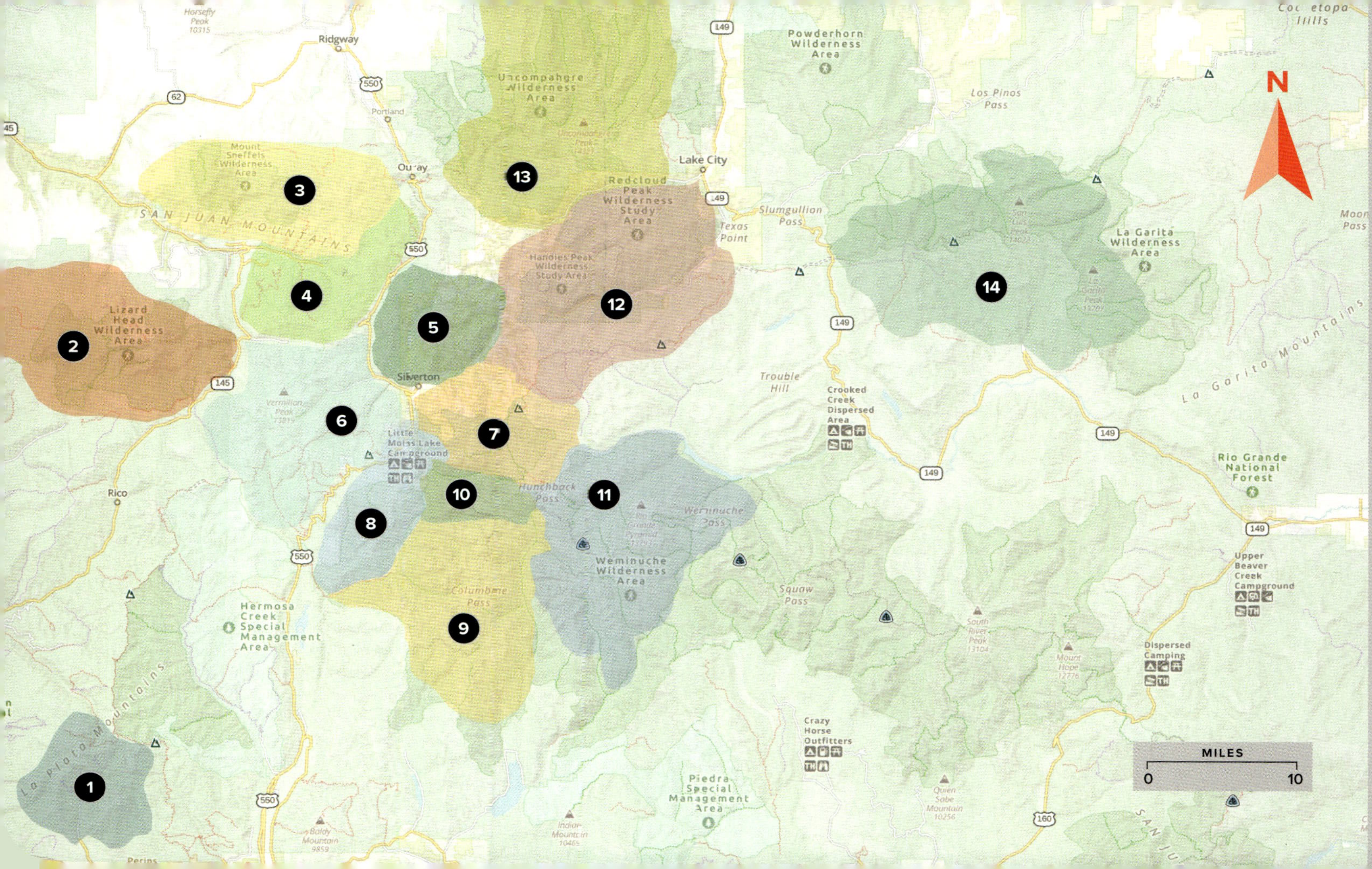

N
MILES
0
10
Ridgway
Ouray
Portland
Lake City
Silverton
Rico
Uncompahgre Wilderness Area
Mount Sneffels Wilderness Area
SAN JUAN MOUNTAINS
Lizard Head Wilderness Area
Redcloud Peak Wilderness Study Area
Handies Peak Wilderness Study Area
Powderhorn Wilderness Area
La Garita Wilderness Area
La Garita Mountains
Los Pinos Pass
Slumgullion Pass
Texas Point
Trouble Hill
Crooked Creek Dispersed Area
Rio Grande National Forest
Upper Beaver Creek Campground
Dispersed Camping
Little Molas Lake Campground
Hunchback Pass
Weminuche Pass
Weminuche Wilderness Area
Columbine Pass
Squaw Pass
Hermosa Creek Special Management Area
Piedra Special Management Area
Crazy Horse Outfitters
La Plata Mountains
Horsefly Peak 10315
149
550
62
145
160
1
2
3
4
5
6
7
8
9
10
11
12
13
14

INTRODUCTION

On the whole, the San Juans are sparsely traveled and infrequently climbed. Crowds tend to congregate on a few popular trails and on the standard approaches and routes to the 14ers (mountains over 14,000 feet in elevation). One reason that this rugged range in the southern Rocky Mountains is not overcrowded in most areas is that there are no large metropolitan areas close by. Another reason is that there is a staggering variety of peaks and trails available. Thirteen of Colorado's fifty-four 14ers and twenty-nine of Colorado's one hundred highest peaks are located in the San Juans. Furthermore, there are hundreds of peaks over thirteen thousand feet in elevation. In fact, of Colorado's 637 ranked peaks over 13,000 feet in elevation, the San Juans are home to 263.

The San Juans offer many different types of climbs, from walk-ups, like San Luis and Redcloud, to severe technical climbs like the east faces of Monitor Peak and Pigeon Peak. We hope that this guide will let hikers and climbers know that they have alternatives to overcrowded areas like Chicago Basin and Yankee Boy Basin. In the San Juans, hikers and climbers can still find the solitude and serenity that we seek in our wilderness ventures.

This guide will give you an idea of where the trails and peaks are, how to get there, and what you will encounter along the way. It is not, however, a "blow by blow" account of what to expect, and furthermore, no guide will allow you to climb something you were not otherwise able to climb. A guide is not a substitute for mountaineering judgment. Good mountaineering means calculating and applying your own capabilities and factoring in associated risks in the mountain setting. Inevitably, you must make decisions based on a variety of factors, including your capabilities, the weather, the time of day, and the season. The bottom line is that you must gain and then apply sound mountaineering judgment.

Read this guide as a way to help you pick new objectives and get a general idea of what to expect. At that point, we suggest you leave the guide behind and let your actions be determined by your own abilities and judgments rather than the pages in this book. Finally, as this guide and other publications make the trails and peaks of the San Juans more accessible, hikers and climbers need to keep in mind that they bear a heavy responsibility to preserve the wilderness for future usage. It is essential not only for ourselves but also for future generations that we both preach and practice an ethic that minimizes our impact on the wilderness we enjoy so much.

BEFORE YOU GO

A Few Words of Advice

The mountains can be an unforgiving place for the inexperienced and ill-equipped. Lightning, avalanches, altitude sickness, hypothermia, rockfall, and many other hazards await the unsuspecting and unprepared. While this guide cannot begin to cover basic mountaineering subjects in depth, this chapter seeks to provide some important hints and cautions. For further reading, an excellent and thorough text on mountain hazards and the dos and don'ts of mountaineering in general is *Mountaineering: The Freedom of the Hills.*

If you lack experience in the mountains, the best way to gain it is to hike or climb with someone who has it. Perhaps you have a friend or relative who is willing to share their experience with you. An alternative is to join an organization, such as the Colorado Mountain Club, which is a gateway to the mountains for both novices and experts and offers a year-round schedule of activities. The Colorado Mountain Club's main office is in Golden, Colorado. Members of the Western Slope Group of the Colorado Mountain Club are located primarily in Durango, Montrose, Grand Junction, and the surrounding communities.

THE TEN ESSENTIALS

The Mountaineers Ten Essentials was formalized in 1974 when the iconic list debuted in the third edition of *Mountaineering: The Freedom of the Hills.* The latest edition presents a thorough modernization to prepare today's mountaineers for adventures. The list has always sought to answer three basic questions:

Can you prevent emergencies? Can you respond positively should one occur? Can you safely spend a night (or more) outside?

Certain equipment deserves space in every pack. Mountaineers will not need every item on every trip, but essential equipment can be a lifesaver in an emergency. Exactly how much equipment "insurance" should be carried is a matter of healthy debate. Whatever your approach to equipment, a checklist will help you remember what to bring in the rush to get ready for a trip. Remember that the Ten Essentials is a guide that should be tailored to the nature of the outing. Weather, remoteness, and complexity should be factored into the selected essentials. This brief list is intended to be easy to remember and serve as a mental pretrip checklist. Note that items within brackets ([ ]) can be shared by a group.

1. Navigation: map, altimeter, compass, [GPS device], [PLB, satellite communicator, or satellite phone], [extra batteries or battery pack]
2. Headlamp: plus extra batteries
3. Sun protection: sunglasses, sun-protective clothes, and sunscreen
4. First aid: including foot care and insect repellent (if required)
5. Knife or multitool
6. Fire: [matches, lighter and tinder, or stove as appropriate]
7. Shelter: carried at all times (can be a lightweight emergency bivy)
8. Extra food: beyond minimum expectation
9. Extra water: in a bladder or bottle(s); beyond minimum expectation, or the means to purify (water filtration)
10. Extra clothes: sufficient to survive an emergency overnight

CLOTHING

Layering is key to dressing for the mountains, allowing the mountaineer to adjust clothing needs by either stripping or adding additional layers of clothing as needed. This is particularly necessary in the San Juans where the southerly latitude and high altitude combine to create a wide range of temperatures and weather conditions.

There are three basic layers. The first layer—undergarments—provides warmth and should also "wick" moisture away from the body. Medium- or lightweight polypropylene underwear works well. The second layer of insulating clothing can consist of a wide variety of materials. Bunting, pile, wool, and quilted polypropylene are all excellent insulators. If possible, cotton should be avoided since it loses its ability to retain body heat when wet and is very difficult to dry. The third, or outer, layer is called the shell and should be made of waterproof materials. There is an ongoing debate over the effectiveness of synthetic shells, which purport to be both waterproof and breathable. It's hard to find a shell that truly accomplishes both goals. To a certain extent, the benefits of breathable materials can be achieved by purchasing waterproof shells that are ventilated. Be wary of "water-resistant" materials. Some simply don't do the job in the high mountains.

Outdoor wear should be comfortable and loose fitting. Fashion should be the last thing on your mind. In addition to the clothing that comprises the three layers, a good pair of warm wool or polyester gloves and a wool hat are necessities in the mountains. Some climbers like to wear leather gloves that have extra grip when engaging on Class 3, 4, and 5 routes. Many climbers also like to use gaiters to seal the boundary between pant legs and boot tops, particularly when climbing in snow or areas with loose scree. Gaiters are a necessity for winter and spring climbing.

FOOTWEAR

The current trend is toward lightweight footwear. Some hiking boots come close to actually being running shoes. Although very comfortable, the lightweight mountain hiking boots are hard to waterproof and are not effective when climbing snow or ice. All-leather boots can be waterproofed but are heavier. If you can wear only one pair of boots in the mountains, it would be hard to beat lightweight plastic hybrid boots with Gore-Tex. In addition to all-around climbing boots, there are several specialized types of climbing shoes. Friction boots are essential for severe technical climbs. Heavy, inflexible plastic boots come in handy when climbing waterfall ice and alpine gullies. If you use friction boots or plastic boots, you will probably want a second pair of shoes to use for the approach.

BACKPACK

The first accessory that any climber or day hiker should consider purchasing is a medium-sized day pack. Without a good day pack, you are extremely limited in what you can do. For climbers, two features to look for are an ice ax loop and a water bladder compartment.

CLIMBING EQUIPMENT

A thorough discussion of climbing equipment is beyond the scope of this guide. It is possible, however, to point out a few of the items that you should consider acquiring as you progress from hiking and "walk-ups" to more difficult climbs. The first of these is an ice ax. It is inevitable that you will encounter snow eventually. An ice ax will allow you to climb on snow safely and facilitate glissade descents. Another early purchase should be a headlamp, which will allow you to make predawn starts. Headlamps free up your hands and are more convenient around a camp than a flashlight.

If you are interested in winter and spring climbing or climbing alpine gullies, crampons are essential. Class 5 climbing requires a rope, carabiners, slings, and a variety of protection devices, such as nuts, chocks, and spring-loaded camming devices. In purchasing a rope, you should consider either acquiring one eleven-millimeter rope either 150 or 165 feet in length or two nine-millimeter ropes, which can be used in tandem. A "dry" rope is worth the extra expense. Another item of climbing equipment that is essential in the San Juans is a good helmet. If you climb long enough in the San Juans, sooner or later a rock will come whizzing past your head.

LEAVE NO TRACE PRINCIPLES

The Seven Principles of Leave No Trace (lnt.org) provide an important framework of minimum-impact practices for anyone visiting the San Juan Mountains. The importance of these principles cannot be overstated, and if we are to continue to enjoy the mountains we love to climb, then we must be role models by following and educating others on these principles and this way of life in the alpine.

1. **Plan ahead and prepare.** Adequate planning and prep before going to the San Juans helps you accomplish your trip goals safely and enjoyably while simultaneously minimizing damage to the land. Poor planning often results in miserable campers and damage to natural and cultural resources. By purchasing and reading this book you are already taking steps toward this principle!
2. **Travel and camp on durable surfaces.** As you travel through the San Juans, your goal should be to avoid damage to the land and waterways as you move through natural areas. Understanding how travel causes impacts is necessary to accomplish this goal. Travel damage occurs when surface vegetation or communities of organisms are trampled beyond recovery. The resulting barren area leads to soil erosion and the development of undesirable trails. Backcountry travel in the San Juans may involve travel over both trails and off-trail areas. Since vegetation in the high alpine is fragile and takes a very long time to recover, it is important when going off-trail that you do so in a spread-out fashion so you don't create new trails that cannot recover. It's also important not to cut switchbacks as this can damage vegetation and encourage erosion.
3. **Dispose of waste properly.** Proper disposal of human waste is important to avoid pollution of water sources, avoid the negative implications of someone else finding it, minimize the possibility of spreading disease, and maximize the rate of decomposition. In most locations, burying human feces in the correct manner is the most effective method to meet these criteria. This is accomplished by digging a cat hole. Cat holes are the most widely accepted method of waste disposal. The holes should be at least 200 feet (70 adult paces) from water, trails, and camp. Select an inconspicuous site where other people are unlikely to walk or camp. With a small garden trowel, dig a hole 6–8 inches deep and 4–6 inches in diameter. The hole should be covered and disguised with natural materials when finished. If camping in the area for more than one night, or if camping with a large group, cat hole sites should be widely dispersed. Toilet paper must be packed out from some places, such as wilderness areas. Land management agencies can advise you of specific rules for the area you plan to visit.

4. **Leave what you find.** Leave the San Juans as you found them. This means you should leave behind the pretty rocks you found while hiking and you should not pick or disturb wildflowers or other plants. Do not dig trenches for tents or construct lean-tos, tables, chairs, or other improvements. If you clear an area of surface rocks, twigs, or pine cones, replace these items before leaving. For high-impact sites, it is appropriate to clean up the site and dismantle inappropriate user-built facilities, such as multiple fire rings and constructed seats or tables. Consider the idea that good campsites are found and not made.
5. **Minimize campfire impacts.** Human-caused wildfires are increasingly common in Colorado, and fire danger has spiked over the past decade due to the impacts of climate change. As a rule of thumb, campfires should probably be avoided in the San Juans due to the increased risk of wildfire; however, campfires can be a life-saving tool if you become wet and cold. The most important consideration when deciding to use a fire is the potential damage to the backcountry. When thinking about building a fire, always consider the following questions:

   - What is the fire danger for the time of year and the location you have selected?
   - Are there administrative restrictions from the agency that manages the area?
   - Is there sufficient wood so its removal will not be noticeable?
   - Does the harshness of alpine growing conditions for trees and shrubs mean that the regeneration of wood sources cannot keep pace with the demand for firewood?
   - Do group members possess the skills to build a campfire that will leave no trace?

6. **Respect wildlife.** We all want to enjoy the many animals that can be found in the San Juans, including mountain goats, marmots, pika, deer, elk, moose, porcupine, and more. The best way to ensure we can all continue to see and appreciate this wildlife is to learn through quiet observation. Do not disturb wildlife or plants just for a "better look." Observe wildlife from a distance so they are not scared or forced to flee. Large groups often cause more damage to the environment and can disturb wildlife, so keep your group small. If you have a larger group, divide into smaller groups if possible to minimize your impacts.
7. **Be considerate of other visitors.** Perhaps the most rewarding aspect of the San Juans is the solitude and wilderness experience that you can enjoy there. This

can be quickly ruined by those who are not respectful of others. It is therefore critical to maintain courtesy toward other visitors. It helps everyone enjoy their outdoor experience. Many people come to the outdoors to listen to nature. Excessive noise, uncontrolled pets, and damaged surroundings take away from the natural appeal of the outdoors. Things to avoid include audible music, large and loud groups, barking dogs, yelling, entering other people's campsites, or violating the other rules on this list.

NATURE FIRST PRINCIPLES

Nature First is a movement for and by landscape and nature photographers, which includes anyone who uses their phone to take photographs in the mountains. It was born out of numerous and sustained observations from professional photographers that the places we love to photograph are quickly becoming degraded and ruined from over-visitation and negative behavior by those who may not be equipped with Leave No Trace ethics or an appreciation for the fragility of these places. A poignant example of this can be found in the San Juan Mountains at Ice Lake Basin. Prior to the advent of social media, very few people knew about or visited Ice Lake Basin, and one could enjoy an alpine experience with perhaps two or three other people nearby. The shorelines of the pristine turquoise lakes were adorned with loads of wildflowers. After about 2016, social media created an explosion of visitation to this location, and it has become overrun with visitors wanting to see and photograph it for themselves. The result of this is well-documented: the shorelines no longer grow flowers, the area is filled with human waste and toilet paper, and the trail is flooded with hundreds of people a day.

As such, a group of photographers, including coauthor Matt Payne, met in 2018 to discuss the problem and create a possible solution. The result of these meetings is the Nature First Photography Alliance (naturefirstphotography.org) and the seven Nature First principles:

1. Prioritize the well-being of nature over photography.
2. Educate yourself about the places you photograph.
3. Reflect on the possible impact of your actions.
4. Use discretion if sharing locations.
5. Know and follow rules and regulations.
6. Always follow Leave No Trace principles and strive to leave places better than you found them.
7. Actively promote and educate others about these principles.

The irony of including fragile locations within this guidebook is not lost on us; however, we believe that the key to combating the degradation of the San Juans is to educate others on how special they are, our obligations when we recreate in them, and how you can help to keep them special for generations to come.

SEASONS

January, February, and March are the most difficult and dangerous months for climbing. Heavy snow cover and winter conditions are inevitable. All approaches must be accomplished by snowshoes or skis. The cold and long approaches make climbing difficult, but the bigger issue during these months is avalanches. Special care should be taken during, or immediately after, storms. During the spring, snow is generally more stable, but snowshoes and skis are still required for approaches. June is unpredictable in the San Juans. The depth of the snowpack from the preceding winter will dictate whether normal hiking and climbing is possible—many years there is still a snowpack down to the 10,000- or 11,000-foot elevations in early June. By July, the snowpack is generally gone except for the north slopes, but the flies and mosquitoes come out and afternoon thunderstorms begin. Thunderstorms continue through August, as does the reduction of the snowpack, which at this point is usually limited to the steep north faces and alpine gullies. July and August tend to be the most crowded months of the year. September is our favorite month for climbing. The thunderstorms typically go away with cooler weather, as do the crowds and insects. Climbing conditions in October vary widely from year to year. You can expect a snowstorm sometime in October and, hence, you should be prepared to walk out through a foot or so of snow. November and December are cold, but they offer the best winter climbing conditions. The lesser snow cover allows you to enjoy winter climbing without as much fear of avalanches.

GEOLOGY

The San Juans are largely composed of volcanic rock from the Tertiary Period. Beginning about forty million years ago, volcanoes erupted violently, pouring massive amounts of ash and lava over the region. In places, deposits built up to depths of 10,000 feet. Actual relief, however, was more like 3,000 or 4,000 feet because of the downward settling of the geologic material. Widespread volcanic activity continued for several million years, centered primarily in the areas north and east of the Needle Mountains. The repeated eruptions emptied the magma chambers under the base of volcanoes, causing them to collapse, thereby forming circular basins bounded by arcuate faults called calderas. The intense volcanic era left several classes of volcanic rock, including lava flows formed from liquid magma, tuff formed from ash, and cinder pellets and breccia made of lava fragments.

The Needles and Grenadiers subranges show no evidence of this volcanic era. Although they undoubtedly received some volcanic spillage from the eruptions, it has now been eroded away. The Needles consist of Precambrian granite and gneiss, while the Grenadiers (called the "Quartzites" by early surveyors) are made up of steeply dipping layers of Precambrian quartzite and slate. The West Needle Mountains are Precambrian metamorphic rock, mostly gneiss. The Animas River, which separates the Needles and West Needles, cuts down through the gneiss into still older metamorphic rock. Continuing west, the highest peaks consist primarily of uplifted and faulted Paleozoic sedimentary layers. On the western fringe of the San Juans, the La Platas and the San Miguels consist of several small masses of Tertiary igneous rock that have intruded into Paleozoic conglomerates, shales, and limestones.

The fire and volcanoes of the Tertiary Period were followed by the ice and glaciation of the Quaternary Period. The glacial era left us with beautiful, U-shaped valleys, cirques, and Matterhorn-shaped peaks, such as Wetterhorn, Golden Horn, and Pigeon.

MAPS

This guide should be used as a supplement to, rather than a replacement for, United States Geological Survey (USGS) maps and US Forest Service maps. In fact, in some instances, route descriptions given here are useless unless read in conjunction with a topographic map. All but a few of the quad maps for the San Juans are 7.5-minute series rather than 15-minute series. USGS maps can be purchased from sport and mountaineering shops in the area or from the USGS website: store.usgs.gov/map-locator. Forest Service maps are of little use for locating climbing routes but are the best method of plotting your approach by road. These maps cover much larger areas than the quad maps, and their road information is generally more current. The San Juan, Rio Grande, Uncompahgre, and Gunnison National Forests all cover portions of the San Juans. Forest Service maps can be ordered from the US Forest Service website: fs.usda.gov/visit/maps. Finally, National Geographic Trails Illustrated maps are good alternative maps and can be purchased from local stores or from National Geographic directly: natgeomaps.com.

There are still an unusually large number of unnamed peaks in the San Juans. When we are aware of them, we have included as many unofficial names as possible. In the headings, the unofficial names are given after designating the peak by elevation. Additionally, we include in parenthesis the location of officially unnamed peaks in relationship to an officially named landmark in the area. Many summits have unofficial names that have sprung up because of local usage or traditional agreement in the climbing community. Examples of these are some of the "T," "S," or "V" designation summits in the San Juans that were first used in *The San Juan Mountaineers' Climber's Guide to Southwestern Colorado* (1932).

Exact elevations are not given for some peaks and passes in the San Juans. In those cases, we have approximated elevations by splitting the difference between contour lines. Almost all the USGS maps for the San Juans are in the 7.5-minute series, which have 40-foot contour lines. Thus, peaks such as the eastern summit of Point Pun are given an elevation of 13,180′ when the highest contour line is 13,160′. As a result, the approximated elevation should be no more than 20 vertical feet off from the exact elevation.

While there is no substitute for a good paper map and compass, we highly recommend the GAIA GPS phone application, which allows you to download topographic maps onto your phone to be used while in airplane mode. This is an invaluable routefinding tool, as it shows your location in real time without the need for cell service. The application also has several layers that can be downloaded to help with planning, such as weather, wildfire smoke, slope angles (great for skiers wanting to avoid avalanche danger), and private property lines. The base "GAIA Topo" layer is fantastic due to its small size for downloading; however, note that it displays peak elevations that are not official USGS elevations. Additionally, you'll find that some of the maps used in this book contain incorrect elevations for peaks since we use the "GAIA Topo" layer, which depends on public input in OpenStreetMap. Elevations can be off by a few feet up to a hundred—corrected elevations are provided when possible. Lastly, the application allows you to download and install other people's routes and record your own. Obtain a discounted subscription by visiting gaiagps .com/mattpaynephoto/.

TERMINOLOGY

There is no accepted standard for defining a mountain. *The Oxford English Dictionary* defines a mountain as "a natural elevation of the earth surface rising more or less abruptly from the surrounding level and attaining an altitude, which, relative to the adjacent elevation, is impressive or notable." One accepted standard in Colorado uses the rule that the mountain must have 300 feet of topographic prominence to be considered a mountain—these summits are considered "ranked." While this metric is good at distinguishing summits from false summits, it fails to recognize summits that are clearly summit-worthy (for example El Diente) or have other features that would lure a person to want to climb or hike to the top of it. Many names of summits are found on the USGS maps. Many high points and peaks that are not named on USGS maps are either provided with nicknames given by local mountaineers or are designated by "Peak" or "point" followed by the elevation of the summit.

Rank

A summit in Colorado is defined as ranked if it rises at least 300 feet above saddles to higher summits. A "soft ranked" designation means the mountain has the *potential* of qualifying as a ranked peak based merely on interpolation, where summit or saddle elevations are not explicitly available from the USGS maps. Here, interpolation is the calculation of the mean of the minimum and maximum possible elevations within a contour interval. For example, a summit on a 40-foot contour map with the highest contour of 12,200 feet has elevation possibilities between 12,200′ and 12,240′ (12,240′ would be the next contour if one were present). The mean of these is 12,220′. If a peak is ranked, this is noted in the book alongside its name and a number. The number is the ranking of that peak according to height (for example, 426 denotes that a peak is the 426th highest peak in Colorado). If a peak does not have sufficient prominence, it is not ranked, and we have placed a designation of "unranked" next to it.

Prominence

The prominence of a mountain is its rise above the highest saddle connecting the summit to higher ground, otherwise known as the prominence saddle. In other words, the prominence of a summit is its height above the lowest contour line encircling it and no higher summit. Prominence is the elevation of the mountain minus the elevation of the prominence saddle.

RATING THE CLIMBS

It has been said that if you ask the same question of three lawyers, you will get three different opinions. The same principle applies to rating the difficulty of climbs. The rating of a climb is ultimately a subjective decision, affected by both the climber's ability and the conditions under which the climb was made. There is, nevertheless, a method to the madness. The most frequently used rating system is the Yosemite Decimal System. The Yosemite Decimal System divides hiking and climbing into six classes:

Class 1. Hiking
Class 2. Off-trail scrambling
Class 3. Unroped climbing requiring the use of handholds
Class 4. Roped climbing where a leader climbs without protection but gives the other climbers a belay
Class 5. Roped climbing where the leader places protection
Class 6. Aid or artificial climbing where equipment is used for advancement as well as protection

Classes 1 and 2 are what most climbers would call a "walk-up." Handies, Sunshine, Redcloud, and Cirque are examples of Class 1 and 2 climbs. Class 3 climbing involves the use of handholds but is not so severe that most climbers feel the need for a rope. Wilson Peak, Vermillion, and Wetterhorn are examples of third-class climbing. The term "third-class climbing" is sometimes used to describe how a climb was made rather than its difficulty. For example, if a climber is able to climb the north face of Storm King, which has been rated 5.7, without a rope, she is said to have climbed the route "third class." The difficulty and rating of the climb remain the same, but the climber's level of ability has allowed her to climb in a manner that most climbers would not consider. Class 4 climbs hover on the borderline and are perhaps the most subjective rating. In some instances, a member of a climbing party will desire the security of a rope, whereas others will not. El Diente, U. S. Grant, Middle Trinity, and Arrow are typically described as Class 4 climbs. Each contains a section on which experienced climbers feel capable of climbing without rope. A beginner or intermediate climber, however, will welcome the security of a rope belay on sections of these peaks.

Class 5 climbing is what is most frequently thought of when one is discussing "rock" or "technical" climbing. Class 5 has a range of subdivisions up to 5.15. Ratings 5.10 and above are further subdivided by lowercase letters *a* through *d* to define the difficulty, with *a* being less difficult and *d* being the most. Wham Ridge, Coxcomb, and Lizard Head are examples of Class 5 climbing.

Class 6 climbing is generally designated by a capital *A* (for aid climbing) and has been subdivided from A-1 through A-5 depending on the stability and load-bearing capacity of the aid placement and the length of the potential fall. Sunlight Spire (the early ascents), the Pope's Nose, and the 1968 route on the east face of Monitor are examples of aid climbing in the San Juans.

Under the Yosemite Decimal System, the rating designates the difficulty of the hardest move on the climb. For example, if a five-pitch climb has four pitches of 5.3 and one pitch of 5.8, the rating given to the climb is 5.8.

When possible, we have identified the easiest route up each mountain, knowing that this is subjective based on a climber's abilities and preferences. For example, some climbers love climbing on steep snow in the spring and find this an easier way to climb than on rock during the summer months. Generally speaking though, snow introduces additional risks that we believe increase route difficulty.

Note: Elevation and mileage—given for every route in the book—are approximate. Mileage given is ONE-way (unless otherwise noted); elevation gain given is the total for the route.

DIGITAL RESOURCES

We are big proponents of doing additional research for your climbs and hikes, and for having at your fingertips as many resources as possible to aid in your success. Studying trip reports can be of huge value, especially since conditions, trails, and access points change. To that end, we've compiled below a list of resources that you may find valuable:

- **Climb13ers.com:** An amazing collection of route descriptions, photographs, and maps compiled by Tim and Carrie Cooney of Grand Junction, Colorado. The site chronicles their climbs, over several decades, of all the ranked 14ers and 13ers in Colorado, and is a treasure trove of information. Many of the "Off the Beaten Path" descriptions in this guide are based on information from Climb13ers.com, with permission from Tim and Carrie. *climb13ers.com*
- **Lists of John:** A massive database of mountains that also allows you to record your climbs and track your progress toward various "lists" of peaks across the country. *listsofjohn.com*
- **14ers.com:** A comprehensive resource for researching everything you need to know about climbing Colorado's 14ers. *14ers.com*
- **Earthline: The American West:** Includes a complete guide to the La Platas, extensive coverage of many other peaks in the San Juans, and exceptional photography. *debravanwinegarden.blogspot.com*
- **Summitpost:** User-curated pages for peaks across the globe. The Colorado climbing community has done an excellent job of creating and maintaining pages for the various Colorado peaks. *summitpost.com*
- **100summits:** A photo-rich site where this book's coauthor, Matt Payne, documents many of his climbs. *100summits.com*
- **13ergirl:** A hidden gem of a website, where climber Sarah Meiser documents her climbs: *13ergirl.com*

THOSE WHO CAME BEFORE

An Overview of San Juans Climbing History

Many San Juan peaks were undoubtedly climbed by Native Americans. The San Juan Mountaineers, an ambitious 1930s climbing group, reported that there was "direct evidence" that Native Americans had carried out hunting expeditions at least to an elevation of 13,000′ on Uncompahgre Peak. Early miners also certainly climbed many of the peaks in the area. The Hayden Survey, led by Ferdinand Vandeveer Hayden, was originally tasked with leading a scientific expedition to Yellowstone in 1871; however, in 1873, Hayden shifted his focus to Colorado due to the heavy expenses of shipping supplies to an area without a railroad as well as the threat of hostile Native American Indians. Hayden divided the Colorado territory into three regions and assigned an expedition party to survey each area. One of these parties was led by photographer William H. Jackson and included an artist and several naturalists. They were given the task of photographing, sketching, and gathering observations for the benefit of both scientists and the public. The Hayden Survey team reported finding prospect holes at 13,500′ on Handies Peak in 1874. Beyond these snippets of information, we are in large measure left to speculate what the Native Americans and miners did or did not climb.

The first climbers to document their achievements were these early surveyors. In 1873, a Hayden Survey team made the first ascent of Stewart Peak. That same year, H. G. Prout climbed Engineer Mountain with a Corps of Engineers party in the San Juans. It was not until 1874, however, that the activities of the surveyors began in earnest and members of both the Hayden and Wheeler Surveys began active exploration in the San Juans.

The Hayden Survey's exploits during the summer of 1874 are one of the most extraordinary chapters in the climbing history of the San Juans. The team was headed by A. D. Wilson, who had made the second ascent of

Dwight Lavender giving Lewis Geisecke a shoulder stand on Kismet during the early 1930s. Photo by Mel Griffiths

Mount Rainier in 1870. The other members of the party were Frederick Endlich and Franklin Rhoda, the half-brother of A. D. Wilson, who wrote the *Report on the Topography of the San Juan Country*, which gave a detailed chronicle of the Hayden team's exploits. Over the course of the summer of 1874, the Hayden party established fifty-four survey stations in the San Juans. A partial list of the peaks climbed by them includes Uncompahgre Peak, Sunshine Peak, Handies Peak, Rio Grande Pyramid, Mount Oso, Vermillion Peak, Mount Sneffels, and Mount Wilson. All but the Rio Grande Pyramid were first recorded ascents. In addition to being the first party to climb many of the major peaks in the San Juans, the Hayden team made a lasting impact by naming many peaks in the area.

Although not as prolific as the Hayden Survey, the Wheeler Survey also made significant achievements in the San Juans over the course of the 1874 and 1875 seasons. The report of the Wheeler Survey's activities by William L. Marshall chronicles ascents of Uncompahgre Peak, Rio Grande Pyramid, Redcloud Peak, and several peaks in the La Platas. The Wheeler Survey's climbs on Rio Grande Pyramid and Redcloud Peak were first recorded ascents.

In the late 1800s, the San Juans began to attract climbers interested in scaling peaks solely for sport. In 1890, Percy Thomas from the Alpine Club of London, England, made a trip to the San Miguels and made a reconnaissance of Lizard Head and the first ascent of El Diente. Frederick Chapin also visited the area in 1890

Left: Fredrick Endlich (left), Franklin Rhoda, and A. D. Wilson of the Hayden Survey, 1874. **Right:** Hayden Survey photographer and tent on the summit of Sultan Mountain. Photos by W. H. Jacskson, courtesy of USGS

Left: Frank (left) and Henry McClintock teamed up with various members of the San Juan Mountaineers and others to make numerous first ascents in the 1930s, 1940s, and 1950s. Photo by Joe Merher **Right:** The San Juan Mountaineers taking a lunch stop on Kismet, 1932. Dwight Lavender (drinking), Gordon Williams, and Mel Griffiths. Photo by Mel Griffiths

and made an early ascent of Mount Sneffels and recorded his climb in the pages of *Appalachia*, the long-running mountaineering journal. The most ambitious of the early alpinists were Williams S. Cooper and John Hubbard. In 1906, Cooper visited the San Juans and climbed Kendall Mountain near Silverton to get a better view of the area. He was particularly struck by the view of the Needle Mountains. Cooper returned in 1908 with John Hubbard and made first ascents of Pigeon Peak, Arrow, Vermillion, Mount Sneffels, Mount Wilson, and Uncompahgre Peak. Cooper and Hubbard were the first reported climbers to purposely seek out some of the most difficult peaks in the area.

One of the most historically significant climbs in the San Juans took place in 1920. In that year, Albert Ellingwood and Barton Hoag did what was previously thought impossible by climbing Lizard Head. At the time of its first ascent, Lizard Head was probably the most difficult climb in America. It is remarkable that the climb was achieved at that point considering the rudimentary equipment and protection devices available to Ellingwood and Hoag.

The next chapter in the climbing history of the San Juans belongs to the San Juan Mountaineers. In the early 1930s, a nucleus of strongly motivated climbers, including Dwight Lavender, Mel Griffiths, Gordon Williams, Chester Price, Henry McClintock, Frank McClintock, Lewis Giesecke, Forrest Greenfield, Carleton Long, and Everett Long, formed the San Juan Mountaineers. The San Juan Mountaineers made over fifty first ascents in the area. Some of the more notable achievements of the San Juan Mountaineers were three routes established during

Left: Bob Ormes. Ormes participated in the first ascent of Chimney Rock, the first traverse of Needle Ridge, and the third ascent of Lizard Head. Photo by Mel Griffiths **Right:** George Bell Sr. on the summit of Sunlight Spire after its first ascent, July 1963. Photo courtesy of George Bell, Sr.

1931, 1932, and 1933 on the north face of Sneffels, culminating in a direct route up the north face, the first ascent of Jagged Mountain, the first ascent of the Index, and the ascents of various pinnacles in the Sneffels area. In addition, the San Juan Mountaineers, in particular Mel Griffiths and Gordon Williams, began making ambitious winter climbs, including Mount Sneffels.

The driving force in the organization was Dwight Lavender. Tragically, Lavender died of polio during the fall of 1934 at the age of 23. During his short life, Lavender participated in over thirty first ascents with the San Juan Mountaineers. He also wrote numerous articles on the group's exploits for *Trail and Timberline*, *American Alpine Journal*, and *The British Mountaineering Journal*, for which he was serving as American editor at the time of his death. Lavender also coauthored, with Carleton Long and contributions from Mel Griffiths, *The San Juan Mountaineer's Climber's Guide to Southwestern Colorado*. Given the brevity of his life, Lavender's achievements were staggering.

After the intense burst of activity generated by the San Juan Mountaineers in the early 1930s, a period of consolidation set in. Significant ascents were made during Colorado Mountain Club outings and by various members of the San Juan Mountaineers who remained active. Several significant climbs made during this era were Chimney Rock and the traverse of Needle Ridge by Mel Griffiths and Robert Ormes; the southeast chimney on Pigeon Peak by Frank McClintock, Henry McClintock, Mary McClintock, and Gordon Williams; and Wham Ridge on Vestal Peak by Rit Burrows, Werner Schnackenberg, and Jim Patterson.

In 1947, Joe Stettner, Jack Fralick, and John Speck made a remarkable ascent of the 1,200′ east face of Monitor Peak. In many respects, this climb was well ahead of its time. While other American climbers were making severe climbs with the assistance of aid, Stettner, Fralick, and Speck free climbed (with the exception of two shoulder stands) what remains even by today's standards an extremely difficult route. Pitons were used for protection only, not for aid. Stettner, who left his mark in the history of climbing in Colorado by climbing Stettners Ledges on Longs Peak in 1927 and the north face of Lone Eagle Peak in 1933, said he felt that the east face of Monitor was far more difficult than his other climbs.

The Needles and Grenadiers became the focus of attention for climbers in the San Juans during the 1960s. In 1962, John Ohrenschall and Doug Ward made technical ascents in the Grenadiers including the east faces of Arrow Peak and Electric Peak. Martin Etter, with various partners, climbed the north face of Coxcomb, the west face of Arrow Peak, the east face of Vestal, and the north face of Wildhorse Peak. George Bell Sr. was also active with several partners and made the first ascents of Sunlight Spire and Ominous Pinnacle. The east face of Monitor Peak was repeated by a more direct route in 1968 by Larry Dalke and Paul Stettner Jr., Joe Stettner's nephew.

The 1960s also saw several difficult winter routes established in the Grenadiers. The Harvard Mountaineers climbed several difficult routes during their 1963 Christmas vacation. One that they missed, Wham Ridge, was climbed in January 1968.

During the 1970s, the emphasis on technical climbing in the San Juans continued to center in the Grenadiers and Needles with various new routes made primarily on the north and east faces of the Grenadiers. Outside of the Grenadiers and Needles, the most significant ascents in the 1970s were made by Jeff Lowe and Paul Hogan on the north face of Wetterhorn Peak and Lowe and Larry Derby on the north face of Half Peak. In 1988, Jeff Achey free climbed Sunlight Spire, which had been climbed using aid in 1966 by George Bell Sr., David Michael, and John Marshall.

The 1970s and 1980s also saw a shift in emphasis. Many skilled climbers began developing rock climbing areas near Telluride (Cracked Canyon, Ophir Wall, Ames Wall), Durango (The Watch Crystal), and the San Luis Valley. In addition, there is challenging ice climbing found in the Telluride and Ouray areas.

The San Juans may probably never again be on the cutting edge of American alpinism as they were when Ellingwood led Lizard Head or Stettner led Monitor's east face. Today, that's not what the San Juans are all about. Rather, the San Juans are a range that offers climbers a lifetime of climbing on varied terrain and a vast menu of mountains that will surely satisfy the appetite of anyone who loves the alpine world.

LA PLATA MOUNTAINS

1

The La Platas are a distinct southwestern offshoot of the San Juans. Although the La Platas were an area of intensive mining activity in the late 1800s, the peaks are seldom visited today except by local climbers and hikers. When climbing or hiking here, you can expect a pleasant day away from the crowds. For climbers, the principal attraction is a cluster of six 13,000′ peaks: Hesperus Mountain, Lavender Peak, Centennial Peak, Mount Moss, Babcock Peak, and Spiller Peak. Hesperus is the highest peak in the group and is located northwest of the other peaks in the range. Hesperus is also one of the four sacred mountains of the Navajo tribe. Named "Dibentsaa" by the Navajos, Hesperus is the Sacred Mountain of the North.

Lavender Peak, named for San Juan Mountaineers' founder Dwight Lavender, is located on the ridge between Hesperus and Mount Moss. The northern flank of Lavender is covered by hundreds of sheer pinnacles. To the northeast of Lavender lies Centennial Peak, which in 1976 was named in honor of Colorado's 100th birthday. Centennial was formerly known as Banded Peak because it is composed of alternating horizontal layers of rust and light-colored rock.

Mount Moss is an enjoyable climb that lies to the north of a rugged ridge separating Owen Basin from Tomahawk Basin. To the south of this ridge lies Babcock Peak, which consists of four separate and rugged summits, with the middle summit being the highest. Directly west of Babcock, at the end of a high rugged ridge called "The Knife," lies Spiller Peak. In addition to the 13,000′ peaks, there are several 12,000′ peaks of interest. To the north of the 13ers lies Sharkstooth Peak; to the east is Diorite Peak; southeast of Spiller Peak is Burwell Peak, each of which is an enjoyable day hike.

The USGS quad map for the La Platas omitted a contour line, which has led to some controversy and confusion over the years about which of the Babcock summits is the highest.

CLIMBING HISTORY

Early explorers were lured into the La Platas by the search for minerals. In the 1870s, the Spaniard Juan de Rivera led a prospecting party into the La Platas and found the silver for which the range is named. The La Platas soon became a scene of intensive mining and milling operations. Parrott City, at the mouth of the La Plata Canyon, was a boisterous mining town, which was not only the county seat but also had the largest population in the county at the time. Undoubtedly, many of the summits in the range were climbed by prospectors of that era.

A panorama of the La Platas from the summit of Babcock Peak.

In 1875, the Wheeler Survey ventured into the La Platas and, from camps on the La Plata River, established two topographical stations in the area. According to George Wheeler's *Annual Report of the Chief of Engineers for 1876,* they selected the "highest of the La Plata Peaks" (presumably Hesperus) for a principal topographical station in their scheme of triangulation but found that it was not accessible from the east. They proceeded west to the Mancos River and located what Marshall termed a very successful survey station.

Hesperus Peak was climbed in 1876 by a Hayden Survey team that included William Henry Holmes. Holmes excelled both in geology and art. From the summit of Hesperus, he made preliminary notes and sketches, which he later transformed into a stunning drawing of the La Platas that was published in *Hayden's Atlas of Colorado.* Of Lavender Peak's north ridge, which is festooned with needles and daggers, Hayden wrote, "It has to be seen to be believed."

ACCESS AND HIKING

Tomahawk Basin

Tomahawk Basin is a great way to access Babcock Peak, Mount Moss, and Lavender Peak. The turnoff to La Plata Canyon and Tomahawk Basin is 11 miles west of Durango and 17 miles east of Mancos. After turning north off US Highway 160, the first 4.5 miles of the road toward La Plata Canyon are paved. After 4.5 miles, the road turns to gravel and continues up the canyon. At 10.5 miles from US 160 (0.4 after crossing Basin Creek), a rugged 4WD road turns off to the left (west) from the La Plata Canyon Road and climbs up the north side of the drainage past the Tomahawk Mine to the old site of the Little Kate Mine. Stay right when the Tomahawk Basin Road splits at 1 mile, pass Tomahawk Mine at 1.4, and park at 1.8 miles, at 10,750′ where the road takes a hard right that takes you away from the cluster of Babcock Peak summits. At 1.8 miles, where the road veers right, a sketchy climbers' trail climbs up the right (north) side of the stream to the high basin and the Babcock Peak summits. The west end of Tomahawk Basin is separated from Owen Basin by a sharply pinnacled ridge between the western summit of Babcock Peak and Mount Moss. A rugged pass on the ridge provides access to Lavender Peak and Mount Moss. Tomahawk Basin and Boren Basin, to the south, both offer excellent spring skiing.

Boren Creek

The turnoff to Boren Creek is located in La Plata Canyon, 8.3 miles up the La Plata Canyon Road from US Highway 160. A 4WD road, FSR 794 turns left shortly after the La Plata Canyon Road crosses Boren Creek and climbs 1,900′ and 2.6 miles to

LA PLATA MOUNTAINS

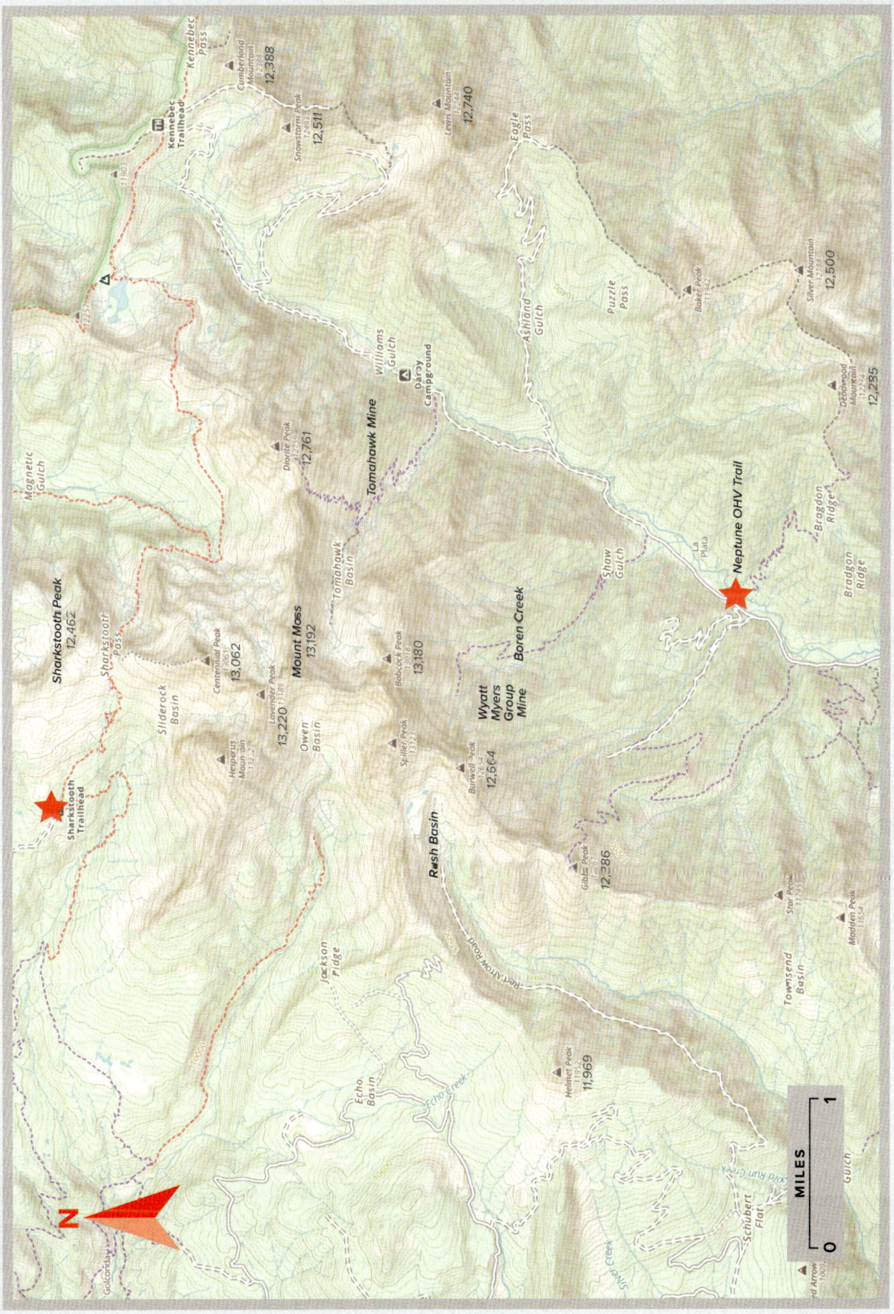

an old mine site at 11,197′. The road is narrow and rugged and has limited pullouts. The high basin above Boren Creek provides access to Burwell Peak, Spiller Peak, the West and Middle Summits of Babcock Peak, and the rugged, exposed ridge between Spiller and the West Summit of Babcock known as "The Knife."

Transfer Campground Road (Sharkstooth Trail)

Transfer Campground Road provides access to the La Platas from the west. The turn-off is located 0.3 mile north of Mancos, on Colorado Highway 184. Turn on the road marked for Jackson Lake. After 10.1 miles, turn right on a road just before Transfer Campground marked "Transfer." From Transfer Campground, drive north on Forest Service Road 561 for 1.6 miles (11.7 from Mancos) and turn right on Forest Service Road 350. Continue on FSR 350 for 6.4 miles (18.1 from Mancos) to a junction. Take the right fork at the junction that is signed for Twin Lakes (1 mile), the Sharks-tooth Trail (1.5 miles from the junction), and the West Mancos Trailhead. The last 1.5 miles to Sharkstooth Trail are rough, and a high-clearance vehicle is necessary. This is the best approach for Hesperus Mountain, Centennial Peak, and Sharkstooth Peak. It's also an alternate approach for Lavender Peak and Mount Moss via steep snow couloirs on the north side of the pass between Lavender and Moss or the rugged southeast ridge from Hesperus.

Early morning panorama of the La Platas from the Needles, from left to right: Babcock and Spiller at center; Moss, Lavender, and Hesperus at right.

Rush Basin

The access road to Rush Basin begins 2.5 miles east of Mancos, where you turn north on Echo Basin Road. At 0.9 mile from US Highway 160, turn right on Forest Service Road 567, which takes you 10.5 miles (11.4 from US 160) to the Doyle Mine in Rush Basin at 11,400'. This approach is long and rocky—and periodically blocked by deadfall and rockfall. The last 4 miles of the road are narrow with limited pullovers and turnarounds. A 4WD vehicle is required, and it's not for the faint of heart; consider hiking the last 4 miles. From Rush Basin, you can climb both Spiller and Burwell from the west.

CLIMBING ROUTES

Babcock Peak

13,180′ RANK 499

Babcock Peak has four separate, distinct summits: East, Shark's Head, Middle, and West. Although closely clustered, it's difficult to get from one of these summits to another. The elevation for East Summit is 13,149′. The elevation for the other summits isn't shown on the quad map, but Middle Summit is now recognized as the highest of the four summits at 13,180′. Shark's Head (between East and Middle Summits) is the shortest of the four summits but, as you would guess from its name, the most difficult to climb.

Babcock Peak from Tomahawk Basin.

East Summit

From Tomahawk Basin Mine at 10,730′: 1.6 miles, 2,400′

East Summit of Babcock, which is the easiest, is frequently climbed by its southeast ridge. Although less technical than the other three summits, the southeast ridge is a Class 3 route on a narrow, exposed ridge. The best approach for the southeast ridge is from Tomahawk Basin. From high in the basin at about 12,000′ or 12,200′, contour around the northeast spur of East Summit and climb to the saddle between the summit and point 12,860′. Once the ridge is gained, you don't have a choice but to follow its narrow course to the summit. In the spring, East Summit can also be gained from Tomahawk Basin by climbing the steep snow couloir on the north flank of the peak to the left (east) of Shark's Head Summit. The couloir is about 40 degrees steep, and crampons and ice axes are required. The safest route to avoid rockfall in the couloir is to stay close to the right wall, which affords points for placing protection once the couloir begins to ice up. From the top of the couloir, there is one pitch of Class 4 climbing, which will place you on the south face of the East Summit, just below the top.

Shark's Head

From Tomahawk Basin Mine at 10,730′: 1.6 miles, 2,400′

From the top of the col separating Shark's Head from East Summit of Babcock Peak, a 40′ pitch of Class 4 climbing on steep, loose rock separates you from easy scrambling to the summit. See the description of how to reach the col in the description for East Summit. Just to the north of the Shark's Head lies an amazing pinnacle. Slings near the top indicate that it has been climbed. It looks terrible.

Middle Summit

From 2WD parking on La Plata Canyon Road at 9,280′: 3.1 miles, 3,869′

From 4WD parking at Wyatt Myers Mine at 11,197′: 0.5 mile, 1,952′

Two routes up to Middle Summit from the Boren Creek side both require fairly challenging Class 3 or Class 4 scrambling over loose rock. From the old Wyatt Myers Group mine site at 11,197′, it's hard to differentiate the Babcock summits. West Summit is the peak with the narrow slotlike feature carved into its south flank. To the right (east) of West Summit, there are three broader gullies. The western gully and the middle gully bracket Middle Summit, and both gullies afford routes to Middle Summit. The western gully combines well with a climb of West Summit and Spiller Peak via the Knife. The gully to the east of Middle Summit works better for a standalone climb of Middle Summit. The western gully doglegs to the left. Near the dogleg, look for a narrow, loose, side gully going right (east) about 200+′ below the col between the Middle and West Summits. The side gully is Class 4 and leads you to cleaner Class 3 climbing as you near Middle Summit. The gully east of Middle Summit takes you almost all the way up to the col between Middle Summit and Shark's Head, where you can exit the gully to the left (west) and angle your way up to the top on a Class 3 route. From Tomahawk Basin, the north-facing snow couloir right (west) of Shark's Head leads to the col separating Shark's Head and Middle Summit. From the col, you can climb the same Class 3 route afforded by the Boren Basin approach. The snow couloir between Middle and West Summits on the Tomahawk Basin side leads to the col separating the Middle and West Summits. From the col, you have to drop 200′ down the southern gully to gain the loose side gully near the dogleg that branches off to the east, described above as part of the Boren Basin routes.

West Summit

From 2WD parking on La Plata Canyon Road at 9,280′: 3.1 miles, 3,900′

From 4WD parking at Wyatt Myers Group Mine at 11,197′: 0.5 miles, 1,983′

West Summit can be climbed from the col connecting it to Middle Summit by steep, rocky Class 3 climbing. The col can be reached by the approaches described above

From left to right: Hesperus, Lavender, and Moss as seen from the slopes of Babcock.

for Middle Summit. West Summit is connected to Spiller Peak by a classic ridge route called "The Knife." The best (and only) route on this notoriously exposed ridge is on the very top of the ridge, except for the pinnacle near the summit of Spiller, which is skirted to the north. The ridge involves some narrow, exposed scrambling, but most experienced climbers will not feel the need for a rope. Once committing to The Knife, there is no escape route. Take a good look at the weather before you set off.

Mount Moss

13,192′ **SOFT RANKED**

South Ridge

From Tomahawk Basin Mine at 10,730′: 1.7 miles, 2,490′

The south ridge of Mount Moss can be gained from Tomahawk Basin. Gaining the ridge involves Class 2+ scrambling to the rugged pass from Tomahawk Basin into Owens Basin and then an ascending traverse of the talus field high on the Owens Basin side of the ridge. Once on the ridge, stay generally to the west until near the summit where the climb turns into an easy walk-up.

Lavender Peak

13,180′ RANK 465

Lavender Peak is a classic climb named after legendary San Juan climber Dwight Lavender. All approaches to Lavender—from Tomahawk Basin over the ridge to Owens Basin, or on the rugged eastern ridge extending from Hesperus, or the steep snow couloir to the saddle between Mount Moss and Lavender—require some real effort.

South Face

From Tomahawk Basin Mine at 10,730′: 2 miles, 2,580′

From Sharkstooth TH at 10,950′ via Hesperus Mountain: 2.5 miles, 2,760′

Lavender Peak has two summits, and the west summit is slightly higher. The west summit is best climbed by a Class 4 scramble up a broad gully on the south face. The north face of Lavender, which is unclimbed, is festooned with slender stone pinnacles. At the notch between the two summits, there was a stunning pinnacle that, at some point after 1988, vanished from view into the chasm below.

Hesperus Mountain

13,232′ RANK 451

Hesperus is the highest peak in the La Platas and one of the four sacred mountains of the Navajo people. It is easily recognized from the west as a pyramid-shaped mountain on the north side of the range.

A piton forged by Dwight Lavender and left in place on Wolf's Tooth, which was later placed on the summit of Lavender Peak in his honor. Photo by Bob Rosebrough

Left to right: Sharkstooth, Centennial, Hesperus, Lavender, Babcock, and Spiller.

West Ridge

From Sharkstooth TH at 10,950′: 2 miles, 2,430′

From the shared trailhead with Sharkstooth Trail, take West Mancos Trail (#621), which descends southeast and crosses the north fork of the West Mancos River 0.6 mile from the trailhead on a log bridge. After the stream crossing, keep an eye out for a cairned climbers' trail that gains elevation and heads south rather than staying on West Mancos Trail that heads west. Once you emerge onto a field of small talus with views of the west ridge (to the south), locate the "black line" in the rock that comes down from the west ridge and marks the most direct line to the ridge. Once you gain the west ridge, there is just under 1,000′ of elevation gain to the summit. As you near the summit, there is one Class 3 scramble through a cliff band on broken but stable rock.

Centennial Peak

13,062′ SOFT RANKED

North Ridge

From Sharkstooth TH at 10,950′: 2.4 miles, 2,112′

The north ridge begins at the 11,935′ saddle between Centennial and Sharkstooth, which is gained by hiking up Sharkstooth Trail. The north ridge is a Class 2 climb on fairly stable talus. The view of Lavender Peak's north face from the summit of Centennial is particularly impressive.

Spiller Peak

13,123′ UNRANKED

Southeast Face and South Ridge

From 2WD parking on La Plata Canyon Road at 9,280′: 3.3 miles, 3,843′

From 4WD parking at Wyatt Myers Group Mine at 11,197′: 0.8 mile, 1,926′

The standard route up Spiller is from the Boren Creek drainage. Climb up the southeast face on talus aiming to gain the southern ridge that connects Spiller to Burwell. The south ridge is Class 3 in spots on broken and, at times, loose rock. It is also possible to climb to the notch, just east of the summit and then climb the last 200′ on the north face. Spiller Peak is the western end of The Knife, which is described in the route description for the West Summit of Babcock Peak.

The Middle and West Summits of Babcock and Spiller from the East Summit of Babcock.

OFF THE BEATEN PATH

Diorite Peak from Babcock Peak.

Diorite Peak

12,761′ RANK 812

1.5 miles east of Mount Moss

From Tomahawk Basin Mine at 10,730′: 1.7 miles, 2,031′

South Face and Southwest Ridge: The standard Class 2+ route up Diorite switchbacks up the south flank to a ridge at 12,360′, which leads to the summit.

Burwell Peak

12,664′ UNRANKED

0.5 mile southwest of Spiller

From 2WD parking on La Plata Canyon Road at 9,280′: 3.25 miles, 3,384′

From 4WD parking at Wyatt Myers Mine at 11,197′: 0.7 mile, 1,467′

East Face: Hike on the old mining road until it ends at about 11,200′, climb the east face to a point north of the summit, and follow the north ridge to the top on Class 2+ terrain.

Sharkstooth Peak

12,462′ RANK 1,025

1.3 miles northeast of Hesperus

From Sharkstooth TH at 10,950′: 2 miles, 1,512′

Southwest Couloir: From the saddle to Centennial, aim for the couloir on the southwest face and a Class 2 route on very loose talus.

Silver Mountain

12,500′ RANK 993

3.88 miles southeast of Babcock Peak

From Neptune OHV Trail on the La Plata Canyon Road at 9,100′: 4.6 miles, 3,710′

West Ridge: Climb the Neptune OHV Trail located 2.7 miles southwest of the Tomahawk Basin Road on the La Plata Canyon Road up and over Deadwood Mountain on steep Class 2 terrain.

SAN MIGUEL MOUNTAINS 2

San Miguels as seen from Dallas Peak. Lizard Head at far left, Gladstone is in front of Mount Wilson with El Diente right of it, Wilson Peak right of center, Fowler, then Boskoff right of Wilson Peak.

The main cluster of the San Miguels is composed of three 14,000′ peaks—Mount Wilson, El Diente, and Wilson Peak—and one peak just under 14,000′: Gladstone Peak. Mount Wilson and El Diente have well-deserved reputations as two of the most difficult 14ers to climb. The rugged, exposed ridge connecting Mount Wilson and El Diente is a "must climb" for serious mountaineers. Neighboring Wilson Peak is not as difficult as Mount Wilson or El Diente but presents all the challenges the average climber cares for. The almost-14er Gladstone Peak (13,913′) is an attractive peak that has been overlooked by climbers intent on the 14ers. Perhaps this is for good reason, however, as the rock on Gladstone is notoriously loose and dangerous.

Two or three miles southeast of the main cluster of peaks lurks the infamous Lizard Head, which has worked hard to gain its reputation as the most difficult and dangerous summit in Colorado to attain. The history of climbing on Lizard Head is replete with stories of broken holds, rockfall, turned ankles, and climbing falls. In sharp contrast to the evil Lizard Head are the more rounded summits of Sunshine Mountain, directly east of the 14ers, and Dolores Peak, Middle Peak, and Dunn Peak, to the west. Lone Cone completes the San Miguels. Aptly named, Lone Cone sits in beautiful isolation several miles to the northwest of the other peaks in the range.

CLIMBING HISTORY

The history of climbing in the San Miguels begins with the Wheeler Survey in 1874. The Wheeler reports concerning Mount Wilson are conflicting. In the survey's *Annual Report of the Chief of Engineers for 1876*, which reflected upon the 1875 field season, William L. Marshall wrote that Mount Wilson "was ascended in 1874 by Mr. Spiller, and in our notes was called Glacier Point." However, an earlier report from the Wheeler Survey by Lieutenant Whipple in 1874 refers to "Glacier Peak, since named Meigs Peak, of the San Miguel Range, which the photographer of the party, Mr. Spiller, occupied with partial success." What did Whipple mean by "partial success"? The Hayden Survey led by A. D. Wilson, after whom the peak was eventually named, did not climb Mount Wilson until late in the year. If Spiller did climb Mount Wilson, his climb would have been a first ascent.

The question of whether Spiller attained the summit was probably resolved by a discovery made by William S. Cooper and John Hubbard in 1908. While downclimbing the difficult south ridge, Cooper and Hubbard passed over a particularly tricky spot in the ridge that forced them to use a rope for the first time during a summer of challenging climbing. In his recently published manuscript, *Mountains*, Cooper wrote, "Just beyond it, something in a crevice caught my eye. It proved to be an exceedingly rusty tin can; in it was a memorandum sheet very dirty and hard to read. I made out the name J. Calvert Stitler and the date 1874; also Corps of Engineers, USA." The location of the tin can along the south ridge led Cooper to believe that "the man who left it was trying to climb Mount Wilson and that his nerve failed him at the cleft." The logical conclusion of these reports is that Spiller (Stitler) did not reach the true summit of Mount Wilson.

The honor of the first ascent has generally been attributed to the Hayden Survey team, which reached the summit of Mount Wilson on September 13, 1874. The Hayden team, composed of A. D. Wilson, Franklin Rhoda, and Frederick Endlich, had developed a great deal of respect for Mount Wilson over the course of the summer. In his account of the 1874 exploration, *Summits to Reach*, Rhoda reported:

> *Only one peak of which we had any dread remained to be ascended, and that was Mount Wilson. From various circumstances, we have reason to believe that this was higher than any station we had yet made, and from its rugged appearance we dreaded its ascent not a little.*

The Hayden Survey team approached Mount Wilson from the southeast and cut steps in a large steep snowbank to reach, according to Rhoda, some "very steep and dangerous rock walls." They straddled and slid across a great stone with its upper part wedged in a notch in the narrow south ridge. More difficult climbing on the south ridge led Rhoda to conclude that Mount Wilson was "by far the most dangerous of all the climbs of the summer."

Early climbers on the north side of Mount Wilson found similar difficulties. In 1921, Carl Blaurock climbed the north face with Dudley T. Smith and William F. Ervin and reported in *Trail and Timberline* (January 1922) that "on the last 200 feet we scrambled like scared cats along a backyard fence."

Like Mount Wilson, neighboring El Diente suffered through an initial period of confusion concerning its first ascent. El Diente was first climbed by Percy Thomas and N. G. Douglas on September 2, 1890. Thomas and Douglas actually thought that they were climbing Mount Wilson.

After a failed attempt on Lizard Head, Thomas and Douglas turned their attention toward what they thought was Mount Wilson. The fact that Thomas and Douglas had actually climbed El Diente rather than Mount Wilson was discovered by Dwight Lavender, who climbed El Diente on July 4, 1930, with Forrest Greenfield and Chester Price. At that time, finding no evidence to the contrary, Lavender assumed that they had made a first ascent. After the climb, however, Lavender read the account of Thomas's climb in the *Alpine Journal.* Lavender and Thomas had both climbed the west ridge of El Diente, and Lavender noted similarities in the description between his climb and one reported by Thomas. In addition, Thomas had written of the "capital view of Mount Wilson" from Dunton. In his *Trail and Timberline* (September 1931) report, Lavender noted that although El Diente is quite striking when seen from Dunton, Mount Wilson "escapes all notice." Thomas did not discover his error upon reaching the summit of El Diente since "the view to the east was entirely blotted out, cutting off all possibility of seeing Mount Wilson."

El Diente, named by Lavender, means "the tooth" in Spanish. Prior to being dubbed El Diente, the peak had been known locally as "The Jag" or "Montezuma Peak." In addition to naming El Diente, Lavender presented a successful case for including El Diente on the list as a separate 14er. He noted that El Diente did not meet some of the criteria set for determining separate summits, such as the

Left: Dwight Lavender (left), Chester Price, and Forrest Greenfield in 1930 with Mount Wilson in the background. Photo by Lavender-Griffiths **Right:** The airy summit of Lizard Head. Photo by Stuart Krebs

combination of horizontal distance and vertical drop from the summit, but concluded that El Diente deserved separate status based on the difficulty of its ascent.

The first recorded climb of Gladstone Peak was made by J. W. Emerson and F. B. Notestein in 1911. Twenty years later, a party of twenty-four climbers led by Dwight Lavender and William F. Ervin made the second ascent of Gladstone on August 20, 1931, during a joint outing of the Colorado Mountain Club and Appalachian Mountain Club.

At the time of its first ascent in 1920 by Albert Ellingwood and Barton Hoag, Lizard Head was probably the hardest rock climb in the United States. Armed with three soft iron pitons, hemp rope, and nailed boots, Ellingwood and Hoag made a few abortive attempts on cracks near the southwest corner before rounding the corner to the west face. Ellingwood reported in *Outing Magazine* (November 1921) that "most of the enticing small holds crumbled at the touch, and large masses of the loosely compacted pebbles would topple dangerously at a slight pull." In spite of the difficulties, they struggled up and placed two rustic pitons in the lower cliff, saving one for the higher cliffs. After spending a half hour at the summit, Ellingwood and Hoag began an epic descent. Ellingwood's rope became stuck on the lower cliff. As he shook it, a rock came loose and hit him on the head, almost knocking him from the wall. Hoag was also hit by rockfall but was on secure footing at the time. After more effort, they had to abandon the rope and begin downclimbing. Ellingwood reported that Hoag "slipped and, leaving a section of his pants behind, drifted relentlessly downward until the wall became vertical and then jumped (perhaps 15′) to the rocks below. I followed with more caution, regretfully saying good-bye to my rope that had served me well for five good seasons."

The fact that Ellingwood and Hoag's climb was well ahead of its time is reflected in the comments of Harold G. Wilm, who made the second ascent on June 9, 1929, with Dobson West. Referring to Ellingwood, Wilm noted in *Trail and Timberline* (August 1931):

> *At the time it was considered an impossible feat, and little credence was given his performance by many who knew the peak. For some time, therefore, Dobson West and I had planned a second ascent, chiefly as a proof of his climb, but also as a mountaineering stunt of our own.*

Wilm and West confirmed the first ascent by retrieving Ellingwood's old rope and finding his old rusty pitons still in place.

ACCESS AND HIKING

Rock of Ages Trail (Silver Pick Basin)

Silver Pick Basin is a popular point of access for climbers interested in tackling the area's 14ers as well as Fowler Peak and Boskoff Peak. For years, this access was lost to the public, until new access was established, which combines a route that starts in Elk Basin before joining Silver Pick Basin higher up. To get to the trailhead from Ridgway, leave US Highway 550 and take Colorado Highway 62 toward Telluride. Drive over the Dallas Divide to Placerville and turn left onto Colorado Highway 145. Drive 6.5 miles from Placerville and turn right onto Silver Pick Road. (From Telluride, drive 9.5 miles west to reach the turnoff or 6 miles west of the Telluride exit on CO 145.) From the turnoff, drive 4 miles to an intersection and turn right onto Forest Service Road 622. Continue 2.2 miles, turn right onto Forest Service Road 645 (6.3 miles from CO 145) and drive 2.3 more miles to the Rock of Ages Trailhead (8.6 from CO 145). The trail, which starts at 10,350′, heads south in Elk Basin before crossing into Silver Pick Basin and, over 4.2 miles, climbs 2,000′ to a 13,020′ pass near the Rock of Ages Mine. Before reaching the pass, the trail traverses a steep talus slope. This pass gives access to the southwest ridge of Wilson Peak, and the northwest ridge of Gladstone Peak, and the north faces of Mount Wilson and El Diente. Those looking to climb Fowler and Boskoff will want to continue south on the Elk Creek Trail at the junction at 11,000′.

SAN MIGUEL MOUNTAINS (EAST)

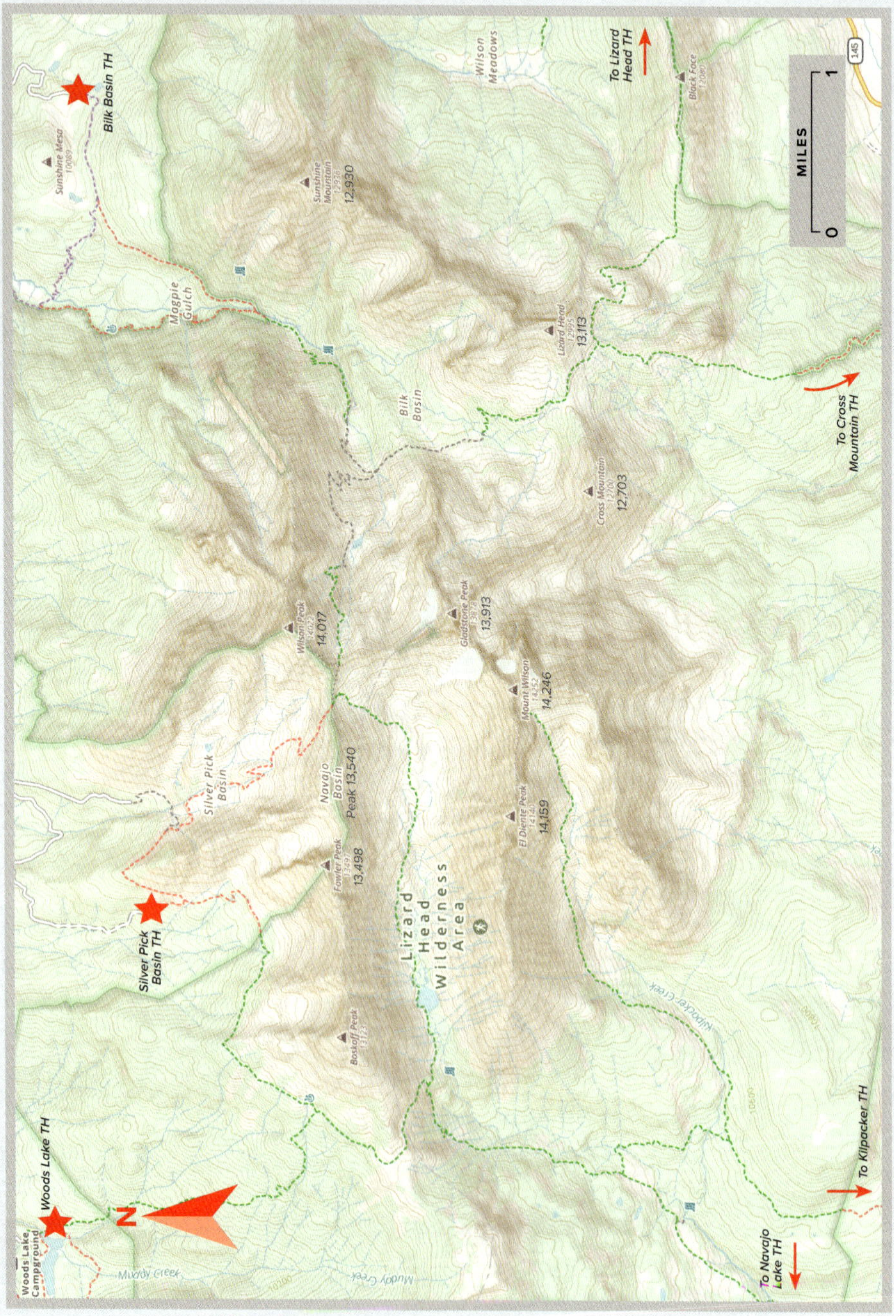

SAN MIGUEL MOUNTAINS (WEST)

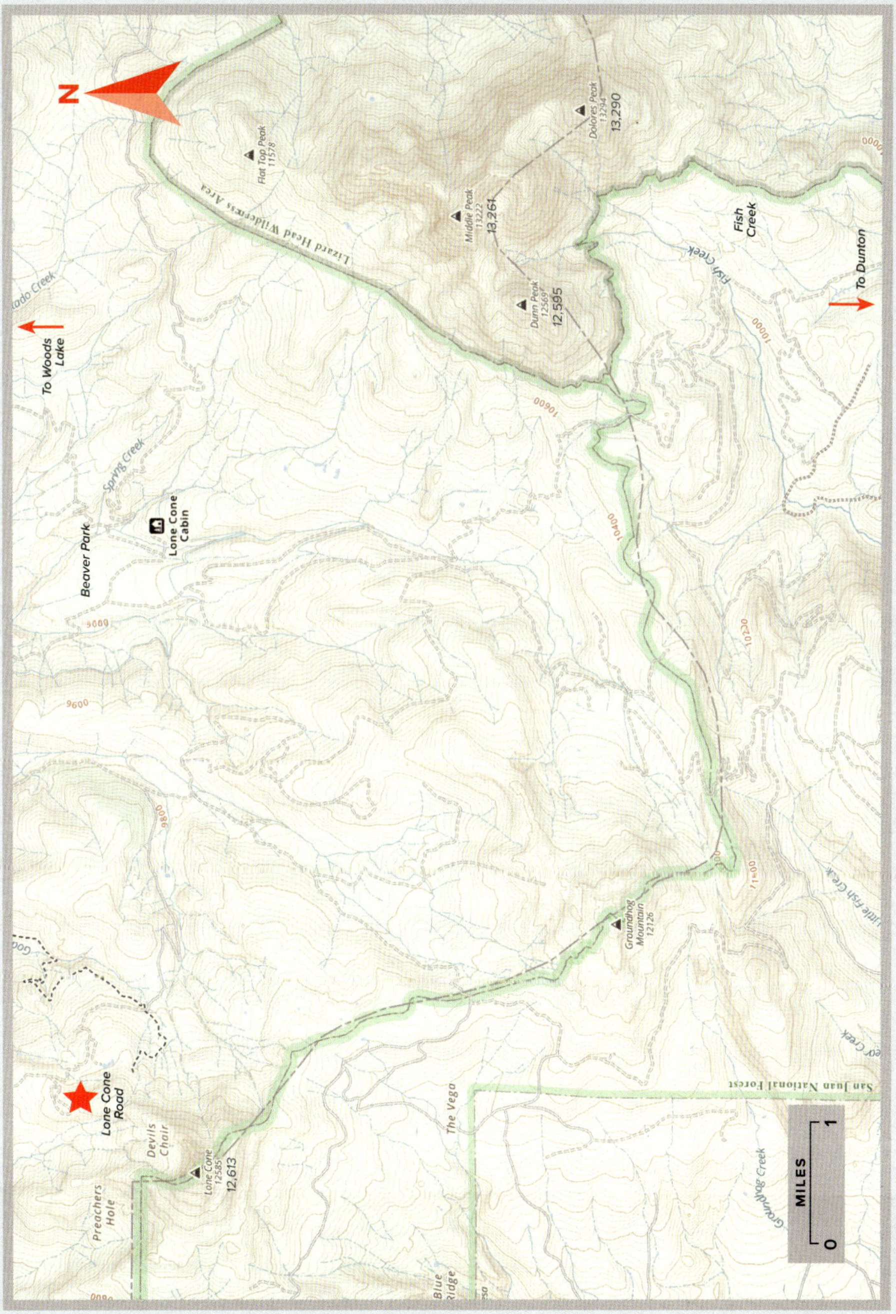

Lizard Head as seen from Bilk Basin.

Bilk Basin

The turnoff to the Bilk Creek Road (4WD recommended) is also located on Colorado Highway 145 between Placerville and Telluride. Ten miles east of Placerville and 6 miles west of Telluride (2.5 miles west of the Telluride exit on CO 145), turn off at the South Fork Road exit. At 2.2 miles from the turnoff, turn right on Sunshine Mesa Road and cross the bridge over the south fork of the San Miguel River. At 5.3 miles, the road steepens and begins switchbacking its way up to Sunshine Mesa. Stay left at 5.9 miles before reaching Wilson Mesa Trailhead (9,750′) at 7.6 miles and a small parking area. From the trailhead, hike west 0.7 mile to a junction where you turn left and head southwest another 1.3 miles to the Morning Star Mine on the west side of Bilk Creek at 10,000′. Bilk Basin provides the most direct access to Sunshine Mountain and alternate access to the southwest ridge of Mount Wilson, the southwest ridge of Wilson Peak, the northwest ridge of Gladstone, and Lizard Head.

Cross Mountain Trail

Cross Mountain Trail starts 2 miles southwest of Lizard Head Pass on Colorado Highway 145 at 10,000′. The trail heads northwest for 1.5 miles where it turns directly north for 1.2 miles and joins Lizard Head Trail at about 11,900′. From the junction of the two trails, there is an easy contour 0.3 mile northwest to the saddle between Cross Mountain and Lizard Head. To the north lies Bilk Basin and Bilk Creek Trail.

This is the most direct approach for Lizard Head and Cross Mountain and an alternate approach for Gladstone Peak and Wilson Peak if you backpack high up in Bilk Basin and set up a camp between the two peaks.

Navajo Lake Trail

This popular trail approaches the highest peaks in the San Miguel Range from the southwest. The trailhead can be reached from several directions. One way is to turn off Colorado Highway 145 13 miles northeast of Dolores and follow a well-maintained gravel road for 23 miles to Dunton. Upon reaching Dunton, continue another 2.5 miles to Burro Bridge, which crosses the West Dolores River. After crossing Burro Bridge, the road switches back and heads north to the well-marked trailhead. Another way to reach the trailhead is via Dunton Road, (Forest Service Road 535), which leaves CO 145 7 miles northeast of Rico and 10.5 miles southeast of Ophir (or 5.5 miles southeast of Lizard Head Pass). Dunton Road is a narrow, high-clearance dirt road with limited pullouts. After 4.5 miles, you will reach the Meadows. Another 3 miles (7.5 from CO 145) brings you to Navajo Lake Trailhead. The trail starts at about 9,300′ and follows the east side of the West Dolores River before crossing the river and passing through large meadows. These meadows offer excellent views of Dolores Peak to the west and El Diente to the east. Once past the meadows, the trail climbs through the forest to tree line at 11,400′ and then drops down to Navajo Lake at 11,154′. The trail is slightly under 5 miles long from the trailhead to Navajo Lake.

Navajo Lake Trail gives excellent access to the west ridge and north face of El Diente. After hiking 2 miles higher into Navajo Basin, the north face of Mount Wilson, the northwest ridge of Gladstone, and the southwest ridge of Wilson Peak are also accessible. The Navajo Lake Trail also can be used as access to Dolores Peak by turning northwest at the meadows about 1.25 miles up the trail.

Gladstone from Navajo Lake.

Kilpacker Creek Trail (Kilpacker Basin)

Kilpacker Creek Trail provides an alternate means of access to Mount Wilson and El Diente. The advantage to this approach is that the backpack is shorter than Navajo Lake Trail—just 4 miles and 1,000′ of elevation gain rather than 5 miles and 2,100′ vertical. The disadvantage is that the trail is more rugged. The initial objective is to reach the Meadows on Dunton Road between Dunton and CO 145. Dunton Road is a narrow, dirt road with limited pullouts. Just west of a seemingly abandoned ranch house (Morgan Camp on the USGS map) at 10,100′, the road starts to lose elevation and eventually switchbacks down at this point. The well-marked parking area for the trailhead angles off Dunton Road to the right, 5.1 miles west of CO 145. From there, the trail, at first an abandoned jeep road, heads west for 1.7 miles, gaining little elevation before it crosses Kilpacker Creek at 10,200′. Once reaching Kilpacker Creek, either continue north to join Navajo Lake Trail or turn right (east) and parallel the creek for a little less than a mile where you cross the creek and head up the north bank of the creek across lush meadows for less than a mile. There is a good camp spot located in pine trees beneath a spectacular waterfall at about 11,000′.

The San Miguels as seen from Beaver Park at sunrise, from left to right: Wilson Peak, Fowler, Boskoff, Mount Wilson, El Diente, Middle Peak, and Dunn.

Woods Lake Trailhead

Woods Lake Trailhead provides alternative access to Navajo Lake and Mount Wilson, Wilson Peak, El Diente, and Gladstone Peak from the northwest. From Colorado Highway 145, turn south onto Fall Creek Road (San Miguel County Road 57P, FSR 618). Continue south and stay right at the junction 4 miles in. Pass two more junctions before reaching the trailhead, continuing straight at both. After 8.9 miles, you will reach the Woods Lake Campground, where you will turn right toward the campground and park at the trailhead. To reach Woods Lake Trail, continue 200 yards southeast from the parking lot to a signed start of the trail.

Fish Creek (FSR 611)

Fish Creek provides the most direct access to Dolores, Middle, and Dunn Peaks. About 0.5 mile north of Dunton, a well-maintained gravel road turns off and heads northwest for Groundhog Reservoir. About 4 miles from the turnoff, you will reach Fish Creek. With 4WD, you can continue up the Fish Creek drainage for another 0.5 mile. If you are interested in the southwest face of Dolores Peak, take the right-hand turn at 0.3 mile.

Lone Cone Road

At 1.5 miles east of Norwood on CO Highway 145, turn south on County Road 44Z S, which is marked as Lone Cone Road. About 10.6 miles after turning off CO 145, the road turns to dirt and is designated Forest Service Road 610. Turn hard left on Beef Trail Road at mile 12 and turn right on 46 M Road at mile 14.5. At mile 19.5, stay straight at the junction with West Beaver Creek Road. Turn right on FSR 612 at 20.9 miles, take a rough, rocky road (avoiding a left-hand turn on a road at mile 23.7), and reach a small trailhead of sorts at 24.9 miles. From the trailhead, follow an old road that has become a trail for a little over a mile, where you reach timberline at a point that puts you in position to view both the northeast and northwest ridges of Lone Cone.

CLIMBING ROUTES

Wilson Peak

14,017′ RANK 48

The iconic Wilson Peak can be seen prominently from many locations and especially from Last Dollar Road near Telluride. It is featured on the Coors beer can. The variety of approaches and solid Class 3 rock on its standard route makes it a beloved classic.

Southwest Ridge

From Rock of Ages TH at 10,350′: 4.5 miles, 3,820′
From Wilson Mesa/Bilk Basin TH at 9,750′: 6.5 miles, 4,600′
From Navajo Lake TH at 9,360′: 7.8 miles, 5,000′
From Navajo Lake at 11,154′: 3.5 miles, 3,000′
From Kilpacker Basin TH at 10,100′: 9 miles; 4,840′
From Woods Lake TH at 9,470′: 7.7 miles, 5,260′
From Cross Mountain TH at 10,040′: 7.5 miles, 5,200′

This is the easiest and most popular route up Wilson Peak. From the Silver Pick Basin area, climb to the 13,020′ pass overlooking the Rock of Ages Mine on the well-established Rock of Ages Trail. From the pass, contour up to the saddle on the ridge between Wilson Peak and Gladstone (if coming from Bilk Basin, your ascent begins here). From this ridge, descend slightly to a climbers' trail that traverses up the right (east) side of the southwest ridge below the ridge to the east, to circumvent cliffs, before scrambling up broken rock to reach the southwest ridge at about 13,450′. It's possible to gain the southwest ridge earlier, but that would involve significantly more difficult climbing and some loss of elevation once the ridge is gained. Once on the ridge, you will need to make a short Class 3+ downclimb on the west side, shortly

A climber summits Mount Wilson's north face; Wilson Peak is at center with Gladstone at right.

below the summit, which involves some exposure. Although this exposure is considerable, it is very solid rock that has been traveled a great deal over the years, so most of the loose rock has been eliminated. A steep but well-broken-up face leads you back to the ridge and summit.

West Face

From Rock of Ages TH at 10,350′: 4.5 miles, 3,820′

This is the most direct route on Wilson Peak, but it requires routefinding and off-trail climbing skills. At 12,560′, the trail up Silver Pick Basin makes a 90-degree turn and begins to contour south toward the pass above the Rock of Ages Mine. Rather than turning right and contouring toward the pass, continue up into the basin below the west face of Wilson Peak. Early in the year, this basin usually has a large snowfield. Once in the basin, there are several Class 3+ variations that lead to the southwest ridge and then to the summit. Later in the year, expect to encounter talus and loose rock. It is also possible to gain the southwest ridge from the west by continuing on the Silver Pick Basin Trail a short distance after it turns south at 12,800′ and then climbing left, up the prominent gully that meets the southwest ridge at 13,700′. Although passable, this gully is a jumble of loose rock.

South Face

From Wilson Mesa/Bilk Basin TH at 9,750′: 6.5 miles, 4,700′

In late spring and early summer, the south face is a moderate (30- to 45-degree) snow climb. From the old miner's cabin in Bilk Basin at 12,800′, head directly up the face to gain the southwest ridge. Once the snow is gone, the route is covered by loose talus and loses its attraction.

Mount Wilson

14,246′ RANK 16

Mount Wilson, the taller of the two Wilsons, offers a variety of mountaineering challenges sure to satiate even the hardiest of climbers. The two Wilsons are 1.5 miles apart and connected via a long ridge extending south and west from Wilson Peak, with Gladstone perched between the two, forming one of the most impressive and rotten ridges in the San Juans. There is debate as to what approach to Mount Wilson is the easiest. We found the approach from Kilpacker via the southwest flank in summer to be the easiest and least traveled.

North Face

From Rock of Ages TH at 10,350′: 5.4 miles, 4,712′

From Wilson Mesa/Bilk Basin TH at 9,750′: 8 miles, 5,840′

From Navajo Lake TH at 9,360′: 7.2 miles, 5,130′

From Navajo Lake at 11,154′: 2.6 miles, 3,000′

From Kilpacker Basin TH at 10,100′: 8.5 miles, 4,950′

From Woods Lake TH at 9,470′: 7 miles, 5,330′

Often considered to be the standard route for Mount Wilson, this approach involves an airy and memorable final pitch sure to excite even the most experienced mountaineer. The north face is accessible either by downclimbing 600′ from the Rock of Ages pass connecting Silver Pick Basin and Navajo Basin or by climbing east from Navajo Lake, high into Navajo Basin following a well-used trail. Until shortly below the summit, the north face is not particularly difficult. Although it does require some scrambling, there are several variations that lead toward the final summit ridge. The last ridge section involves exposed and at times precarious Class 4 climbing along a thin ridge that, although it appears unstable, is relatively firm.

Southwest Flank

From Kilpacker Basin TH at 10,100′: 6 miles, 4,200′

In winter or spring, from high and far east in Kilpacker Basin via Kilpacker Creek Trail, the southwest flank of Mount Wilson presents (when snow conditions are right) a moderate snow climb that's not possible later in the year when it's more of a talus slog. Aim for a narrow couloir that leads you up to a spot about 100′ north to the summit where you finish on the same narrow, exposed ridge that completes the north face route. In summer and autumn, this route has a very well-established trail leading up from the Kilpacker Creek Trail that is Class 1 until the final 1,000′ of the climb, where it begins to cross several boulder fields, a snow field, and some easy Class 3 sections of rock directly below the summit. To gain the summit, you will partially ascend a well-traveled gully, cross a solid rock rib and ascend another short gully to a notch and then up to the summit. An airy but easy Class 3 move is required on the summit block itself. This route combines well with the south flank route of El Diente for those looking to avoid the more technical traverse while completing both in a long day with a solid weather window. The junction for both climbs is at the 12,640′ cairn.

Mount Wilson—El Diente Traverse

This classic 0.8-mile traverse is undoubtedly one of the most difficult ridges between 14ers and has claimed many lives, so extreme caution should be given. The ridge is 0.8 mile long. The low point is 346′ below Mount Wilson and 259′ below El Diente. When these 14ers are climbed together, via the ridge, it is best to climb Mount Wilson first. The first two-thirds of the ridge involves some scrambling and exposure but is not unreasonably difficult. At this point, however, you are confronted with a 30′ rappel or a severe Class 4 downclimb. After the rappel, it's best to drop off the ridge to the south (left) to avoid a series of rock pinnacles called the Organ Pipes before regaining the ridge shortly below the El Diente summit. The rock on the ridge is hard, highly fractured, and fairly stable; however, in years of extreme moisture, the rock becomes more unstable.

Topping out on the summit of El Diente, with Gladstone and Mount Wilson in the background.

El Diente

14,159′ **UNRANKED**

El Diente, located just 0.8 mile west of Mount Wilson, is Spanish for "the tooth." Anyone who has seen it from the summit of Mount Wilson or from the safety of Beaver Park to the west can recognize the resemblance.

North Flank

From Rock of Ages TH at 10,350′: 5 miles, 4,360′

From Navajo Lake TH at 9,360′: 7.5 miles, 5,230′

From Navajo Lake at 11,154′: 2.6 miles, 3,000′

From Woods Lake TH at 9,470′: 7 miles, 5,610′

There are a couple of routes on the north side of El Diente for climbers who are comfortable on both snow and rock. These are best accessed via Navajo Lake Trail or Rock of Ages Trail. The Class 4 north buttress route climbs directly up to El Diente's summit from the north on rock. Another Class 4 route climbs the snowfield northeast of the summit, aiming for the notch in the Mount Wilson–El Diente ridge east of El Diente and then finishes on the steep, highly fractured, but solid Class 4 climbing from the notch to summit. A tromp or glissade down the steep snow field is usually the preferred descent and requires an ice ax.

South Flank

From Kilpacker Basin TH at 10,100′: 5.7 miles, 4,230′

This is the easiest route up El Diente. Using the Kilpacker Creek approach affords a safer route that requires slogging a scree field on El Diente's south flank after the

El Diente from near Beaver Park to the west.

snow has melted off for the season. Make an ascending traverse high up into Kilpacker Basin until you are east of El Diente's summit and the notch in the Mount Wilson and El Diente ridge. At a cairned location at 12,640', climb north-northwest up an established trail through a large scree field. Care and attention in routefinding should be given to stay below the dangerous overhangs to the north and west to gain the notch in the ridge at 13,840'. Finish with a Class 4 climb from the notch to the summit to the west following a well-established but loose trail. This route combines well with the southwest flank route of Mount Wilson for those looking to avoid the more technical traverse while completing both in a long day with a solid weather window. The junction for both climbs is at the 12,640' cairn.

Gladstone Peak

13,913' RANK 67

Gladstone Peak is easily recognized from many angles due to its pyramid shape. It is found on a connecting ridge between both of the Wilsons and is one of the least enjoyable climbs in the area due to its loose and dangerous rock.

North Ridge

From Rock of Ages TH at 10,350': 5 miles, 3,830'

From Wilson Mesa/Bilk Basin TH at 9,750': 6.7 miles, 4,450'

From Navajo Lake TH at 9,360': 8.2 miles, 5,070'

From Navajo Lake at 11,154': 3.7 miles, 2,900'

From Woods Lake TH at 9,470': 8 miles, 5,240'

The Gladstone approach from Bilk Basin.

The north ridge is the easiest way to climb Gladstone; however, the route is filled with loose rock and large boulders that are easily toppled on climbers below, so great care should be given on this route, especially in early-season conditions when snow has not fully melted and rocks can slide down snow fields. From either Navajo Lake or Bilk Basin, gain the ridge between Gladstone and Wilson Peak at its lowest point and follow it directly to the summit. Some routefinding is required to avoid loose and nasty rock. The Bilk Basin approach to here is particularly beautiful and offers a full alpine experience with excellent views of Lizard Head. The ridge is narrow and covered with large blocks, some of which are not stable. At Class 3, Gladstone's north ridge is not technically difficult, but it can be unsettling and, in at least one case, has proved to be fatal. About 200′ below the summit, you will be forced left (east) from the ridge by a narrow spot; however, the rest of the climb from here is straightforward.

The San Miguels as seen from Beaver Park at sunset, from left to right: Wilson Peak, Fowler, Boskoff, Mount Wilson, El Diente, and Middle Peak.

Fowler Peak—"Big Bear Peak"

13,498′ **RANK 256**

Fowler Peak is located on a connecting ridge 1.5 miles west of Wilson Peak and 1 mile east of Boskoff Peak. Charlie Fowler and Chris Boskoff were residents of Norwood, Colorado, at the time of their tragic deaths during an alpine climb in Tibet in 2006. The bill renaming these two peaks was passed in January 2019.

East Ridge

From Rock of Ages TH at 10,350′: 2.75 miles, 3,090′

This is the most direct route for Fowler Peak. From Rock of Ages Trailhead, hike to the trail junction at 11,000′ and instead of going left (northeast) for Wilson Peak, continue south on Elk Creek Trail. At approximately 11,400′, turn left (south) up an old winding mining road, climbing into the basin between Fowler Peak and Peak 13,540′. Continue up the road to its end at 12,820′. From here, continue up loose and dangerous Class 2+ talus to the saddle. The route up Fowler from here is quite challenging. Head west on the ridge toward Fowler's summit, avoiding the highest section of the ridge for the last 300′ of climbing, where you'll want to traverse across talus to a gully just left (south) of the ridge. This gully contains Class 3+ moves that should be tested due to the looseness of the rock here. The summit is a short scramble from the top of the gully.

Boskoff Peak—"Woods Peak"

13,123′ **RANK 548**

Boskoff Peak is connected via a ridge 1 mile west of Fowler Peak. Many brave mountaineers may find the traverse from Fowler to Boskoff to be tempting; however, it is fraught with loose and unsafe Class 5 terrain. The more sensible approach is from Elk Creek Trail via Rock of Ages TH or from Woods Lake TH.

West Ridge

From Rock of Ages TH at 10,350′: 4.1 miles, 3,020′

From Woods Lake TH at 9,470′: 3.25 miles, 3,260′

From either Woods Lake or Rock of Ages, head to the intersection of Elk Creek Trail and Woods Lake Trail. From here, continue southeast for 0.1 mile, where you will leave the trail and head left (east) up the Class 2 slopes of Boskoff until you reach the summit.

Lizard Head Peak and the Milky Way core.

Lizard Head

13,113′ RANK 556

Lizard Head is one of the most recognizable peaks in Colorado. The summit block is the remnant of an ancient volcano and rises 300 vertical feet. Lizard Head is often considered the most difficult 13,000+′ peak to climb in all of Colorado. The most direct access to Lizard Head is from Cross Mountain TH.

South Dihedral (aka South Chimney)

From Cross Mountain TH at 10,040′: 3.7 miles, 3,073′

From Lizard Head TH at 9,870′: 5 miles, 3,760′

For many climbers, Lizard Head is a once-in-a-lifetime crucible. The first pitch starts near the large dihedral on the south face of the summit block. Initially, the route follows the right side of the dihedral for nearly 80′ to a platform. From the platform, cross to the left side of the dihedral and then finish with an exposed traverse to the left, high on the wall. The first 80′ is around 5.6 on seriously loose rock. Above the platform, the climbing is 5.7 on better rock. From the top of the first pitch, a talus-strewn ramp leads to the second pitch on the west side of the upper cliff band. The second pitch starts in a 75′ vertical chimney. The crux (5.8) is a small overhang, or bulge, low in the chimney. Above the overhang, you can traverse left out of the chimney into a gray-colored gully to finish. A #4 camming device works well to protect the overhang.

Lone Cone

12,613′ **RANK 927**

In 1876, William L. Marshall, of the Wheeler Survey, reported in the survey's *Annual Report of the Chief of Engineers for 1876* that Lone Cone "is the most beautiful peak I have ever seen. It is entirely detached from the other mountains, and rises, a solitary, graceful peak, 3,000 feet above its base. It was named by me, West Point. This is the last peak to the west [in Colorado]."

Northeast Ridge

From Lone Cone Road at 10,950′: 1.38 miles, 1,600′

The lower section of the Class 4 northeast ridge is made up of small, loose spires, which you work your way over and around on exposed terrain. Many climbers break out a rope at this point. The lower section of the ridge is dark and extremely loose, and the upper section is gray and more stable than the lower section. Once on the upper ridge, some difficulties can be bypassed to the left (east).

Northwest Ridge

From Lone Cone Road at 10,950′: 1.43 miles, 1,600′

The Class 2 northwest ridge is composed of stable talus. Getting to the ridge requires crossing the huge rock glacier that forms the seat of the Devil's Chair, which is the formation created by the northern face of Lone Cone being the seat back and the northeast and northwest ridges being armrests. The northwest ridge is frequently used as a descent route for parties who have climbed the northeast ridge. It is easier, more stable, and less exposed than the northeast ridge.

Lone Cone from Beaver Park.

OFF THE BEATEN PATH

Sunshine Mountain

12,930′ RANK 696

1.8 miles northeast of Lizard Head

From Wilson Mesa/Bilk Basin TH at 9,750′: 2.8 miles, 3,250′

Northwest Ridge: From tree line, a Class 2 route on the northwest ridge curves its way to the summit.

Cross Mountain

12,703′ UNRANKED

1 mile west-southwest of Lizard Head

From Cross Mountain TH at 10,040′: 4.3 miles, 2,770′

From Lizard Head TH at 9,870′: 5.9 miles, 3,810′

East Ridge: A climbers' trail takes you on an ascending traverse to a 20′ steep, gravelly Class 3 section that places you on easier terrain above.

Dolores Peak

13,290′ RANK 409

5 miles west of El Diente

From Fish Creek Road at 10,210′: 2 miles, 3,000′

Southwest Face: A Class 2 route on the southwest face leads you to the summit over loose scree and talus.

Middle Peak

13,300′ RANK 393

5.8 miles west of El Diente

From Fish Creek Road at 10,210′: 2.8 miles, 3,120′

Northwest Ridge: As part of a traverse from Dunn Peak, the northwest ridge is a Class 2 route on steep, broken rock.

Wilson Peak, Gladstone, and El Diente at upper left; Middle at right.

Dunn Peak

12,595′ RANK 915

1.7 miles west-northwest of Dolores Peak

From Fish Creek Road at 10,900′: 1.3 miles, 1,700′

South Ridge: A Class 2 walk-up along the south ridge is an easy snow climb in late spring or early summer. Later in the year, the route is composed of stable scree.

SNEFFELS RANGE 3

Left to right: Mount Ridgway, Reconnoiter, Teakettle, Cirque, Kismet, and Sneffels.

The Sneffels Range is, with the exception of the Needles-Grenadiers, the largest concentration of high, rugged peaks in the San Juans. The monarch of the range, Mount Sneffels, is a beautiful mountain and certainly one of the most interesting not only in the San Juans but in Colorado.

Sneffels offers an excellent variety of climbing from the moderate standard route up the southeast couloir to the rugged north face with its steep snow and ice couloirs. Other interesting aspects of Sneffels are the rock pinnacles that flank its northwest and western ridges. On the lower portion of the northwest ridge, three spectacular pinnacles—The Hand, The Penguin, and The Thumb—are closely clustered. Higher on the ridge is the prominent Purgatory Point. To the southwest lie the Wolf's Tooth, Blue Needle, and The Monolith.

Although Sneffels is the only 14,000′ peak in the group, both Dallas Peak and Teakettle Mountain exceed 13,800′ in elevation. Dallas is regarded by many climbers to be the most difficult of the highest one hundred peaks (the Centennials) in Colorado to climb. Teakettle is also a very challenging climb. Its summit pinnacle is an interesting geological formation with what looks like the handle of a teakettle formed by a perfectly circular hole.

Teakettle is one of a series of high peaks that extend east from Mount Sneffels to the north of Yankee Boy Basin. Just east of Sneffels lies Kismet. Kismet is separated from Mount Sneffels to the west by Scree Col and from Cirque Mountain to the east by Dike Col. The ridge culminates to the east with Potosi, whose flat summit is guarded by spectacular 200′ cliffs.

Yankee Boy Basin is bounded on the south by Gilpin Peak, Mount Emma, and Mendota Peak. Spectacular Saint Sophia Ridge is a rugged line of rotten rock pinnacles, which separates Mount Emma and Mendota Peak. Dallas Peak, West Dallas Peak, and "T-0" lie to the west of Gilpin Peak at the head of Blue Lakes Basin.

CLIMBING HISTORY

Undoubtedly, many peaks in the Sneffels group were climbed by miners who did not record their exploits. During a climb of Gilpin Peak in 1952, John Filsinger found an old hand-forged miner's pick just below the summit. The first recorded ascent in the area was Mount Sneffels by the Hayden Survey on September 10, 1874. The team reached the southwest ridge, which, according to Franklin Rhoda's *Summits to Reach,* they "had to climb with care" since it "was quite steep in some places."

Sneffels's present name is a corruption of the name given by the Hayden Survey after the Icelandic volcano described in Jules Verne's *Journey to the Center of the Earth*. Standing in the basin below the north face of Sneffels, a member of the survey team accompanying Frederick Endlich compared the chasm to the great hole described by Verne. Endlich agreed and pointed to the peak above exclaiming, "There's Snaefell!"

The first recorded ascent of a peak in the group other than Sneffels was made in August 1929, when Charles Rolfe and Alonzo Hartman climbed Teakettle Mountain. Although Rolfe and Hartman were with a party of four, the other two climbers stopped at the base of the summit pinnacle.

In the early 1930s, one of the primary objectives of the San Juan Mountaineers was the north face of Sneffels, which they climbed by different routes in 1931, 1932, and 1933. In his report of the 1931 climb in *Trail and Timberline*, Dwight Lavender noted that "the taunting north face of Mount Sneffels, untrodden by men, had beckoned to us for years."

Lavender, Mel Griffiths, Charles Kane, and Gordon Williams climbed the lower portion of the north face on July 16, 1931, by the east couloir. On July 6, 1932, Lavender, Griffiths, and Williams returned to the north face and chose a route up the right, or northwest, couloir. Lavender reported in *American Alpine Journal* that "the couloir proved to be a veritable hell of snow: hard snow, crusted snow, soft snow, and soggy snow."

The San Juan Mountaineers achieved a direct route on the north face in 1933. In August of that year, Lavender, Griffiths, Lewis Giesecke, Henry McClintock, Mary McClintock, and Frank McClintock climbed directly up to the great cliff that splits the center of the face. At one point, the party narrowly avoided disaster. Griffiths was leading and had taken a detour around an overhang. Lavender was climbing behind Griffiths, and the two climbers were having difficulty hearing each other. Griffiths thought that Lavender was planning to climb the overhang directly. Unknown to Griffiths, who was giving a shoulder belay, Lavender was actually planning to do a pendulum swing to a crack. Griffiths reported in *Trail and Timberline* (January 1941):

> *Before I was ready, his full weight came swinging down on the ropes and I was fighting to keep my balance on the narrow ledge. For an instant I let the rope slide over my shoulder while I dug in my heels. Then I clamped down tight. The shock brought me half to my knees before I could stop his fall. A moment later he was dangling free below the overhang, and I was thanking my lucky stars that we had spent some hours during the summer in belay practice.*

After the early difficulties, the group made better time higher on the face and reached the summit after ten hours of climbing.

Another objective of the San Juan Mountaineers was the pinnacles to the northwest and west of Sneffels: The Hand, Wolf's Tooth, and The Thumb in July 1932 and Blue Needle, The Monolith, and Penguin in 1933. Although the San Juan Mountaineers conducted a reconnaissance of Purgatory Point, it appears to be the only major pinnacle on the northwest or west side of Mount Sneffels that they did not climb in the early 1930s. That honor was apparently left to Henry and Frank McClintock, whose report in the May 1958 *Trail and Timberline* indicates that they climbed Purgatory Point some time prior to 1958.

The climbers of the 1934 Colorado Mountain Club did not limit themselves to the pinnacles on Mount Sneffels. They also made several notable ascents of high peaks in the area. Don McBride and Everett Long reached the summit of Dallas Peak after "extremely careful and delicate climbing," which at one point involved a shoulder stand. After climbing T-0—which was first climbed in July 1933 by Griffiths—A. C. Bartlett and Robert Blair traversed the east ridge of West Dallas Peak to make its first ascent.

After the intensive activity of the early 1930s, it seemed as if there was not much to do in the area. Virtually all the first ascents were taken up by the San Juan Mountaineers' burst of activity. Over twenty years passed before there were reports of new routes in the area. In 1958, *Trail and Timberline* reported that David Lewis and Frank McClintock climbed the difficult northwest ridge of Mount Sneffels, which, as far as the men knew, was "the only major ridge or face route upon the peak that had not yet been climbed."

Interest was renewed in Dallas Peak in 1976 when Spencer Swanger made a solo climb of the peak, which was the last of the hundred highest peaks in Colorado that he had not climbed. Swanger reported in *Trail and Timberline* (September 1976) that of the nearly three hundred climbs he had made, "perhaps . . . this had been the toughest." Swanger had reviewed the *San Juan Mountaineer's Climber's Guide to Southwest Colorado*, written two years prior to McBride and Long's ascent of Dallas in 1934. Since he did not find either a cairn or register on the peak, Swanger incorrectly speculated that he had made a first ascent. In fact, his ascent was probably a third ascent. Stuart Krebs also made a solo climb of Dallas in July 1956.

The first winter ascent of Sneffels was accomplished in February 1934 by Mel Griffiths and Gordon Williams. They approached Sneffels from Blaine Basin, climbed up Scree Col, and then the couloir on the southeast face to the summit. In January 1983, Kitty Calhoun and Lyle Dean climbed the north face of Sneffels. Per a 1984 report in *American Alpine Journal*, Calhoun and Dean climbed the "eastern couloir of the north face for 100 feet and traversed on to the main face," which they then climbed directly to the summit. They reported that the climbing "varied from excellent 60-degree snow to several mixed rock pitches. One open bivouac was made about halfway up the face."

ACCESS AND HIKING

Yankee Boy Basin

Yankee Boy Basin is the most popular point of access to the Sneffels Range. To reach the basin, turn west off US Highway 550 just south of Ouray on a well-maintained gravel road. After leaving US 550, the road heads up spectacular Canyon Creek toward Camp Bird. When you reach the Camp Bird turnoff at 4.7 miles, stay right and follow the road as it travels past the old town of Sneffels. Shortly after the Camp Bird turnoff, you encounter a point where the road was actually dug into the side of the cliff, with part of the cliff overhanging the road. At 6.7 miles from US 550, you reach the parking spot for 2WD vehicles at 10,700′. At 7.7 miles, you reach the lower 4WD parking at 11,350′. Hardcore 4WDers can drive to a point 9.4 miles from US

SNEFFELS RANGE (WEST)

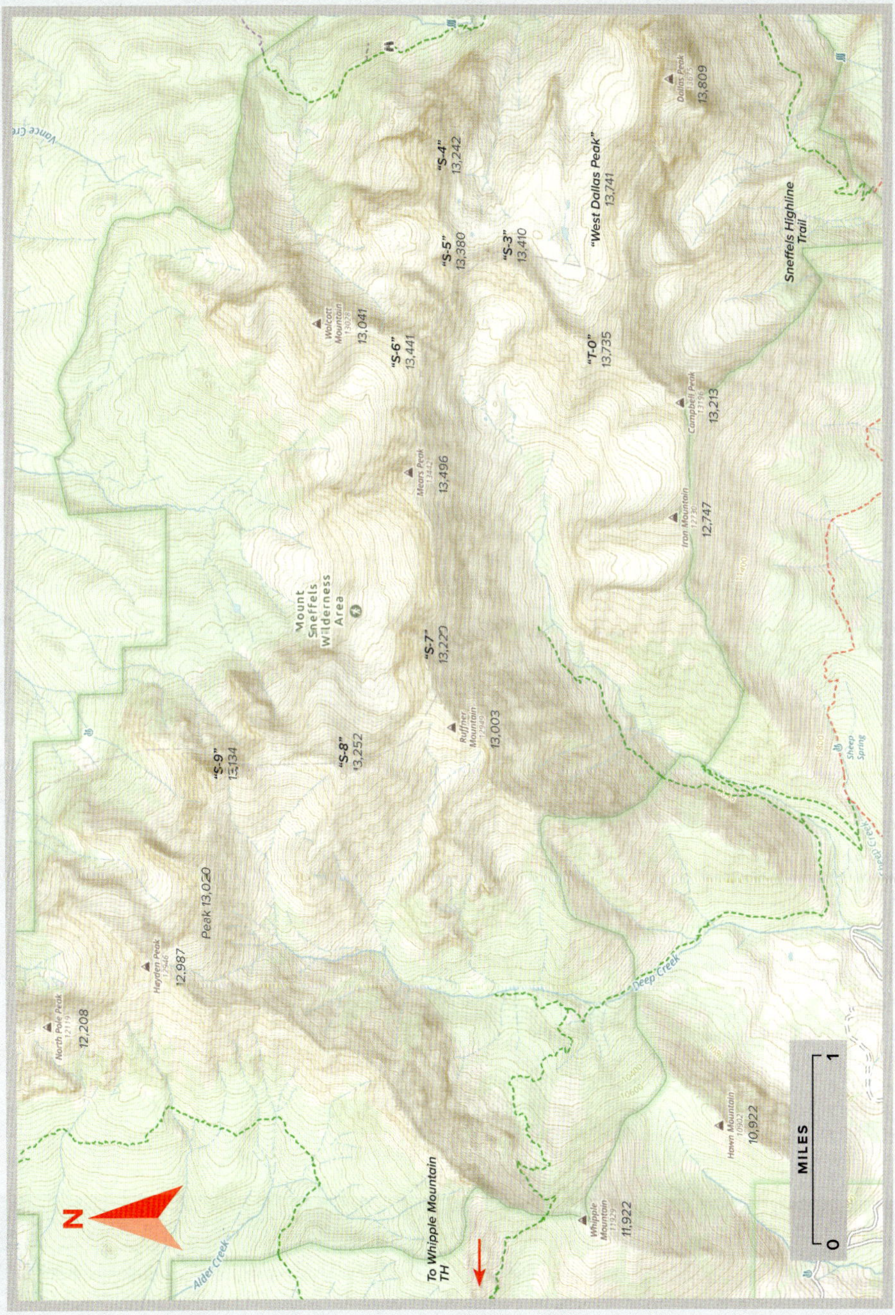

SNEFFELS RANGE (EAST)

550 at 12,460′ directly south of Kismet. Yankee Boy Basin is the best means of access for climbing Sneffels by the southeast couloir and southwest ridge, Kismet, Cirque, Teakettle, Potosi, and Gilpin. Blue Lakes Pass, at 12,980′, connects Yankee Boy Basin and Blue Lakes Basin. Lavender Col at 13,580′ between Sneffels and Kismet and Dike Col at 13,060′ between Kismet and Cirque connect Yankee Boy Basin with Blaine Basin to the north. Even as overcrowded as it is with vehicles and people, Yankee Boy Basin is a beautiful, awe-inspiring place.

Governor Basin

The initial access for Governor Basin is the same as that for Yankee Boy Basin. After driving past Camp Bird on Forest Service Road 361 up Canyon Creek, continue for a total of 6.9 miles where the 4WD road takes off to the right for Yankee Boy Basin. Rather than taking a right, continue straight ahead on the 4WD road on the right side of Sneffels Creek. At mile 7.2, turn left (south) and cross over Sneffels Creek where you head southwest until you take a left at a junction crossing over to the east side of Governor Basin and switchback your way up to the upper basin. Governor Basin provides the best means of access for Mendota Peak, Mount Emma, and "T-5."

Blaine Basin

The initial turnoff to Blaine Basin is located 5 miles west of US Highway 550 (Ridgway) on Colorado Highway 62 where you turn left (south) on East Dallas Creek Road. After leaving CO 62, stay right at 2.1 miles and continue for a total of 9.2 miles until you reach Blue Lakes Trailhead. The best approach for Blaine Basin follows Blue

Right to left: Sneffels, Cirque, Teakettle, and Ridgway.

Left to right: Dallas Peak, West Dallas Peak, and T-0, all above Blue Lakes.

Lakes Trail for 100 yards before angling off to the left (east) on an abandoned road and crossing the stream on what is left of an old bridge. After crossing the stream, the trail gains a bit of elevation and contours to meet Wilson Creek, which you cross to the north and then parallel for a half mile before crossing the stream again. Stay on the south side for another half mile before switching back to the north for good. There are a total of four stream crossings. Depending on time of year, it may be necessary to wade the stream at one or two of the crossings. Most of the elevation is gained over the last mile. The total distance to Blaine Basin is 2.5 miles with a gain of 1,400′. There are several good camping spots in the flats of the basin. Both the Forest Service and USGS maps show a road that leaves the main road about 7 miles from CO 62 and angles up to reach Wilson Creek. Although this road used to provide more direct access, it is now closed by a locked gate. Blaine Basin provides an excellent campsite for those interested in the north face of Mount Sneffels or the northeast couloir of Kismet. It is also possible to climb Cirque from Dike Col or the standard route on Sneffels from Scree Col. Dike Col is much steeper on the Blaine Basin side than the Yankee Boy Basin side.

Blue Lakes Trail

The initial access to Blue Lakes Trail is the same as that for Blaine Basin. The trailhead is 9.2 miles south of Colorado Highway 62 on East Dallas Creek Road. Lower Blue Lake is 3.5 miles and 1,600′ from the trailhead. From the lakes, the trail continues up to Blue Lakes Pass and Yankee Boy Basin. Blue Lakes Basin provides access to Gilpin Peak, "T-0," West Dallas Peak, and the southwest ridge of Sneffels. It also provides access to several seldom climbed "Off the Beaten Path" peaks west of Blue Lakes, including "S-3," "S-4," "S-5," "S-6," "S-7," and Mears Peak.

Mill Creek Road—Deep Creek Trail

Mill Creek Road is the standard beginning point for access to Dallas Peak, West Dallas Peak, T-0, and Campbell Peak. The turnoff to Mill Creek Road is 1 mile west of the roundabout at the western entrance to Telluride and 1.8 miles east of the roundabout on Colorado Highway 145. Initially Mill Creek Road heads north before turning left (west) and climbing a narrow section of the road with limited pullouts. At 0.7 mile, the road turns sharply to the right (west) near an access point to Elder Creek Trail and continues for a total of 1.6 miles to the trailhead near the Telluride Waterworks at an elevation of 9,400′. From the trailhead, hike north 0.4 mile on the west (left) side of Mill Creek to a junction where you turn left (west) and hike an additional 1.4 miles, for a total of 1.8 miles to a trail junction with Sneffels Highline Trail. Hike 0.6 mile north up Sneffels Highline Trail through a series of switchbacks to 11,200′, where the trail heads east-northeast and contours to the basin southwest of Dallas. As you round the south ridge of Dallas, near tree line, Mill Creek Basin comes into sight, and you are on Dallas Peak and ready to start climbing in earnest.

Whipple Mountain Trail

Whipple Mountain Trailhead is found on Last Dollar Road, a 4WD road that cuts through the Dallas Divide between Ridgway and Telluride. The trail provides access to some of the "Off the Beaten Path" peaks for this section, including Hayden Peak, Peak 13,020′, S-9, S-8, S-7, and Mears Peak. From Ridgway, head west on Colorado Highway 62 toward the Dallas Divide. After 11.3 miles, turn left (south) onto Last Dollar Road. Whipple Mountain Trail is 10.7 miles up Last Dollar Road on the left (north) near the top of the road. From Telluride, drive 2.75 miles west on Colorado Highway 145 and take a right (north) on Airport Road/ Last Dollar Road. Continue 9.7 miles on this 4WD road to the top of the pass and find the trail on your right (north).

Miller Mesa—Dallas Trail

Dallas Trail offers alternative access for a few peaks found in the "Off the Beaten Path" section, including Corbett Ridge, Whitehouse Mountain, and Mount Ridgway. From Ridgway, drive west on Colorado Highway 62 to Amelia Street. Go 0.25 mile and turn right on County Road 5. Drive 10.2 miles on an easy 4WD road to the trailhead.

CLIMBING ROUTES

Mount Sneffels

14,150′ **RANK 27**

One of the most recognizable peaks in the San Juans, Mount Sneffels is photogenic from every angle.

South Slopes/Lavender Couloir

From Yankee Boy Basin TH at 10,700′: 3.9 miles, 3,450′

From Yankee Boy Basin 4WD parking at 12,440′: 1.2 miles, 1,710′

From Blue Lakes TH at 9,410′: 6 miles, 5,050′

This route is not quite Class 3 but is more difficult than a standard Class 1 or Class 2 walk-up. It is a great way to get a taste of what some of the more difficult Class 3 peaks are like on this Class 2+ route. From Yankee Boy Basin TH, this is considered the standard and easiest route up Mount Sneffels. Hike up the road for 0.2 mile and continue 1.2 miles northwest on the trail to a junction at 11,415′. Continue 0.4 mile west up a rugged 4WD road to another junction at 11,760′. Leave the road and continue west for 0.6 mile and then north to 12,200′. Continue 0.3 mile and rejoin the road at its highest point (also known as the 4WD parking) where the Blue Lakes Trail starts at 12,440′. From the Blue Lakes Trail junction, hike 0.5 mile west through scree to 12,640′. Continue up the trail to 12,700′ just before it begins switchbacking up Blue Lakes Pass. Note: If coming from Blue Lakes TH, you will climb up and over Blue Lakes Pass and join the route at this point. Here, you leave Blue Lakes Trail and climb 0.4 mile north up the eastern side of the slope to the infamous 13,500′ Scree Col, which is well named. From Scree Col, the large, prominent southeast couloir known as Lavender Couloir lies to the northwest. The couloir is filled with large boulders and, until midsummer, a large snowbank. Near the top of the couloir, exit to the left by a Class 2+ V-shaped slot in the wall. The summit is a short scramble from this exit. From Scree Col, it is also possible to climb to the left of the couloir out onto the southeast face and follow a steep but well-broken, sustained Class 3 route that generally parallels the couloir. The route on the southeast face is clear of snow much earlier in the year than the couloir.

Class 3 terrain on the Sneffels northwest ridge route.

Southwest Ridge

From Yankee Boy Basin TH at 10,700': 3.9 miles, 3,450'

From Yankee Boy Basin 4WD parking at 12,440': 1.2 miles, 1,710'

From Blue Lakes TH at 9,410': 6 miles, 5,050'

From Yankee Boy Basin, the southwest ridge Class 3 route looks impossible because of the jagged pinnacles just north of Blue Lakes Pass; however, this route is an absolute classic. The easiest way to reach Blue Lakes Pass is by the trail in upper Yankee Boy Basin. It is also possible to reach the pass from Blue Lakes Trail, but this is much longer. From the pass, the pinnacles low on the ridge are easily passed to the left (west). Once past the pinnacles, climb into the prominent notch in the ridge, located just north of the pinnacles. Once in the notch, a south-facing gully leads up the upper ridge. The gully contains loose rock and involves some scrambling. Once on the ridge, stay directly on the ridge or just to the east in spots; there is a great deal of exposure to the west. In the spring and early summer, it is possible to gain the ridge by cramponing up to the notch from the east.

Starting the upper section of Snake Couloir. Photo by Bob Rosebrough

Northwest Couloir (Snake Couloir)

From Blaine Basin at 11,100′: 1.3 miles, 3,050′

The northwest couloir is on the right (west) side of the north face. When snow conditions are right, this is a classic Class 3 snow climb, one the best in the San Juans. When conditions aren't right, it's not a place you want to be. The right-slanting couloir at the base of Sneffels meets another couloir coming down from the summit, which is hidden from below. In winter, spring, and early summer (depending on snowfall), the route is all snow and ice until 100′ below the summit. The steepest portion of the couloir (45 to 50 degrees) is the 200′ just below the junction of the two couloirs. Helmets, crampons, and a couple of ice tools are essential. The route gets progressively more difficult over the course of the season as the snow turns to ice water.

North Buttress

From Blaine Basin at 11,100′: 1.3 miles, 3,050′

This direct Class 5 route climbs the central buttress on the north face, which is gained by traversing from the snowfield on a narrow ledge to the right. The lower part of the route is the most difficult section, following a broken, left-leaning ramp (5.6) that leads to easier ground above. Rockfall can be a problem on this route.

East Slopes

From Blaine Basin at 11,100′: 1.3 miles, 3,050′

This is the easiest (Class 2+) route from Blaine Basin, on the north side of the peak. Climb 1 mile south under the east face to 12,400′. Continue 0.15 mile southwest to 12,500′ and turn right (west) to begin climbing up a wide gully for 0.4 mile to Scree Col. From here, follow the standard south slopes route.

Peak 13,694′—"Kismet"

UNRANKED

Peak 13,694′ or "Kismet" is located 0.5 mile southeast of Mount Sneffels.

East Ridge

From Yankee Boy Basin TH at 10,700′: 3 miles, 3,000′

From Yankee Boy Basin 4WD parking at 12,440′: 1 mile, 1,530′

The initial objective on this route is Dike Col (13,060′ between Kismet and Cirque Mountain; see next entry). From Yankee Boy Basin, the climb up to Dike Col is easy. From Blaine Basin, it is steep and covered by a large snowbank. The summit of Kismet can't be seen from most points in Yankee Boy Basin. The false summit you see is the east shoulder of the peak. From Dike Col, the ridge gets progressively harder. The upper portion of the ridge is a Class 4 scramble over loose rock.

Cirque Mountain

13,686′ **RANK 155**

From Yankee Boy Basin TH and via Dike Col, Cirque Mountain is one the easier climbs in the area, located just 1.1 miles east of Mount Sneffels.

Southwest Ridge

From Yankee Boy Basin TH at 10,700′: 3.2 miles, 2,986′

From Yankee Boy Basin 4WD parking at 12,440′: 1.2 miles; 1,250′

From Dike Col, which splits Cirque and Kismet, bypass point 13,500′ to the left (north). The southwest ridge is a walk-up until you encounter a very short section of scrambling at 13,400′, just below the summit.

Teakettle Mountain

13,819′ **RANK 98**

The summit formation of Teakettle is spectacular and classic. Located 0.6 mile southeast of Cirque Mountain, Teakettle is one of the most recognizable and iconic peaks in the San Juans.

Author Matt Payne standing in the handle of Teakettle, gazing out at Dallas Peak.

Southeast Face

From Yankee Boy Basin TH at 10,700′: 2.25 miles, 4,000′

From Yankee Boy Basin 4WD parking at 11,300′: 1.35 miles, 3,400′

This is the standard and safest route. Traverse to the right (east) of the south basin and climb the southeast face of Teakettle directly below Coffeepot, a 13,568′ point located on the ridge between Teakettle and Potosi. Traverse left (west) below the base of Coffeepot and then climb a couloir with dark rock (called The Black Gully by many) to gain the southeast ridge, which is composed of loose volcanic scree. The summit pinnacle is climbed by a steep, 30′ pitch that culminates with a near-vertical 12′ Class 5.3 chimney on the east side. The summit is flat, airy, and comfortable for two to three climbers, but not more.

South Couloir

This route saves you 800′ of climbing, but most avoid it due to risk of rockfall on the approach. For most of the year, every way to get there is a slog up talus, with one exception: During a small window in late spring/early summer when the south-facing routes described here are covered with consolidated snow that you can climb with crampons and ice axes, both the approach and the summit pitch are great. For most of the year though, you have a choice between talus slogs. A point of reference for sorting out approach routes on Teakettle is the large basin south of the summit, bounded on the left (west) by the jutting southwest ridge and on the right (east) by the more rounded southeast face. Just to the right of the southwest ridge is the steep south couloir. Climb directly up the couloir, hugging the wall to your left. A helmet is essential, as you may encounter rockfall from above. Near the top of the couloir, exit to the right and gain the southeast ridge and continue the same way up as the southeast face route.

Coffeepot

13,568′ UNRANKED

Coffeepot is the unofficial name for the block aiguille located between Teakettle and Potosi.

Northwest Ridge

From Yankee Boy Basin TH at 10,700′: 1.8 miles, 3,750′

From Yankee Boy Basin 4WD parking at 11,300′: 1 mile, 3,150′

The initial approach is described under the southeast face route for Teakettle. The summit block is split by several off-width cracks and chimneys on the east face. The best alternatives are the 30′ chimney on the left (south) or the 20′ off-width crack that is 6 to 8 inches wide on the right (north). Both are lower Class 5 but hard to protect.

Potosi Peak

13,786′ RANK 113

Potosi Peak, one of the easternmost mountains in the Sneffels Range, is recognized by its flat-topped summit.

Teakettle, Coffeepot, and Potosi.

Coffeepot towers high with Potosi behind it, as seen from near the summit of Teakettle.

Southeast Flank

From Yankee Boy Basin Road at 10,700′: 1.5 miles, 3,200′

The starting point is located on Yankee Boy Basin Road, 6.2 miles from US Highway 550, where Imogene Pass Road turns to the left. The southeast flank starts out as a steep climb over grassy slopes that gives way to loose talus fields. From below, what appears to be the summit is not. The true summit is several hundred vertical feet above the false summit that you see. Once you pass the false summit and gain the base of the true summit block, contour right (east) to the east face. In contrast to the vertical cliffs surrounding the other side of the summit block, the east face is an enjoyable, well-cairned, Class 2+ scramble. The flat, spacious summit of Potosi is a pretty special place.

Southwest Flank

From Yankee Boy Basin Road at 11,190′: 1.5 miles, 2,600′

The route starts 700 vertical feet higher than the southeast flank route; it is less direct, however, and involves a contour around the peak to gain the east face. To begin, hike or drive up Yankee Boy Basin Road for about a mile after it turns to 4WD, and park where the road makes a turn to the left as it crosses a stream. From here, climb the rust-colored talus slope and then begin the contour around Potosi to the east to gain the summit by the same well-cairned, Class 2+ scramble described for the southeast flank. If you plan to ascend by the southwest flank, make sure to take a good look around when you top out on the first couloir after climbing the rust-colored talus slope. On your return, you need to be sure that you return by the same route. Several of the other couloirs on the lower portion of the southwest flank can be difficult.

North Couloir

From Weehawken TH at 8,770′: 4.5 miles, 5,000′

The north couloir on Potosi is a classic San Juan snow climb. It's shorter, at 900′, than the northwest couloir on Sneffels and not as difficult, at 40 degrees. It also avoids the talus slopes of the southside routes on Potosi. Primary access is from Weehawken Trail, 2.5 miles up Yankee Boy Basin Road from US Highway 550. The trade-off to avoiding the talus of the southside talus slopes is that the Weehawken Trail starts at around 8,770′, resulting in a total elevation gain on the climb of 5,000′.

Mendota Peak

13,275′ **UNRANKED**

Mendota Peak is located at the southeast end of Saint Sophia Ridge, 1.2 miles southeast of Mount Emma.

Left to right: Cirque, Teakettle, and Potosi, all rising above Yankee Boy Basin.

North Face and East Ridge

From Governor Basin Parking at 12,060′: 1.25 miles, 1,300′

Mendota Peak is located at the southeast end of Saint Sophia Ridge. After hiking or driving up the road into Governor Basin, climb into the basin northeast of the peak. From the basin, you will see twin points at 13,220′. Climb the western summit and then follow Mendota's east ridge, at Class 2+, to the summit. Remember that Mendota is the high point extending from Saint Sophia Ridge so as not to be confused by the rounded points (Peak 13,337′ and Peak 13,436′, aka T-5) located to the east, which are actually higher.

Peak 13,436′—"T-5"

RANK 293

T-5 is located 1 mile east of Mendota Peak.

Northwest Ridge

From Governor Basin parking at 12,060′: 1.3 miles, 1,376′

The approach for T-5 is by 4WD or on foot up Governor Basin aiming first for the Virginius Mine and then the saddle on the ridge between the summit of Mendota—the high point at the southern end of Saint Sophia Ridge. The talus slope below the saddle consists of large, loose rock. Once you gain the saddle, climb up and over point 13,337′ and follow T-5's Class 2+ northwest ridge to the summit.

Emma and the peaks east of Telluride, as seen from Gilpin.

Left: Gilpin (left of center) from Blue Lakes Pass. **Right:** Chossy rock found on the standard route for Gilpin Peak, a hallmark of the San Juans.

Mount Emma

13,581′ **RANK 197**

Mount Emma is connected by a ridge 0.8 mile south of Gilpin Peak and is one of the more recognizable peaks in the area due to a pyramid shape that's cut off on the top. It is also the craggy summit on the northern end of Saint Sophia Ridge.

East Face

From Governor Basin parking at 12,120′: 1 mile, 1,461′

From Governor Basin, climb northwest to gain the east flank of Mount Emma, which is composed of loose scree and talus. The summit block is an amalgamation of gullies and volcanic pillars presenting several Class 3+ and Class 4 route options that will challenge your routefinding skills.

Gilpin Peak

13,694′ **RANK 149**

Gilpin Peak is connected by a heinous ridge 1.2 miles south of Mount Sneffels and offers spectacular views of the entire subrange.

Northwest Ridge

From Yankee Boy Basin TH at 10,700′: 4.1 miles, 3,000′

From Yankee Boy Basin 4WD parking at 12,440′: 1.4 miles, 1,250′

From Blue Lakes T at 9,410′: 6.6 miles, 4,290′

Access this route from Blue Lakes Trail or Yankee Boy Basin. From Blue Lakes, it is recommended to descend partially into Yankee Boy Basin and begin from below the ridge connecting Mount Sneffels and Gilpin, as the ridge consists of Class 5 terrain and is very loose. From upper Yankee Boy Basin, leave Blue Lakes Trail at approximately 12,740′ and head south. Aim for the low point on the ridge that separates Blue Lakes Basin from Yankee Boy Basin. Early in the summer, it is possible to crampon up the 40-degree snowfield just east of the ridge to gain the upper ridge. Obstacles on the ridge are generally bypassed to the left (east). The rock is loose, but there is an obvious and well-traveled Class 2+ climbers' trail that makes an ascending traverse through loose boulders and talus. Once the upper portion of the ridge is gained, it is a walk-up to the summit, where your view of Sneffels is magnificent.

Dallas Peak

13,809′ **RANK 100**

Dallas Peak, the one-hundredth highest peak in Colorado, is one of the most difficult of the Centennial Peaks (highest one hundred) to climb.

East Ridge/North Face of Summit Block

From Mill Creek TH at 9,420′: 4.7 miles, 4,590′

From Mill Creek Basin, climb toward the middle section of the ridge that extends east from Dallas between the prominent couloirs. Climb directly up the flank of the

Dallas, West Dallas, and T-0, from Blue Lakes Pass.

east ridge angling up to the left. After topping out above the couloirs to your left (west), traverse below the east ridge on a climbers' trail and angle up toward the summit block. From below, you will see two prominent summit blocks. The north summit block appears higher and is the true summit. Although the route up to the east ridge involves some scrambling, the real difficulties do not begin until the last 200′, where climbers are faced with two separate pitches of Class 5 climbing. The first objective is to gain the ledges on the north side of the peak, below the summit block. At the base of the summit block is a small snowbank, which is the highest snowbank on the southeast face. To the right of the snowbank, between two blocks, is a short couloir, which is the best way to gain the ledges. At least one move in the short couloir is strenuous, and if you have a rope, you might as well break it out at that point. It is also possible to crampon up the snowbank, which appears to dead-end under large boulders. There is an exit to the right from the top of the snowbank, hidden from view when seen from below. Either variation will lead you to the ledge on the north face of the summit block, which you should traverse about 50′ to 75′ to a crack system that takes you directly up to the summit. The ledges leading to the crack system are broken up and wide enough that you do not feel the full extent of the exposure on the north face. The last 100′ of the crack system above you is lower Class 5 climbing. The amount of snow on the ledges and in the crack system is a variable that affects the route's difficulty. In mid- to late summer, the route is often snow-free. Once on the summit, you can downclimb the ascent route or rappel off the northeast face of the summit block down through a hole between two large dihedrals.

"T-0"

13,735′ **RANK 134**

T-0, located 1.4 miles west of Dallas Peak, is yet another high remote peak in the Sneffels Range that requires a long approach.

Southwest Ridge

From Eider Creek TH at 9,120′: 4.75 miles, 5,065′

From Eider Creek TH (see Mill Creek Road access, p. 63), hike 1.6 miles to Deep Creek Trail and head west (left). About a quarter mile after crossing Eider Creek, after coming to a ridge of sorts, leave the trail and head northwest through thick trees and downfall aiming for the steep, grassy, southeast flank of Campbell Peak. High up on Campbell, a cliff band is scaled by 80′ of Class 3 climbing to the right (east). Once through the cliff band, climb to the summit of Campbell Peak, descend 235′ to the saddle with T-0, and climb T-0's Class 2 southwest ridge on a climbers' trail over dinner-plate talus to the summit.

OFF THE BEATEN PATH

Mount Ridgway

13,468′ RANK 275

1 mile northeast of Teakettle Mountain

From Weehawken TH at 8,770′: 4.6 miles, 5,310′

East Ridge: From the Ridgway-Whitehouse saddle, it's an enjoyable Class 2+ scramble to the summit on talus.

Whitehouse Mountain

13,492′ RANK 260

3.5 miles west of Ouray and 1.9 miles northeast of Teakettle Mountain

From Weehawken TH at 8,770′: 5 miles, 5,510′

Southwest Slopes: From the Ridgway-Whitehouse saddle, it's a simple Class 2 walk-up.

"Corbett Ridge"

13,100′ RANK 571

0.5 mile northeast of Whitehouse Mountain

From Dallas TH at 9,890′: 2 miles, 3,090′

North Ridge: An off-trail scramble up steep Class 2+ talus.

"Reconnoiter Peak"

12,980′ RANK 650

0.7 mile northwest of Mount Ridgway

From Weehawken TH at 8,770′: 5.3 miles, 5,660′

West Gully: Often climbed with Mount Ridgway, the crux is the descent on chossy and dangerous Class 3 rock to a grassy ledge.

"S-4"

13,242′ RANK 445

1.4 miles north-northeast of Dallas Peak

From Blue Lakes TH at 9,410′: 5.3 miles, 4,170′

West Ridge: From west of Blue Lakes, a lower Class 4 route ascends to the west ridge up a red gully followed by loose talus to the summit.

"S-6"

13,441′ RANK 292

0.84 mile east of Mears Peak and 0.8 mile west of S-4

From Blue Lakes TH at 9,410′: 6.4 miles, 5,320′

Southeast Ridge: From the saddle between S-6 and S-3 descend west to 12,600′ and gain the southeast ridge up a Class 3 scree gully.

On the ascent of Dallas Peak, with West Dallas and T-0 behind.

"West Dallas Peak"

13,741′ **SOFT RANKED**

0.5 mile west of Dallas Peak

From Mill Creek TH at 9,420′: 4.5 miles, 4,296′

West Ridge: From the saddle with T-0, the Class 2+ west ridge is moderately exposed and requires some scrambling in a couple of spots.

Campbell Peak

13,213′ **UNRANKED**

1.7 miles west of Dallas Peak

From Eider Creek TH at 9,120′: 4.5 miles, 4,090′

Southeast Flank: Climb up steep, grassy slopes on the southeast flank. The cliff band high on the peak is scaled by an 80′ Class 3 climb.

Hayden Peak

12,987′ **UNRANKED**

3 miles northwest of Mears Peak

From Whipple Mountain TH at 10,700′: 5.9 miles, 4,090′

South Slopes: Climb Whipple Mountain Trail up Deep Creek, leave the trail, and climb Class 2 terrain up the south slopes.

Peak 13,030′

RANK 625

0.3 mile southeast of Hayden Peak

From Whipple Mountain TH at 10,700′: 6.2 miles, 4,280′

Northwest Ridge: A steep but short Class 2 climb on talus from Hayden Peak.

"S-9"

13,134′ RANK 543

0.85 mile east of Peak 13,030′

From Whipple Mountain TH at 10,700′: 7.1 miles, 4,860′

South Face: From Peak 13,030′, traverse below the southwest face and up the south face on Class 3 talus and rock.

"S-8"

13,252′ RANK 440

0.7 mile south of S-9

From Whipple Mountain TH at 10,700′: 7.9 miles, 5,300′

North Ridge: A Class 1 walk-up from below the south face of S-9.

"S-7"

13,220′ RANK 464

0.75 mile southeast of S-8

From Whipple Mountain TH at 10,700′: 7.9 miles, 5,300′

West Ridge: Downclimb the southwest ridge of S-8 to the saddle between S-8 and S-7 and up the summit on Class 2 terrain.

Mears Peak

13,496′ RANK 259

3.8 miles west of Mount Sneffels

From Whipple Mountain TH at 10,700′: 9.8 miles, 6,450′

Southwest Ridge: From S-7, the approach is on dangerous, loose Class 3 talus through cliff bands and then up Class 2 talus to the summit.

TELLURIDE EAST

4

The peaks south and east of the town of Telluride.

While some of the well-known trails close to Telluride are overwhelmed by tourists and day hikers, the high mountain basins with stunning turquoise-blue lakes south of Telluride, north of Ophir Pass Road, east of Colorado Highway 145, and west of US Highway 550 are captivating and rarely overcrowded. Lookout Peak is the most frequently climbed peak in this group, but it's rare to encounter more than another party or two on other peaks in the area.

TELLURIDE EAST

ACCESS AND HIKING

Blixt Trail

In the late 1800s, a miner from Ophir, Oscar Blixt, built a seriously impressive road connecting the Ophir Mining District with Bridal Veil Basin to the north. That road is now a steep trail that starts around 10,500′ and switchbacks up 2.8 miles, through forest, grassy slopes, and rust-red talus slopes to Oscars Pass at about 13,150′. There isn't a trailhead or sign on Ophir Pass Road (aka Forest Service Road 630) to mark the start of Blixt Trail. From the turnoff to Ophir on Colorado Highway 145, drive east on Ophir Pass Road, through the town of Ophir, and look for a two-track angling to the left around 3.9 miles east of CO 145. There is limited parking on Ophir Pass Road in this area, and there are other unmarked two-track roads angling left in the vicinity. It works well to pass the turnoff to Blixt Road/Trail and continue east to cross a shallow stream at mile 4.1 and then pull off to the left (north) 4.2 miles east of CO 145 (1.8 miles west of Ophir Pass and 5.9 miles west of US 550), where there is space for several vehicles. This isn't the start to Blixt Trail, but a well-defined walking trail crosses the stream here heading north, and after a short climb, the trail curves west and levels out before connecting to Blixt Trail where you begin a long, steep climb. Once at Oscars Pass, you are within striking distance of Oscars Peak (Peak 13,432′) and San Joaquin Ridge to the west, Wasatch Mountain to the north, T-12 (Peak 13,614′) to the southwest, and Bridal Peak (formerly T-11, or Peak 13,510′) to the northeast. Blixt Trail connects with Wasatch Trail and the old Bridal Veil Basin Road just north of Oscars Pass.

Bear Creek Trail

Bear Creek Trail is the San Juan's equivalent of the autobahn, the busiest, fastest trail around. Peakbaggers, ultra-distance runners, hikers, mountain bikers, and an occasional horseback rider all compete for space and speed on the trail that at some points is 10′ wide and rocky. Bear Creek Trail starts on the south end of Pine Street in Telluride at 8,820′ and climbs 1,000′ while paralleling Bear Creek to the west until it reaches Bear Creek Falls. Two miles from the trailhead, Wasatch Trail angles off to the right, 0.25 mile short of Bear Creek Falls. Bear Creek Trail doesn't reach the peaks or high basins; it's a stem trail that connects to the Wasatch Trail that takes you up high.

Wasatch Trail

From Bear Creek TH to the 13,050′ pass that separates the Bear Creek drainage from Bridal Veil Basin is 6.2 miles with 4,250′ of elevation gain. Wasatch Trail angles off to the right 2 miles from Bear Creek Trailhead. At 3.2 miles from the trailhead,

East Fork Bear Creek Trail veers off to the left to cross Bear Creek (before rejoining Wasatch Trail in the upper basin), and at 3.7 miles from the trailhead, the Wasatch Connecter comes in from the right. East Fork Bear Creek Trail is a shorter, steeper variation of Wasatch Trail. But the main attraction here is the lush, flower-filled high basin, above tree line. Wasatch Trail provides access to Wasatch Mountain, Silver Mountain, San Joaquin Ridge, and Oscars Peak (Peak 13,432′).

Bridal Veil Basin

Where you start a hike up Bridal Veil Basin depends on whether you have a 4WD vehicle. Without 4WD, start at the lower parking lot 2 miles east of Telluride (9,000′). With 4WD, drive past Bridal Veil Falls to the hydroelectric power plant above the falls (4 miles east of Telluride, at 10,400′). The road forks above Bridal Veil Falls, where you'll find limited parking. Black Bear Pass Road heads left (east) and the Bridal Veil Basin Road heads right (south). East-bound vehicular travel is prohibited on Black Bear Pass above the power plant. Travel on the Bridal Veil Basin Road is blocked by a barrier above the power plant. From the power plant, it's a 4.9-mile hike up to the 13,050′ pass that separates Bridal Veil Basin from Wasatch Trail in the Bear Creek drainage. The road progressively turns from a narrow, gravelly road to a rugged two-track road and then to a trail. At about 1.7 miles from the power plant, look for an unmarked turnoff to the left of Blue Lake. The Bridal Veil Basin Road provides access to La Junta, Wasatch Mountain, Oscars Peak (Peak 13,432′), T-12 (Peak 13,614′), Bridal Peak (formerly T-11), and Three Needles.

Black Bear Pass Road

The portion of road east of Black Bear Pass (12,820′) that is approached from US Highway 550 between Silverton and Ouray provides access to a row of 13ers on the crest that separates the South Mineral drainage to the east and from Ingraham and Bridal Veil Basins to the west. From the top of the pass to the power plant above Bridal Veil Falls near Telluride, Black Bear Pass Road is one-way from east to west by vehicle and is deadly in spots due to the narrowness of the road and the steep drop-offs. Yet, the road is safe on foot and comes in handy to connect multipeak loops. From the Telluride side, the Black Bear Pass Road can be accessed on foot by taking the left (east) fork in the road near the power plant above Bridal Veil Falls. From the Ouray side, the road turns off US 550, 13 miles south of Ouray just south of Red Mountain Pass. Black Bear Pass is straddled by Trico Peak to the northeast and the north summit of T-10 (Peak 13,477′) to the southwest. From the power plant above Bridal Veil Falls, Ajax Peak, Peak 13,230′, Telluride Peak, Peak 13,510′, and Trico Peak, or some combination thereof, can be strung together in a full day with the

Looking north into the Sneffels group from the summit of Chicago Peak. Photo by Kiefer Thomas

Black Bear Pass Road providing a route up to the Ajax Mountain Trail at the beginning of the day and a return route after the last peak of the day to the east is climbed.

Imogene Pass Road

Imogene Pass is a rugged 4WD road that can be accessed from Telluride or Ouray. From Telluride, head north on North Oak Street, which dead-ends at Tomboy Road, where you will take a right to head up Imogene Pass. From Ouray, turn south on Camp Bird Road off US Highway 550 as if going to Yankee Boy Basin. After 4.6 miles, stay left to begin the ascent of Imogene Pass. Imogene Pass offers access to Trico Peak, Peak 13,510′, Telluride Peak, Peak 13,230′, Ajax Peak, Chicago Peak, "Tomboy Peak," T-7, and T-8.

Richmond Trail

Richmond Trail provides access from the east to the northeast end of this section and offers backpacking options into the Imogene Pass area for those without 4WD, and access to Hayden Mountain North, Hayden Mountain South, T-8, and T-7. From Ouray on US Highway 550, drive 8.3 miles south past Crystal Lake and Ironton to a turnoff on your right. After turning off the highway, follow the road to the left, past an old mine on the right, for less than 100′ to the trailhead. The trailhead can be tricky to find; the sign sits off to the side of the road and is partially obscured from view.

Porphyry Basin from near the summit of Three Needles, with T-10 at far left. Photo by Kiefer Thomas

Porphyry Basin

With four turquoise lakes, swaths of flowers and grass, and large rock slabs that have been worn smooth, Porphyry Basin has the feel of a Zen garden. The basin is located at 12,600′ to 12,800′ and can be accessed from US Highway 550 by turning west on Forest Service Road 822, 0.7 mile south of Red Mountain Pass. A rugged, narrow 4WD road climbs 2.7 miles and 1,400′ to a parking area (12,300′). The road is so narrow in some spots that two vehicles can't pass, and it's not fun to back up. Consider parking at the sharp switchback, 1.8 miles from US 550 (11,700′) to avoid coming nose to nose with another vehicle on the last 0.9 mile of the route. Porphyry Basin provides the best access for the south summit of T-10 (Peak 13,477′) and Three Needles. Bridal Peak (formerly T-11, or Peak 13,510′) can also be reached from Porphyry Basin by contouring south and then west.

Columbine Lake Trail

This trail is located off a small road 0.7 mile north of the Ophir Pass turnoff on Highway 550. The road ends at the Imogene Mine, where your adventure begins. This trail climbs 2,500′ in 3 miles while switching back up steep terrain before it reaches the shores of idyllic Columbine Lake. This is a good backcountry access point for Bridal Peak, Peak 13,300′, and Peak 13,159′.

Ophir Pass Road

Ophir Pass Road (called Forest Service Road 679 on the west side of the pass and Forest Service Road 630 on the east side of the pass) once transported ore to smelters in Silverton. While not as dangerous as Black Bear Pass or Imogene Pass, it should not be taken lightly, especially the portion of road on the west side of the pass. Two-way traffic is permitted, and etiquette calls for vehicles headed downhill to yield to vehicles going uphill. The east end of Ophir Pass Road is 5 miles north of Silverton and 17 miles south of Ouray. The west end of the road is 13 miles south of Telluride. The top of the pass is 4.1 miles east of US Highway 550 and 6 miles west of Colorado Highway 145. Ophir Pass is the best spot to begin a climb of Lookout Peak. Most climbers park in an area 0.2 mile east of the high point on the pass.

Alta Lakes Road

The turnoff to Alta Lakes is 5.7 miles south of Society Turn outside of Telluride on Colorado Highway 145. From Telluride, turn left (east) and drive 4.5 miles up to Alta Lakes Road on a narrow dirt road that requires you to pull over for other vehicles in some spots. A 2WD high-clearance vehicle will work. Alta Lakes Road provides access to Palmyra Peak.

Saint Sophia Gondola and Telluride Ski Area

Telluride's free, in-town gondola transports you from 8,750′ to 10,544′. From the Saint Sophia lookout, follow the See Forever ski run, or paralleling roads, past Lift #9 but short of Gold Hill to access the Wasatch Connector Trail, which contours across Revelation Bowl before dropping into the Bear Creek drainage and connecting with Wasatch Trail. The Wasatch Connector is 1.6 miles and drops 620′ from the ski area before reaching Wasatch Trail. Another ski area option that provides access to Silver Mountain or San Joaquin Ridge is to continue up and past Gold Hill toward Palmyra Peak, but at the top of the metal stairs on Palmyra's northeast shoulder, traverse east at 12,700′ before diagonally descending into Lena Basin, from which Silver Mountain can be accessed.

CLIMBING ROUTES

Ajax Peak

12,785′ UNRANKED

South Face

From Black Bear Pass Road at 11,360′: 1.5 miles, 1,400′

Ajax Peak, which dominates the view from most points in Telluride, isn't really a peak. By the standard route on this Class 2 climb, you *descend* a ridge to reach the summit. The grassy, sloped trail up Ajax turns off Black Bear Pass Road just above the deadly section of the jeep road above Ingram Falls and an abandoned mining structure. A well-designed trail with long, sweeping switchbacks leads you up the

Ajax Peak as seen from Telluride. Photo by Kiefer Thomas

grassy slopes south of Ajax. Up high, the trail forks, with the left fork being a steeper, more direct route to the summit and the right fork leading you to the ridge between Ajax and Peak 13,230′, which you downclimb to the summit of Ajax. The views of Telluride from Ajax's summit are fantastic.

Peak 13,230′

UNRANKED

Peak 13,230′, frequently mistaken for Telluride Peak, is located 0.75 mile east-southeast of Ajax Peak.

West Ridge

From Black Bear Pass Road at 11,360′: 1.7 miles, 1,870′

Once you gain the ridge between Ajax and Peak 13,320′, follow the ridge up a rocky section of Class 2+ climbing that gives way to a grassy walk-up above.

East Ridge

This Class 3 climb connects with the west ridge of Telluride Peak. Several spots on the two ridges require scrambling on exposed terrain. The east ridge allows you to do a long loop connecting Ajax Peak, Peak 13,320′, and Telluride Peak—and if that's not enough, Peak 13,510′ and Trico Peak as well—before descending the Black Bear Pass Road back to Telluride.

Telluride Peak

13,509′ SOFT RANKED

Telluride Peak is 1.25 miles east-southeast of Ajax Peak and 0.5 mile south of the summit of Imogene Pass.

Northeast Ridge

From Imogene Pass at 13,120′: 0.6 mile, 420′

From the summit of Imogene Pass, the northeast ridge is a straightforward Class 2 climb that allows jeep parties to reach a 13er summit with barely over 400′ feet of elevation gain.

West Ridge

From Black Bear Pass Road at 11,360′: 2.4 miles, 2,300′

The west ridge of Telluride Peak is reached by a downclimb of the east ridge of Peak 13,230′ The west ridge is a Class 3 climb requiring a few exposed moves. From the west ridge, you get a bird's-eye view of the traffic on Imogene Pass Road.

Southwest Ridge

From the summit of Black Bear Pass at 12,830′: 2.1 miles, 1,320′

The Class 2 climb works well if you are approaching from the summit of Black Bear Pass to climb Telluride Peak via Peak 13,510′ and Trico Peak.

Telluride Peak (right of center) from north of Imogene Pass. Photo by Kiefer Thomas

Black Bear Pass and Trico Peak, from the north slope of T-10. Photo by Kiefer Thomas

Peak 13,510′

RANK 249

Peak 13,510′ is 1.25 miles north of Trico Peak. Both the northwest ridge and the south ridge of Peak 13,510′ are rounded Class 2 climbs with expansive views well above tree line.

South Ridge

From the summit of Black Bear Pass at 12,830′: 1.5 miles, 1,050′

The south ridge combines well with an approach from Black Bear Pass and Trico Peak.

Northwest Ridge

From Imogene Pass at 13,120′: 1.25 miles, 680′

The northwest ridge combines well with an approach from Imogene Pass and Telluride Peak.

Trico Peak—"T-9"

13,321′ RANK 376

The summit of Trico Peak is the point at which San Miquel, Ouray, and San Juan Counties connect.

Southwest Ridge

From the summit of Black Bear Pass at 12,830′: 0.5 mile, 400′

From the summit of Black Bear Pass, a distinct but unmaintained trail provides a Class 2 route up Trico Peak.

Northwest Face/Ridge

From Imogene Pass at 13,120′: 2.2 miles, 1,100′

This Class 3+ route can be used as part of a loop climb that includes peaks north of Trico or as a ridge traverse from Imogene Pass via Telluride Peak and Peak 13,510′. The northwest flank of Trico is steep and strewn with boulders and talus. This side of Trico looks terrible but is more stable than it appears. Go slow and test each hold and step.

Note: Ajax Peak, Peak 13,230′, Telluride Peak, Peak 13,510′, and Trico Peak can be done as a loop.

From Black Bear Pass Road at 11,360′: 8 miles, 3,450′

Peak 13,477′—"T-10" North Summit

RANK 269

T-10 is a peak with twin summits that are both 13,477′ high and separated from each other by an unclimbable ridge. For all practical purposes, T-10 is two peaks rather than one.

Northeast Flank

From the summit of Black Bear Pass at 12,830′: 0.4 mile, 550′

From Black Bear Pass, the north summit of T-10 can be climbed by a Class 3 route on the northeast flank that is a slog up talus and scree slopes that leads to some scrambling near the summit. It's possible to drop down and contour across the loose, talus-strewn east face of T-10 from one summit to the other, but this isn't recommended. The east face is difficult and unstable.

T-10's north summit from the top of the south summit. Photo by Kiefer Thomas

Peak 13,477′—"T-10" South Summit

RANK 269

Southeast Ridge

From Porphyry Basin 4WD parking at 12,360′: 0.6 mile, 1,110′

From parking on Porphyry Basin Road, gain the southeast ridge of T-10's south summit by climbing north-northeast up a steep grass clustered slope. From there, it is a straightforward Class 2+ climb to the summit where you can look across the chasm that separates you from the north summit. From each summit, the other summit looks higher. The south summit of T-10 is rounded and spacious, a good place to take in a 360-degree panorama of the San Juans.

Southwest Ridge

From Porphyry Basin 4WD parking at 12,360′: 0.9 mile, 1,110′

The southwest ridge can be gained by climbing higher up into Porphyry Basin to gain the saddle between Three Needles and the south summit of T-10 at about 13,000′. The left (west) side of the ridge drops off sharply into Mud Basin, while the right (east) side of the ridge has a gentler slope. A Class 2+ route on the ridge or just to the east of the ridge leads up to the south summit through rugged, fractured blocks of rock.

T-10's south summit from Black Bear Pass. Photo by Kiefer Thomas

Ascending Three Needles. Photo by Kiefer Thomas

Three Needles

13,481′ RANK 266

Three Needles rises above the terminus of Porphyry Basin and offers excellent scrambling opportunities for those looking for a climb that's a bit spicy.

East Face

From Porphyry Basin 4WD parking at 12,360′: 0.9 mile, 1,120′

From Porphyry Basin, you can see two U-shaped notches on the ridge south of the summit of Three Needles. The climbing route goes through the notch closest to the summit. At some points on the climb, the notch is obscured, but as you get closer, you can't miss it. Once you gain the ridge extending south from the summit, you get a great view of Blue Lake in the Bridal Veil Basin drainage. The climb up the vast talus slope to the notch is a slog, but the summit block on Three Needles offers several Class 4 routes, all of which involve friable volcanic gravel on moderately exposed terrain. One of the summit routes is a 10′ near-vertical crack with excellent holds. A couple of other summit routes are south of the 10′ crack and follow right (south) slanting ramps that then turn diagonally left (north) to cross exposed slopes that lead left (north) to the summit. A rope on the summit block would be handy.

Left: Bridal Peak from the south ridge. **Right:** Near Columbine Lake with Lookout Peak (left) and T-12 (right) in the distance. Photos by Kiefer Thomas

Bridal Peak—"T-11"

13,510′ **RANK 250**

Bridal Peak was unofficially named T-10 by Dwight Lavender in the 1930s but designated Bridal Peak by USGS in 2014. The summit rises 0.6 mile south of Blue Lake and 1 mile north of Columbine Lake.

South Ridge

From Columbine Lake at 12,310′: 1.5 miles, 1,160′

From Columbine Lake TH at 10,430′: 3.9 miles, 3,080′

From Bridal Veil Falls parking at 10,360′: 5.4 miles, 3,450′

Bridal Peak is best accessed from Bridal Veil Basin or Mill Creek Basin (Columbine Lake). From either direction, the initial objective is to reach Columbine Pass to the south of Bridal Peak. Once on the pass follow a Class 2 climbers' trail up the south ridge to the summit.

Lookout Peak

13,661′ **RANK 166**

The top of Ophir Pass at 11,720′ is the beginning point for a climb on Lookout Peak. Lookout doesn't combine well with other peaks, but because you start at high elevation, you will probably have time for other exploits in the afternoon, if the weather holds.

South Ridge

From Ophir Pass at 11,720′: 1 mile, 1,940′

The best spot to start this climb is 0.2 mile east of Ophir Pass. This allows you to bypass the rounded hill (12,187′) to the east. Avoid the steep, rotten sections on the lower portion of the south ridge by heading up into the broad basin southeast of the peak on a climbers' trail. High in the basin at 12,600′, contour to the left (west) to gain the south ridge of Lookout, which involves some Class 3+ scrambling on steep, gravelly rock and ledges.

Peak 13,614′—"T-12" "North Lookout"

UNRANKED

From Ophir Pass Blixt TH at 10,310′: 3 miles, 3,300′
From Bridal Veil Falls parking at 10,360′: 6 miles, 3,250′
From Bear Creek TH at 8,820′: 6.8 miles, 5,200′

Northwest Ridge

A good place to begin a climb of this infrequently visited peak is at the top of the Blixt Trail at Oscars Pass. Initially, most obstacles on the ridge are bypassed to the right (southwest), but as you gain elevation, there are a few false summits where you are forced left (northeast). As you near the summit, you'll encounter points on this rocky, broken Class 4 climb where a belay would be welcome. The summit is broad and roomy. The ridge between Lookout Peak and T-12 is spectacular and unclimbable. There is a broad cliff not far south of the T-12 summit. Alternate routes to gain the northwest ridge near the top are from the pass between Tempest Peak (Peak 13,440′) and T-12.

Peak 13,432′—"Oscars Peak"

SOFT RANKED

Oscars Peak is located 1.2 miles northwest of Lookout Peak and is one of the easiest mountains to climb in the San Juans due to the ease of the trail and the slow and steady elevation gain.

From Ophir Pass Blixt TH at 10,310′: 3 miles, 3,120′
From Bridal Veil Falls parking at 10,360′: 6 miles, 3,070′
From Bear Creek TH at 8,820′: 6.8 miles, 4,610′

North Ridge

From the pass between Bridal Veil Basin and the basin north of Wasatch Mountain, a Class 2 social trail leads to the summit.

Southeast Ridge

Although there is not a social trail from Oscars Pass to the summit of Oscars Peak, it is also an easy Class 2 hike up the southeast ridge to the summit.

San Joaquin Ridge

13,460′ RANK 284

The high point recognized as the summit of San Joaquin Ridge is on an east-west ridge between Oscars Peak and the eastern summit of Silver Mountain. The summit is east of the feature on topo maps that is labelled San Joaquin Ridge and not to be confused with the 13,446′ point on the southern terminus of the San Joaquin Ridge. The summit can be reached from a variety of approaches, all of which require basic route-finding skills. The San Joaquin Couloir is on the west flank of the San Joaquin Ridge.

Bear Creek Approach

From Bear Creek TH at 8,820′: 5.5 miles, 4,640′

San Joaquin can be approached from the north by Bear Creek Trail or the Wasatch Connector Trail and climbed by circumventing the San Joaquin Ridge by hiking up the high basins either west or east of the ridge. Near the summit on the west side, there is a 10′ near-vertical Class 3 climb with good holds.

East Ridge

From Ophir Pass Blixt TH at 10,310′: 3.8 miles, 3,520′

From Bridal Veil Falls parking at 10,360′: 6.8 miles, 3,470′

From Bear Creek TH at 8,820′: 7.6 miles, 5,000′

From Oscars Peak, an east-west ridge leads to San Joaquin. The rocky ridge is generally stable but requires Class 3 scrambling near the summit as the ridge narrows.

South Flank

From Carbonero Mine Road at 10,600′: 1.8 miles, 2,860′

From a locked gate at 10,600′ on the Carbonero Mine Road located on the northeast side of the town of Ophir, hike up the switchbacking road to the mine at 11,500′. From there, you face a tough slog up steep, loose Class 2+ rock while aiming to gain the east-west ridge between point 13,446′ and the summit to the east.

San Joaquin Couloir

From Bear Creek TH at 8,820′: 7.6 miles, 5,000′

The San Joaquin Couloir is a startlingly steep, straight, narrow, aesthetic line that holds snow well into summer and is easily accessible. The couloir can be approached by Bear Creek TH and Wasatch Trail, or the Wasatch Connector. Including the bottom apron, the couloir is 1,000′ high, 45- to 50-degrees steep, and 25′ to 30′ wide with a couple of choke points that are about 12′ wide. Ice axes and crampons are required, and snow pickets, a rope, and an early start are recommended.

Silver Mountain B

13,470′ RANK 274

There is no "standard" route up Silver Mountain, and the many options all require off-trail routefinding. However you find your way to the top of Silver Mountain, once you arrive, you are in for a treat. The twin summits (east at 13,463′ and west at 13,470′) are a half mile apart and separated by an airy, rounded ridge with a few fun Class 3 moves that make up for all you endured to get there.

Lena Basin

From Bear Creek TH at 8,820′: 5.7 miles, 4,650′

From Telluride Ski Area–Gold Hill at 12,540′: 1.5 miles, 1,170′

Lena Basin, to the south of Silver Mountain, can be accessed by Bear Creek Trail and Wasatch Trail. When you reach the point where Wasatch Trail intersects with the Wasatch Connector, start looking for ways to bushwhack up the west fork of Bear Creek. Alternatively, you can hike past Gold Hill going south at the Telluride ski area to the top of the metal staircase on the northern flank of Palmyra Peak. From the top of the staircase, immediately head east to catch a faint social trail and a descending traverse into Lena Basin. From Lena Basin, head for the Y-shaped couloir below the west summit of Silver Mountain and take the left (east) branch of the couloir filled with loose talus that will put you in position for the final Class 2+ scramble up to the west summit.

South Flank

From Carbonero Mine Road at 10,600′: 2.1 miles, 2,870′

Silver Mountain can also be climbed by long, steep, talus sufferfest approaches up Staatsburg Basin or the Carbonero Mine Road. Both approaches involve unrelenting elevation gains from the Ophir side of the peak. If you gain the ridge between the eastern summit of Silver Mountain and San Joaquin Ridge, you can make a Class 2+ or 3 traverse around the eastern summit of Silver Mountain to the north by dropping about 100′ below the cliffs on the eastern summit. The traverse puts you in a position to climb a talus-filled couloir on the north flank of Silver to gain the ridge between the two summits where you can then climb either one or both summits.

Palmyra Peak

13,319′ UNRANKED

The terrain north of Palmyra Peak is known for its harrowing ski chutes. To the south, an outrageously difficult ridge connects Palmyra Peak to the west summit of Silver Mountain.

Alta Lakes

From Alta Lakes TH at 11,460′: 0.75 mile, 1,860′

From Alta Lakes, the object is to gain the gentle ridge that forms the Telluride ski area boundary as it extends northeast from Palmyra Peak. Once on the ridge, you climb first on grassy slopes, then solid, rocky terrain, and ultimately on steep, loose gravel. The summit block is steep and exposed in spots, and gravelly all over. Several variations lead to the summit, which range in difficulty from Class 3+ to lower Class 5. The easiest route traverses out on the east flank of the summit block on an exposed gravel-strewn ledge that switchbacks to the right before reaching the top. Some fixed bolts appear to afford protection for at least one Class 5 route.

Wasatch Mountain

13,555′ RANK 214

Wasatch Mountain is located 1 mile north of Oscars Peak on the western side of Bridal Veil Basin.

South Ridge

From Ophir Pass Blixt TH at 10,310′: 4 miles, 3,250′

From Bridal Veil Falls parking at 10,360′: 6.5 miles, 3,200′

From Bear Creek TH at 8,820′: 7.3 miles, 4,730′

Start at the 13,060′ pass north of Oscars Peak between the east fork of Bear Creek drainage and Bridal Veil Basin. The ridge climbs over two prominent subpeaks, 13,420′ and 13,500′, on orange and red dinner-plate rocks. The ridge is mostly Class 2 with a few Class 3 sections thrown into the mix. When necessary, difficulties are skirted to the east. The final section of the ridge from 13,500′ to the summit is Class 2+, high, and airy.

Northeast Ridge

From Bridal Veil Falls Parking at 10,360′: 4.25 miles, 3,200′

From the 12,860′ pass between La Junta Peak and Wasatch, a Class 2+ social trail leads you through the talus to the summit.

La Junta Peak

13,472′ RANK 273

La Junta Peak is located 0.67 mile northeast of Wasatch Mountain.

Southwest Ridge

From Bridal Veil Falls Parking at 10,360′: 3.25 miles, 3,200′

At around 12,200′ on Bridal Veil Trail, turn off and head west, aiming for the 12,860′pass between La Junta and Wasatch. A steep, gravel-covered, Class 2+ user trail switchbacks up the southwest ridge to the summit and climbs through one cliff band via a gully.

Peak 13,145′—"Jackass Point"

RANK 529

Jackass Point is located 0.5 mile north of La Junta Peak on the west side of Jackass Basin and is usually climbed in conjunction with La Junta Peak.

South Ridge

From Bridal Veil Falls parking at 10,360′ via Jackass Basin: 2.5 miles, 2,790′

From Bridal Veil Falls parking at 10,360′ via La Junta: 3.8 miles, 3,550′

If ascending only Jackass Point, you can do so from the saddle between La Junta and Jackass Point. The south ridge is a steep Class 2 walk-up and can be accessed from Jackass Basin to the east. If climbing La Junta first, the challenge is to get to the saddle from La Junta. There are three obstacles on the descent of the north ridge of La Junta to the saddle. The first two obstacles are circumvented by veering left (west) out onto steep gravel covered slopes. The third involves a Class 3+ or 4 downclimb where a short rope belay would be handy.

Ballard Mountain

12,804′ UNRANKED

South Ridge

From Bridal Veil Falls parking at 10,360′ via La Junta and Jackass Point: 4.3 miles, 3,680′

The south ridge of Ballard, which finishes a traverse from La Junta and Jackass Point, is a walk-up. The challenge is getting to the base of the south ridge that, if you are completing a loop from the south, includes the three obstacles on the south ridge of La Junta described in the south ridge route to Jackass Point.

Silver Lake Basin

From Bridal Veil Falls parking at 10,360′: 2.5 miles, 2,440′

A well-used tourist trail splits off Bridal Veil Trail about a half mile after you pass through the pipe gate and leads to Silver Lake. From Silver Lake, hike up the lush basin above the lake, aiming to gain the northeast ridge of Ballard to complete a Class 2 climb.

OFF THE BEATEN PATH

Chicago Peak, looking northwest from near Imogene Pass. Photo by Kiefer Thomas

Chicago Peak—"T-6"

13,385′ RANK 325

0.9 mile northwest of Imogene Pass

From Imogene Pass at 13,120′: 0.9 mile, 500′

Southeast Ridge: After bypassing rough terrain north (right) of the ridge, T-6 is a Class 2 walk-up.

"Tomboy Peak"

13,095′ RANK 573

1.4 miles northwest of Imogene Pass

From Imogene Pass at 13,120′: 1.7 miles, 740′

East Slopes: Climb steep Class 2 talus from Chicago Peak.

"T-7"

13,359′ RANK 350

0.7 mile east-northeast of Imogene Pass

From Imogene Pass at 13,120′: 0.7 mile, 460′

West Slopes: A simple Class 2 walk-up from Imogene Pass. Often climbed with T-8.

Left: Tomboy Peak. **Right:** T-7 and Ptarmigan Lake, from near the summit of Peak 13,510′. Photos by Kiefer Thomas

Left: T-8 from Richmond Pass. **Right:** Peak 13,159′. Photos by Kiefer Thomas

"T-8"

13,317′ RANK 378

0.65 mile northeast of T-7

From Imogene Pass at 13,120′: 1.4 miles, 950′

Southwest Ridge: A tricky Class 3–4 traverse can be done from T-7 by navigating around pinnacles.

Northeast Slopes: A Class 2 route up grassy slopes can be done from Richmond Basin to the north or from Richmond TH to the east near Ironton.

Hayden Mountain South

13,206′ RANK 479

1.1 miles northeast of T-8

From Richmond TH at 9,900′: 3.1 miles, 3,400′

South Slopes: A Class 2 walk-up from Richmond Pass northeast of T-8.

Hayden Mountain North

13,139′ RANK 539

1.2 miles northeast of Hayden Mountain South

From Richmond TH at 9,900′; 4.6 miles, 4,700′

South Ridge: A ridge traverse from Hayden Mountain South involves intricate routefinding on Class 3 terrain with significant elevation loss.

Peak 13,300′

SOFT RANKED

0.9 mile east-southeast of Lookout Peak

From Columbine Lake at 12,310′: 0.5 mile, 390′

West Ridge: A Class 2 walk-up from the south shores of Columbine Lake.

Peak 13,159′

RANK 514

1.3 miles east of Lookout Peak

From Columbine Lake at 12,310′: 0.5 mile, 390′

West Ridge: An easy Class 2 climb from the saddle between Peak 13,300′ and Peak 13,159′ east of Columbine Lake.

SILVERTON NORTH GROUP

5

The view of Storm Peak and the Silverton West group, from Tower at sunset.

This group of seldom-climbed peaks, located just a few miles north and east of Silverton, offer excellent solitude and a mixture of mountaineering challenges. The area both benefits from and is plagued by its rich mining history. Due to the mining, lots of high-elevation roads crisscross the area; expect to encounter large groups of loud ATVs all summer, which may detract from your overall experience until you are deep into the wilderness away from roads. This area spans a rectangular area that is 70 square miles (10 north to south, 7 east to west). The southern section offers exciting climbs and wilderness experiences on Storm Peak, East Storm Peak, Tower Mountain, and Dome Mountain. The northern area includes peaks that are easily accessed via 4WD with short approaches including Emery Peak; "Proposal Peak"; Bonita Peak; Red Mountains 1, 2, and 3; Hurricane Peak; Hanson Peak; California Mountain; Tuttle Mountain; Brown Mountain; and Abrams Mountain.

SILVERTON NORTH

ACCESS AND HIKING

Boulder Gulch

Boulder Gulch provides access to Storm Peak, East Storm Peak, Tower Peak, and Dome Peak via a steep trail with backpacking possibilities. From Silverton, take the main road (Greene Street/Colorado Highway 110) to the north end of town, past the city park. Just past the park, the road becomes Colorado Highway 110A and heads left (northwest). There's a fork here, with the left (main) road providing access to Velocity Basin while the right heads to Hillside Cemetery and Boulder Gulch Trailhead. The road quickly forks three times; stay left each time to find the gated trailhead 0.5 mile from the Velocity Basin fork.

Velocity Basin (South Fork Cement Creek)

Velocity Basin is a popular ATV destination due to its stunning views of Storm Peak and the abundance of wildflowers in July. It provides great access to East Storm Peak, Tower Peak, and Dome Peak. From Silverton, take the main road (Greene Street/Colorado Highway 110) to the north end of town, past the city park. Just past the park, the road forks and becomes Colorado Highway 110A and heads left (northwest). Continue northwest on the road. The pavement ends after 0.5 mile, but the road is well maintained. Drive up the road for 6.5 miles to the Gladstone townsite and a junction at the infamous Gold King Mine, which in 2015 dumped toxic metals into the Animas River, turning it a sickly yellow. Continue right (west) for 0.25 mile and then turn right (south) at a junction on County Road 52, which continues up an easy 4WD road for 1.5 miles, ending at the base of Tower Peak and a turquoise lake.

Velocity Basin and Storm Peak en route to Tower Mountain and East Storm.

Minnehaha Gulch

Minnehaha Gulch offers access from the west for Bonita Peak, Emery Peak, and Proposal Peak. For access to Minnehaha Gulch, follow the instructions for Velocity Basin; however, when reaching the Gladstone townsite, instead of turning right at the junction for CR 52, continue 200′ and turn right at the next junction to climb up into Minnehaha basin on a 4WD road.

Corkscrew Gulch

Corkscrew Gulch provides access to Red Mountain 1, 2, and 3 from the north off US Highway 550 at Ironton. Those with 4WD can drive all the way to the summit of Corkscrew Pass at 12,230', which can also be accessed from the southeast from the Gladstone townsite. From Ouray, drive south on US 550 for 7.6 miles and turn left (east) into Ironton Park where 2WD vehicles can park. Four-wheel-drive vehicles may continue up into Corkscrew Gulch, which saves 3.45 miles of hiking and 2,590′ of elevation gain.

Eureka Gulch

Eureka Gulch provides access to Dome Mountain and Tower Mountain via a 4WD road, as well as several "Off the Beaten Path" peaks, including Proposal Peak, Emery Peak, Bonita Peak, Hanson Peak, Hurricane Peak, California Mountain, and Peak 13,075′. From Silverton, follow the main road (Greene Street/Colorado Highway 110) and turn right where CO 110 forks at Seventeenth Street. Continue on CO 110 northeast for 8.2 miles past Howardsville and Eureka. At 10,000′, the road forks. For Eureka Gulch and access to Dome and Tower Mountains, turn left (southwest). Here the road gets more difficult, and a high-clearance vehicle is advised. Continue 1.1 miles to another fork and take a left down the hill. Continue for 0.8 mile to where the road crosses the Eureka drainage creek. Park or continue an additional 0.3 mile across the creek to a campsite and the end of the road, where the trail begins. For upper Eureka Gulch and access to the "Off the Beaten Path" peaks, stay right at the 10,000′ junction and continue northwest on the 4WD road.

Animas Forks

Access to the Animas Forks townsite follows the same road for Eureka Gulch from Silverton on a 4WD road; however, instead of turning left after 8.2 miles on CO 110, continue straight for an additional 3.9 miles, passing Grouse Gulch Trailhead (described in the Lake City West section, p. 253). From the Animas Forks townsite, you can access several "Off the Beaten Path" peaks, including Proposal Peak, Emery Peak, Bonita Peak, Hanson Peak, Hurricane Peak, California Mountain, and Peak 13,075′. Note: The road intersection at Animas Forks offers access to Cinnamon Pass to the east and Engineer Pass to the north. From Animas Forks, you can also continue driving higher to gain higher access to a variety of peaks in the area via California Gulch on County Road 19, which connects with California Pass and Hurricane Pass.

CLIMBING ROUTES

Storm Peak

13,487′ **RANK 265**

Storm Peak, located 3 miles north-northeast of Silverton, towers above the terminus of the well-traveled Velocity Basin, from which it looks nearly unclimbable. But as with many peaks in the San Juans, looks are deceiving, and this peak can be climbed via a Class 3 route from Boulder Gulch.

South Face

From Boulder Gulch TH at 9,500′: 6 miles, 4,000′

This climb can be done in a day or makes for a nice overnight backpack to the upper basin below Storm Peak. In spring and early summer, you will want an ice ax and crampons or microspikes; however, in mid- to late summer, the route is mostly clear of snow. From Boulder Gulch Trailhead, hike east along the old road until you reach the creek in Boulder Gulch. Once at the creek, search on the east (right) side of the creek near old mining remnants; the trail is above the creek to the right and switchbacks up Boulder Gulch through varied terrain. The drainage splits at 11,400′, and the trail crosses the main creek above the confluence and turns left (northwest) toward Storm Peak. Instead of switching back to the right (east) on the main trail, continue on a faint trail to the left above the creek on the north side to a small lake at 11,880′. From the lake, continue up the northwest creek to the base of Storm and two more small lakes. Continue northeast to a couloir that comes from the right (western) side of the summit. Hike up a talus slope and enter the couloir. The terrain is difficult here, and the rocks are loose; a helmet is recommended. Eventually the couloir splits, and you will take the right fork. It ends abruptly at a small saddle, where you will climb over blocks of rock on Class 3 terrain to the summit, which affords intense views down into Velocity Basin.

East Storm Peak

13,325′ **RANK 373**

East Storm Peak is located 0.5 mile east of Storm Peak and can be climbed on its own or in combination with Tower Peak on a long day. Theoretically, you could climb it from Storm Peak or vice versa, but the route would be on nearly impassable Class 5 garbage that only the bravest person would attempt. The most direct route is from Velocity Basin. There are also backpacking possibilities in the basin to the east of East Storm that can be accessed from Velocity Basin or Boulder Gulch.

Left: Storm from the summit of East Storm. **Right:** East Storm and Storm as seen from the east.

Northeast Ridge

From Velocity Basin TH at 11,300′: 2.6 miles, 2,110′

From Boulder Gulch TH at 9,500′: 5.2 miles, 4,040′

From Velocity Basin TH, weave west-northwest up a nice but steep trail to a switchback at 11,290′. From here, the true trail contours north around the mine at 12,110′ and becomes tricky to follow, fading into a small game trail as it climbs north just shy of point 12,263′. Here, the trail turns sharply to the right (southeast) and follows the ridge up and over points 12,601′ and 12,931′ on Class 2 terrain where it finally gains the summit of point 13,060′. Here, either continue southeast toward Tower Mountain (next entry) or west toward East Storm. From the 13,060′ point, continue south for 250′ and follow the ridge to your right (west) across point 12,978′ up gentle terrain. Eventually, you will reach a tower at 12,970′ that you will want to bypass to the left on a faint trail and continue up Class 2+ terrain to the summit of East Storm, where you will be blown away by the view down to Velocity Basin. To descend, pick your poison: you can avoid downclimbing the steep and chossy Class 2+ terrain by dropping off the east face on loose dirt and scree and reconnecting with your ascending route by wrapping around the face to 13,020′.

Tower Mountain

13,552′ **RANK 219**

Aptly named given the large metal tower on its summit, Tower Mountain is 1.3 miles east-southeast of Storm Peak. It offers great views of the entire area and is the easiest peak to climb in this section if approached from Velocity Basin. The route from Eureka Gulch offers two possibilities: one is to ascend Dome Mountain (next entry) and traverse to Tower's summit on Class 2 terrain; the other is to continue deep into the scenic South Fork Animas River basin on a long trail that eventually joins up with the standard route for East Storm and Tower at point 12,931′. This makes for

Tower Mountain approach from Velocity Basin.

excellent backpacking, as there are idyllic tarns located in the upper basin to the north of Tower. If approaching from Eureka Gulch, you could do a large loop by doing Tower first and descending via Dome. The mileage listed below is for the latter.

Northwest Slopes

From Velocity Basin TH at 11,300′: 2.9 miles, 2,440′

From Eureka Gulch TH at 10,550′: 4.25 miles, 4,050′

From Boulder Gulch TH at 9,500′: 5.4 miles, 4,090′

Follow the route from Velocity Basin as described in East Storm, but instead of turning west (right) from just below point 13,060′, continue southeast toward Tower on a serviceable Class 2 trail that crosses a small talus field and several areas of tundra while gaining the summit. From here, you could continue to Dome Mountain, which would add 1.5 miles one-way.

Dome Mountain

13,370′ RANK 344

Dome Mountain, located 1.3 miles east-northeast of Tower Mountain, is adorned with green tundra and offers excellent Class 2+ scrambling opportunities. It can be accessed via a traverse from Tower Mountain or on its own via Eureka Gulch.

West Ridge

From Velocity Basin TH at 11,300′ via Tower Mountain: 4.2 miles, 3,130′

From Boulder Gulch TH at 9,500′ via Tower Mountain: 7 miles, 4,900′

The route is approached via a Class 2 traverse from Tower Mountain and requires a long day of weather-exposed ridge walking. While only 1.3 miles from Tower as the crow flies, don't be fooled: this is a long ridge where you will lose 750′ of elevation and climb nearly 1,000′—and that's one-way.

North Ridge

From Eureka Gulch TH at 10,550′: 2.3 miles, 3,000′

This route has many variations, each offering a different challenge. The route detailed here gains the ridge of Peak 12,540′, offering a fantastic ridge climb all the way up to Dome's summit. From the trailhead prior to the creek crossing, walk west, passing old mining structures. Turn sharply right (north) on the road at the turnaround and campsite and look for a pack trail on the left marked with a sign indicating that the trail is for hikers only. At 0.5 mile, find a well-worn footpath on the south side of the south fork of the Animas River, where you will cross (which will be a challenge in early summer due to snow runoff). Continue west below a north-facing slope and through a forest of short trees. After 0.8 mile, at 10,880′, leave the trail and climb the left side of the avalanche slide path above. After 200 vertical feet, find a faint trail switchbacking up the slide path, which continues northeast to avoid a ravine. Gain the ridge for Peak 12,540′ at 1.3 miles at approximately 11,800′. Climb up and over Peak 12,420′ where you will see the rest of the route. Continue to Peak 12,641′ and drop down to the saddle between Peak 12,641′ and Dome, where the route continues up loose dirt, tundra, and scree on Class 2+ terrain.

Dome Mountain from Tower Mountain.

OFF THE BEATEN PATH

"Proposal Peak"

13,330′ RANK 369

2 miles northeast of Storm Peak

From Minnehaha Gulch at 11,600′: 0.8 mile, 1,660′

West Ridge: A Class 3 ascent via a steep gully on the north side of the west ridge on solid rock. Often climbed as the first peak in conjunction with Emery Peak and Bonita Peak.

Emery Peak

13,310′ UNRANKED

0.45 mile north-northeast of Proposal Peak

From Minnehaha Gulch at 11,600′: 1.3 miles, 2,110′

South Ridge: A challenging traverse from Proposal Peak on Class 2+ talus. Descend 200′ onto the east side (right) of the connecting ridge and up steep talus to the summit.

Bonita Peak

13,286′ RANK 410

1 mile north of Proposal Peak

From Minnehaha Gulch at 11,600′: 2 miles, 2,500′

South Ridge: From Emery Peak, the traverse is simple except for the need to downclimb a Class 3 chimney en route; otherwise, it can be kept at Class 2.

Houghton Mountain

13,052′ RANK 607

1.1 miles northwest of Animas Forks

From Animas Forks at 11,170′: 1.1 miles, 1,880′

Southeast Slopes: A great starting or ending peak on a loop that can include up to nine 13ers from Animas Forks, all Class 2, including Tuttle, Hurricane, Bonita, Emery, Hanson, California, and Peak 13,075′. From Animas Forks, climb the Class 2 slope to the top.

Tuttle Mountain

13,203′ RANK 486

1.5 miles west-southwest of Houghton Mountain

From Animas Forks at 11,170′: 2.65 miles, 2,560′

Northeast Slopes: A Class 2 walk-up from the Tuttle-Houghton saddle.

Hurricane Peak

13,447′ UNRANKED

1.4 miles south-southwest of Tuttle Mountain

From Animas Forks at 11,170′: 4 miles, 2,430′

Northwest Slopes: From Tuttle, traverse south and meet California Gulch Road. Descend west (right) toward Brown Mountain on Hurricane Pass Road and turn left (south) to ascend the northwest slopes at around 12,740′ up Class 2 terrain.

Hurricane Peak from Brown Mountain.

Hanson Peak

13,454′ RANK 286

1.1 miles northeast of Bonita Peak

From Animas Forks at 11,170′: 4 miles, 2,430′

Northeast Slopes/South Slopes: From Animas Forks, either take the northeast slopes (from the Hurricane-Hanson saddle) or the south slopes (from Bonita) on Class 2 terrain.

California Mountain

13,220′ SOFT RANKED

0.8 mile east of Hurricane Peak

From Animas Forks at 11,170′: 4 miles, 2,430′

Southwest Slopes: A Class 2 walk-up from the California-Hanson saddle.

Peak 13,075′

RANK 589

1 mile east-southeast of Hanson Peak

From Animas Forks at 11,170′: 4.1 miles, 2,030′

Northwest Slopes: A Class 2 walk-up on grassy slopes with a short Class 2+ cliff band at the summit.

Brown Mountain

13,339′ RANK 364

1 mile northwest of Hurricane Peak

From Hurricane Pass spur road at 12,900′: 0.5 mile, 440′

Northeast Ridge: Most people choose to climb Brown from near the summit of Hurricane Pass. From Hurricane Pass, continue west 0.15 mile, turn right (north) on a spur road, which takes you to the northeast ridge of Brown and an easy Class 2 slope to the summit.

Red Mountain 1

12,592′ RANK 939

3.6 miles north-northwest of Storm Peak

From Corkscrew Pass at 12,230′: 0.3 mile, 320′

Southeast Ridge: An easy Class 2 walk-up that can also be done off trail from tarns to the east for those looking for a longer approach. Often climbed with Red Mountain 2 and 3.

Red Mountain 2

12,219′ UNRANKED

1.1 miles west of Red Mountain 1

From Corkscrew Pass at 12,230′: 1.8 miles, 850′

South Ridge: A Class 2 walk-up from Corkscrew Pass via the saddle between Red Mountain 2 and Red Mountain 3.

Red Mountain 3

12,890′ RANK 723

0.86 mile south-southwest of Red Mountain 2

From Corkscrew Pass at 12,230′: 1.8 mile, 1,210′

East Ridge: A Class 2 walk-up from Corkscrew Pass via the saddle between Red Mountain 2 and Red Mountain 3.

Panorama from Red Mountain 1, left to right: East Storm, Storm, Grand Turk, Sultan, Red Mountain 3, Red Mountain 2.

SILVERTON WEST GROUP

6

Vermillion, Golden Horn, and Pilot Knob in early winter, from Sultan.

This vast group of peaks is located west and south of Silverton and east and south of Trout Lake and Ophir. To the west, the group is bounded by Colorado Highway 145 between Rico and Ophir and to the east by US Highway 550 from Coal Bank Pass north to Silverton. Although there are no 14,000′ peaks in this group, there are many high, rugged 13ers. Nine of the 200 highest peaks in Colorado are located here. Vermillion Peak (13,894′) is the highest. It is clustered near Ice Lake Basin with Fuller Peak, Golden Horn, Pilot Knob, and U. S. Grant Peak. Pilot Knob is one of the more difficult major mountains in Colorado to climb. The summit of Pilot Knob is formed by a long, narrow ridge with steep 20′ cliffs on all sides. Less than 4 miles to the southwest of the Ice Lake Basin peaks lie San Miguel Peak, Grizzly Peak, and Rolling Mountain. Although these three peaks are located within 2 miles of each other, they are best approached from three separate directions. Northeast of Ice Lake Basin, South Lookout Peak stands to the south of Ophir Pass. On the eastern edge of the group are several lower peaks of interest: Engineer Mountain, Jura Knob, Grand Turk, and Sultan Mountain. Several rugged 13ers designated by V-nomenclature are interspersed throughout the group.

CLIMBING HISTORY

The first survey climb made in the San Juans was a climb of Engineer Mountain in June 1873 by H. G. Prout, who was topographic assistant with a US Army Corps of Engineers party led by E. H. Ruffner.

Prout climbed the northeast ridge of Engineer and was impressed by the difficulty and exposure, reporting in Ruffner's *Reconnaissance in the Ute Country* that "the feelings of a solitary man toiling on hands and knees up this edge are not cheerful." Prout was also impressed by the view of the San Juans from Engineer's summit, saying he doubted that "any other mountain region in the world displays so extensive a mass of such increasing variety of form and so wholly grand."

The following year, a Hayden Survey team led by A. D. Wilson made the first reported ascents of Vermillion Peak and Sultan Mountain. In *Mountains*, William S. Cooper reported that the top of Vermillion Peak was so small that when the "tripod was set up, we could not pass around it, but had to crawl under it."

The next reported climb in the area was the 1908 climb of Vermillion by Cooper and John Hubbard. Cooper and Hubbard approached Vermillion from Ice Lake Basin and attempted the ridge connecting Vermillion to Golden Horn. In *Mountains*, Cooper describes a 20′ vertical ledge high on the ridge that forced Hubbard to "cut foot holds with his pocketknife" in a "60-degree snowbank frozen solid." Ice axes had not been introduced in Colorado as of 1908. Cooper learned to climb under the guidance of Enos Mills, who used a hatchet to cut steps on Longs Peak.

The early 1930s saw numerous first ascents. In August 1931, T. T. Ranney and Jess Wood of the US Geological Survey made the difficult climb of South Lookout

The entirety of the Silverton West group from near V-7.

Peak. In 1932, the Colorado Mountain Club held its annual summer outing at Ice Lake Basin. During the outing, first ascents were made of U. S. Grant Peak and the western summit of Rolling Mountain. Second ascents were made of Pilot Knob and South Lookout Peak. On Pilot Knob, Dwight Lavender led a party of five, which rounded the summit ridge to the west after not finding a route on either the east or north side and climbed the first chimney that they encountered on the west that looked possible. Once on top, they were disappointed to discover that there was an easier route up the east face to the middle summit from which the true summit to the north could be reached.

Shortly before the 1932 Ice Lake Basin outing, four students from the Michigan School of Mines—Robert Jones, Jerome S. Baer, K. Spencer, and Charles Speer—made what was probably a first ascent of Golden Horn via the south face.

ACCESS AND HIKING

Ice Lake Basin

In order to reach Ice Lake Basin, the initial objective is South Mineral Campground. At 2 miles west of Silverton on US Highway 550, turn left and drive 4.5 miles on a well-maintained gravel road to South Mineral Campground. Where the campground entrance turns off to the left, turn right and park on the right side of the road. The trail to Ice Lake Basin (9,800′) starts about 100 yards farther up the road and angles up the hillside to the right (northeast). Two miles of steep hiking brings you to Lower Ice Lake Basin at 11,500′. Lower Ice Lake Basin affords the last wooded campsites. After another mile and 750 vertical feet, reach Ice Lake at 12,257′. The

SILVERTON WEST (NORTH)

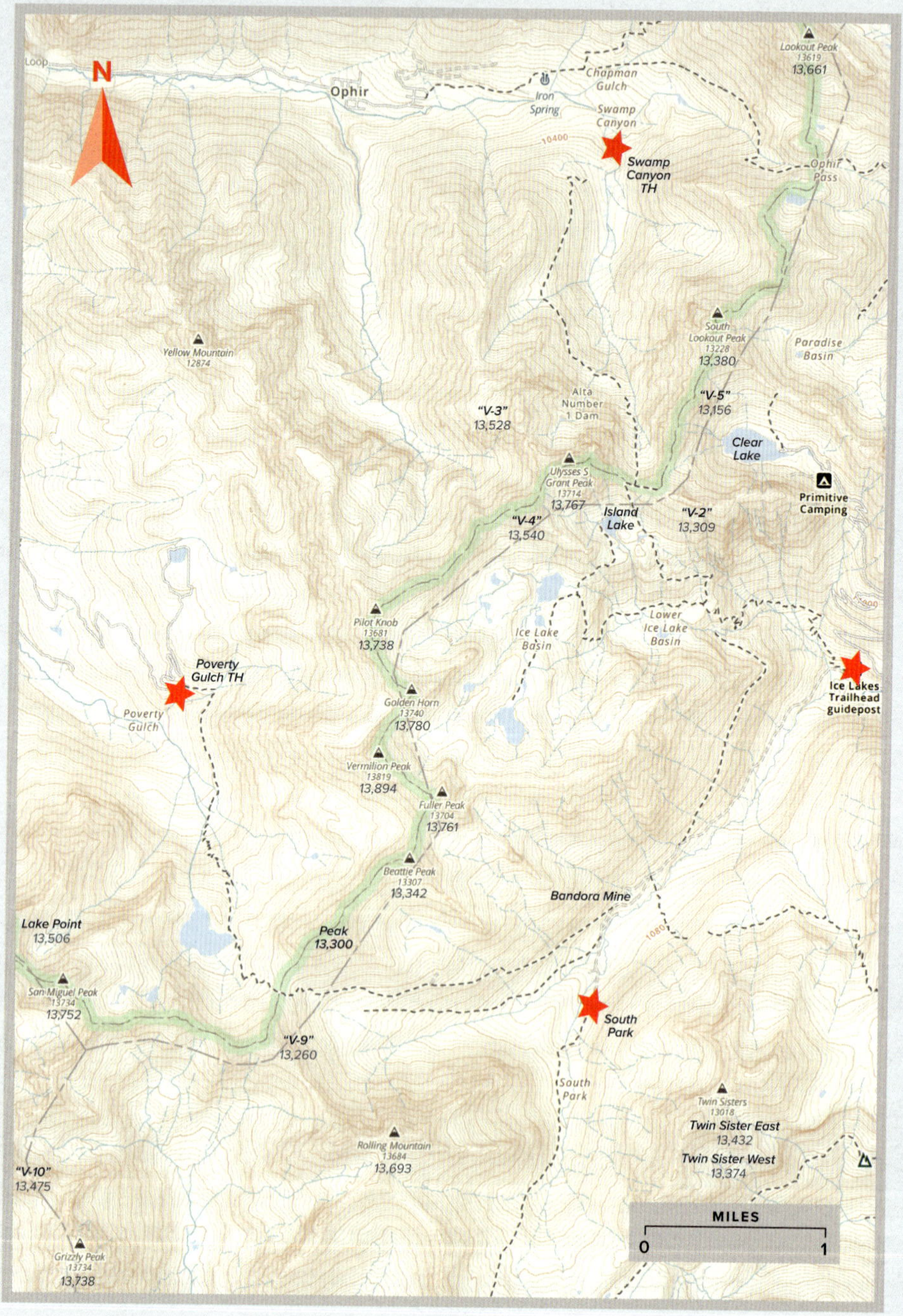

SILVERTON WEST (SOUTH)

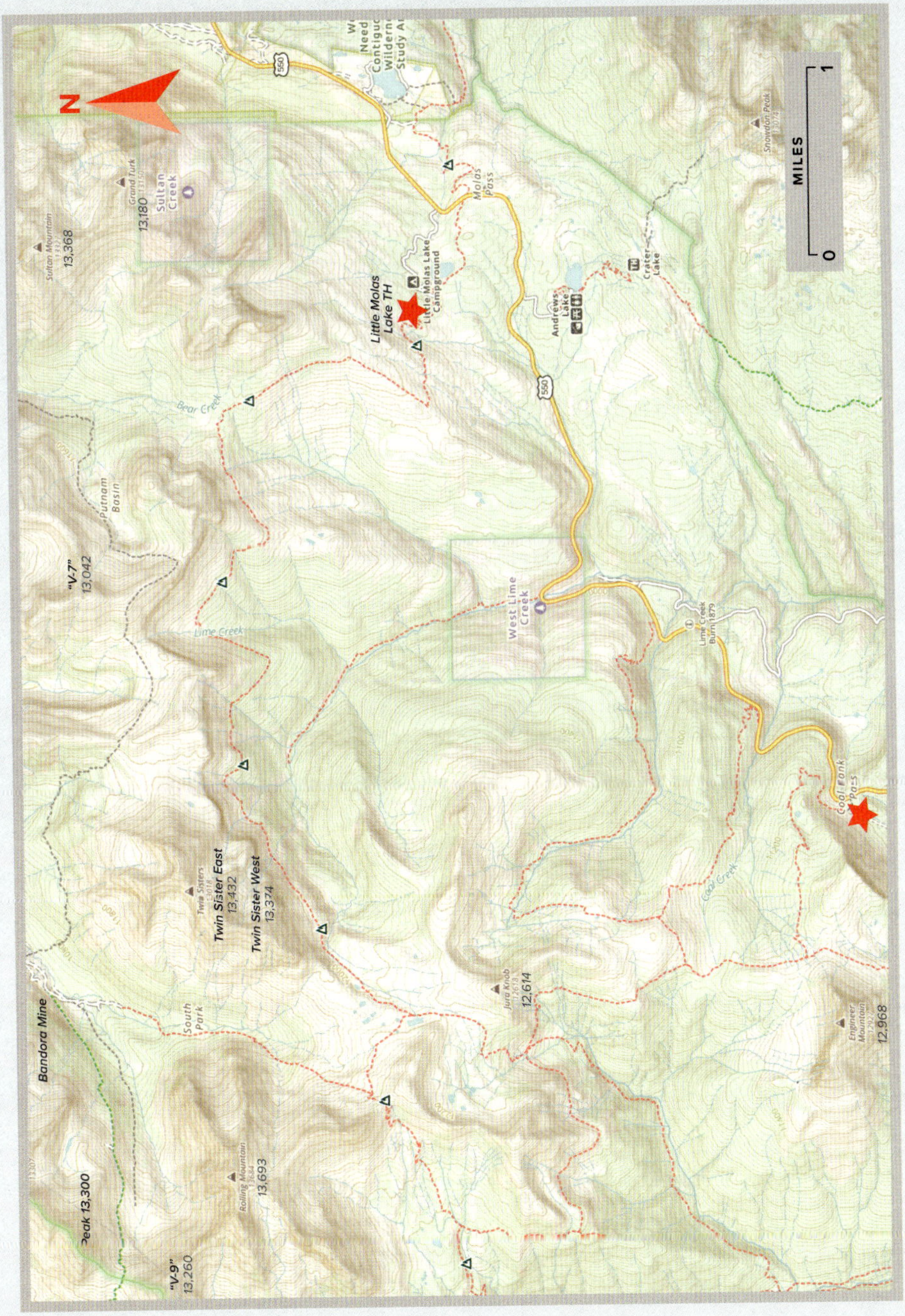

named peaks rimming Ice Lake Basin from south to north are Fuller Peak, Vermillion Peak, Golden Horn, Pilot Knob, and U. S. Grant Peak. Note: The US Forest Service has considered plans to implement a permit system for Ice Lake Basin, so bear this in mind and check with the Forest Service before heading there.

South Park

South Park is a lush meadow located between Rolling Mountain and Twin Sisters. To reach South Park follow the 4WD road that continues past South Mineral Campground. About 2.3 miles past the campground, turn left at Bandora Mine and descend to cross the stream at 2.5 miles past the campground. The Rico-Silverton Trail #507 to South Park starts 0.3 mile after crossing the stream at about 10,700′ and heads through timber before reaching South Park. From the trailhead, the trail climbs 2.7 miles to 12,600′. From the top, the trail skirts Peaks 12,766′ and 12,703′ to the west and follows the ridge between Cascade Creek and Engine Creek down to the bottom of Cascade Creek. From South Park, Rolling Mountain rises to the right (west) and Twin Sisters to the left (east). Additionally, Peak 13,300′ can be accessed just shy of this trailhead by following a trail heading southwest from Bandora Mine into the basin between Rolling Mountain and Peak 13,300′.

Clear Lake Road

The turnoff to Clear Lake is 3.8 miles from US Highway 550 on the South Mineral Campground Road. A well-maintained 4WD road takes you up to the lake at 11,940′. South Lookout Peak and U. S. Grant Peak can each be climbed from Clear Lake as well as "V-2" and "V-5," which rim the basin. Although you start out high, the route for U. S. Grant Peak from Clear Lake involves losing and then regaining elevation.

Trout Lake Road—Lake Hope Trail—Poverty Gulch

The road from Trout Lake and Lake Hope Trail provides access from the west for Pilot Knob, Golden Horn, and Vermillion Peak. Lake Hope Trail also provides the most direct route for San Miguel Peak. To reach Lake Hope Trailhead, take the turnoff to Trout Lake, which is 3 miles south of the Ophir turnoff on Colorado Highway 145 or 15 miles northeast of Rico. After turning off CO 145, skirt Trout Lake to the northeast. Turn left at 1.7 miles on Hidden Lakes Road (#627), which takes you another 2.5 miles to the trailhead (4.2 miles from US 550). Lake Hope Trail starts at about 10,300′, a few hundred yards west of Poverty Gulch. If you are interested in Pilot Knob or Golden Horn, head up Poverty Gulch. The western ridge of Vermillion is gained just after crossing the creek in Poverty Gulch. If your goal is San Miguel Peak or Beattie Peak, continue up Lake Hope Trail almost to the lake and then head east for Beattie or west for San Miguel. From the trailhead, it is 2 miles and 1,600 vertical feet to Lake Hope. Another 0.5 mile and 600 vertical feet bring you to the 12,445′ pass overlooking the South Mineral Creek drainage. From Lake Hope Trailhead, the road continues up to an unnamed lake at 11,200′ in Groundhog Gulch. This road enters private property, but if not posted for trespassing or locked, provides a higher point of beginning for the west face of Pilot Knob.

Ophir Pass Road/Swamp Canyon Trailhead

A 4WD road over Ophir Pass connects Colorado Highway 145 with US Highway 550. The turnoff on CO 145 is located at the Ophir Loop 12 miles south of Telluride or 18 miles northeast of Rico. From the CO 145 turnoff, the road continues 2 miles to Ophir and then a total of 6 miles to the top of the pass at 11,789′. The turnoff on US 550 is located 5 miles northeast of Silverton or 5.2 miles south of Red Mountain Pass. From the US 550 turnoff, 4.1 miles brings you to the top of the pass. The Ophir Pass Road provides access to Lookout Peak to the north and "V-3" to the south. The best place to start for Lookout Peak is 0.2 mile east of the pass. For "V-3," turn south 3.7 miles east of CO 145 onto the road into Swamp Canyon.

Cascade Divide Road

The best approach for Grizzly Peak B is a long, dirt road that starts at Purgatory ski area, 26 miles north of Durango or 24 miles south of Silverton. Turn west into Purgatory ski area and 1.1 miles after turning off US 550, look for a sign for Hermosa Park Road. At 3.2 miles from US 550, turn right at a sign that directs you toward Hermosa Creek Trail. At 3.7 miles, turn right (away from Hermosa Creek) on Relay Creek Road and Cascade Divide Road. At 4.9 miles, turn right on Cascade Divide Road (FSR 579). At 6.6 miles, the road becomes rocky and more difficult with occasional stream crossings and steep spots until you grind to a halt at the trailhead at 15.5 miles. A short hike from the trailhead puts you on the Continental Divide Trail that contours south of point 12,695′ and provides access from the south to Grizzly Peak.

Little Molas Lake

The turnoff to Little Molas Lake is located on US Highway 550, 7 miles south of Silverton and 43 miles north of Durango. This is 0.5 mile north of Molas Pass. From US 550, Little Molas Lake is about a mile from the highway on a well-maintained gravel road. Little Molas Lake is a good point of beginning for climbs of Grand Turk, Sultan Mountain, "V-7," or Twin Sisters. The trail for Grand Turk and Sultan, which serves as a point of beginning for these climbs, starts from the gravel road on the west side of the lake, whereas the Colorado Trail parking lot is used for Twin Sisters.

CLIMBING ROUTES

Vermillion Peak

13,894′ RANK 74

Vermillion Peak can be approached from South Mineral Campground and Ice Lake Basin or Lake Hope Trail. From Ice Lake Basin, Vermillion combines well with Fuller and Golden Horn in a single day's climb. From Lake Hope Trail, Vermillion combines well with Peak 13,300′, Beattie Peak, and Fuller Peak in one long day.

Southeast Ridge

From Ice Lake Basin TH at 9,820′: 4.3 miles, 4,070′

From Lake Hope TH at 10,740′: 4 miles, 3,150′

The best way to gain the southeast ridge of Vermillion from Ice Lake Basin is to aim for the low point on the ridge between Vermillion Peak and Fuller Peak. If coming from Lake Hope Trail, ascend the trail just shy of Lake Hope at 11,750′ and traverse northeast and up to the saddle between Vermillion and Fuller. Once on the ridge, avoid difficulties by skirting the large blocks on the ridge to the southwest (left). In a few spots, the large blocks on the ridge are circumvented to the south (left). One spot on the ridge requires an exposed Class 2+ scramble around a tower. A 100′ steep, U-shaped, Class 2+ gully leads to the summit, which is composed of loose rock. Take care not to dislodge rocks on other climbers while in the gully or on the summit.

The view from the summit of Vermillion, including Golden Horn, Pilot Knob, and Fuller.

Vermillion, Fuller, and Beattie, from Peak 13,300'.

East Couloir

From Ice Lake Basin TH at 9,820': 5 miles, 4,070'

A steep couloir lies directly below the summit to the east and is a classic Class 3 snow climb when conditions are right. The couloir is best reached by climbing toward the saddle between Golden Horn and Vermillion Peak and then traversing south toward the couloir. Crampons, helmet, an ice ax, and a few snow pickets are recommended.

Golden Horn

13,780' RANK 116

Approach Golden Horn from either Ice Lake Basin or Poverty Gulch. It combines well with Vermillion or Pilot Knob but usually not both due to the time and effort required.

Southeast Face

From Ice Lake Basin TH at 9,820': 4.3 miles, 3,960'

From Poverty Gulch at 10,740': 1.75 miles, 3,040'

From either Ice Lake Basin or Poverty Gulch, climb toward the saddle between Vermillion and Golden Horn. From the saddle, follow the southwest ridge about halfway up before moving out on to the southeast face to the right. There are two summits on Golden Horn. The western, or left-hand summit, is slightly higher. Although Golden Horn looks extremely difficult from most angles, the climb up the southeast face is generally Class 2+ with a couple of Class 3 moves.

Vermillion, Golden Horn, and Pilot Knob at sunrise.

Fuller Peak

13,761′ UNRANKED

Fuller is usually approached from Ice Lake Basin. An alternate approach is from Lake Hope Trail. Fuller combines well with Vermillion from the Ice Lake Basin side, Beattie, and Peak 13,300′ from the Lake Hope side, or climb all three in a long day from the Lake Hope side.

Northwest Ridge

From Ice Lake Basin TH at 9,820′: 4.3 miles, 3,940′

From Lake Hope TH at 10,740′: 3.75 miles, 3,020′

From Ice Lake Basin: The north face of Fuller Peak is covered by a large snowfield. The snowfield can be climbed directly to gain the 13,500′ saddle between Fuller Peak and Vermillion Peak. In late summer, the snow is gone, making for an unenjoyable climb up Class 2 scree. Once the ridge is gained, it's an easy Class 2 walk-up to the long, flat, comfortable summit.

From Lake Hope Trail: Ascend the trail just shy of Lake Hope at 11,750′ and traverse northeast and up to the saddle between Vermillion and Fuller. Once the ridge is gained, enjoy the easy walk-up to the summit.

Pilot Knob

13,738′ RANK 132

Pilot Knob is traditionally approached from Ice Lake Basin to the east. The easiest route on this challenging peak, however, is on the west face, which can be approached from Lake Hope Trail and Poverty Gulch or, if not posted for trespassing, the road on private property in Groundhog Gulch. From either approach, Pilot Knob combines well with Golden Horn.

West Face

From Ice Lake Basin TH at 9,820′: 4.75 miles, 3,920′

If approaching Pilot Knob from Ice Lake Basin, climb up loose talus and scree to the right (north) of Pilot Knob, pass the summit block to the north, and then turn left (south) to make an ascending traverse to reach the base of the west face near its midpoint. Look for cairns and climb the west face at this point to gain the summit ridge. There are two prominent summits on Pilot Knob: the northern summit, which is the highest, and the central summit. Between these summits are two irregularly shaped obstacles on the summit ridge. The notch between the two intermediate obstacles is the low point on the summit ridge. The notch can be gained from the west without technical difficulty. Once on the ridge, the heftier challenges begin as you encounter Class 4 climbing on exposed, loose ground. The most difficult spot is the irregularly shaped tower just south of the true (north) summit, where you make an exposed

Pilot Knob at sunrise.

Left: On the crux pitch during a winter climb of Pilot Knob. Photo by Bob Rosebrough **Right:** Left to right: V-4, U. S. Grant, and V-2.

downclimb on loose ground to the left (west). Most people will want a rope belay. A half-length rope works well on the summit ridge. Once around the obstacle just south of the summit, the difficult ground is over.

East Face Couloirs

From Ice Lake Basin TH at 9,820′: 4.9 miles, 3,920′

From Poverty Gulch at 10,740′: 2 miles, 3,000′

Pilot Knob's east face, which you view from Ice Lake Basin, is more difficult than the west-face route, which is out of view from Ice Lake. To climb Pilot Knob by either of the east-face couloirs, the beginning point is the saddle between Golden Horn and Pilot Knob, reached from either Ice Lake Basin or Poverty Gulch. From the saddle, traverse below the summit block past the central summit. The first yellow couloir north of the central summit has a lower section that is loose and rotten but not particularly difficult. The last 10′ to 15′ are both rotten and lower Class 5 climbing—protection should be employed. The first couloir tops out at the notch between the central summit and the intermediate summit just to the north. Once on the summit ridge, it is generally better to traverse or downclimb obstacles to the left (west). A half-length rope and several camming devices are recommended. When looking for the yellow couloirs, be sure to distinguish between a chimney and a couloir. There are a couple of steep yellow chimneys just north of the central summit that should be avoided.

The San Juans and Island Lake, from the summit of U. S. Grant.

U. S. Grant Peak

13,767′ RANK 119

Ulysses S. Grant Peak is usually approached from South Mineral Campground, Ice Lake Basin, and Island Lake Basin. It combines well with Peak 13,520′ ("V-4").

Southwest Ridge

From Ice Lake Basin TH at 9,820′: 4 miles, 3,950′

The southwest ridge is a Class 4 climb that begins at the 13,220′ saddle separating U. S. Grant from "V-4." To reach the saddle, climb up Ice Lake Basin Trail to 11,200′, where you will find the Island Lake Trail. Continue up to Island Lake and climb northwest into the Island Lake Basin and then directly to the saddle. If coming from Upper Ice Lake Basin, use the easy-to-find Ice Lake–Island Lake cutoff trail located at 12,260′ just east of Ice Lakes. Follow the ridge to a point where you climb a 15′ cliff with good holds that gains a narrow ledge with some exposure. The ledge leads horizontally right (east) for about 150′ to 200′ until it reaches the south face where a gully leads you to the summit. A rope belay is advisable for the cliff and at least one exposed section on the ledge.

Northeast Ridge

From Ice Lake Basin TH at 9,820′: 4 miles, 3,940′

The rock band on the lower portion of the ridge is skirted by going out onto the east face. After reaching the top of the rock band, it is quicker to contour back over to gain the ridge, rather than fighting the loose rock on the east face. Once back on the ridge, the best route climbs just to the right (west) of the ridge. As you near the top, you encounter some Class 2+ scrambling.

South Lookout Peak

13,380′ RANK 333

South Lookout Peak is best approached from Clear Lake. Note that from Clear Lake, the summit of South Lookout is not visible; what you see is a high point on the ridge due west of Clear Lake. The three clustered high points of South Lookout are actually right (north) of that visible high point. South Lookout can be combined with "V-5" or "V-2" or both, but it deserves to be the primary focus of your attention, as it is one of the most challenging peaks in the San Juans and a difficult routefinding test.

Southeast Flank and Upper East Face

From Clear Lake at 11,940′: 1 mile, 1,440′

From Clear Lake, it's easy to reach the southern summit of South Lookout Peak. There are three summits on South Lookout, and the middle summit is the high point and can't be reached directly via the south summit. To reach the middle summit, it's necessary to do a jagged descending and then ascending traverse on the upper east face of the peak on exposed, steep, and, at times, loose rock via challenging Class 4 terrain. You will cross the tops of several couloirs and rock ribs that are closely clustered and soon reach the steep flank of the true (middle) summit, which you ascend right to left (east to west). Climb13ers.com does a great job of describing this difficult-to-explain route:

> *From the east side and below the false south summit, descend via a contouring angle down the east flank of the mountain, crossing one branch of a larger scree-filled couloir then a very minor rib of rock and entering the second branch of the wide couloir. Continue angling down and arrive at a vertical wall of rock. Total elevation loss to this point is less than 100′. At the wall of rock, continue to descend some until you reach a section of the wall that is less vertical. Ascend here via a 30′ Class 4 scramble on loose rock to a small perch on the rib crest. From here, change directions to the left and cross over the crest of the rib. On the rib crest, you can see your next objective: an extremely steep couloir just a few feet away. A rock ledge, about 4″ wide and 3′ long, leads into this narrow couloir. Enter the couloir. In early summer, it will most likely be filled with snow and require the security of an ice ax to cross. Ascend the couloir 5′ to 10′ in order to exit the couloir on the right and scramble up a few*

Left to right: South Lookout, Bear Mountain (in front), and Lookout.

feet to find a good exit point. Walk out onto the more stable but steep slope above the couloir and locate a faint trail. Hike northwest along the slope of rock ledges and tundra, cross the next minor ridge, and then ascend west on yet another flat scree slope to a flat area immediately below the middle summit block. From here, it's just another easy Class 3 scramble up the blocky cliff to the summit on secure rock. If taking rope, you don't need more than 100′ and some slings to set up an anchor.

San Miguel Peak

13,752′ **RANK 124**

San Miguel Peak, located 2.4 miles southwest of Vermillion Peak, is impressive from all angles. A climb of San Miguel combines well with Lake Point.

Northeast Flank/Ridge

From Lake Hope TH at 10,740′: 3.75 miles, 3,010′

To reach the northeast ridge, leave Lake Hope Trail before it reaches the lake and traverse toward the lake's outlet. To bypass the large, jutting buttress on the lower portion of the northeast flank, gain the ridge from the east at about 12,500′. Once on the ridge, follow it directly toward the summit on Class 2+ terrain. Near the summit, you will find yourself rock hopping on large boulders and downclimbing a gap in the summit ridge with some Class 3+ moves.

San Miguel, Lake Point, and Lake Hope, from Peak 13,300'.

West Ridge

From Lake Hope TH at 10,740': 3 miles, 3,010′

The west ridge begins at the 13,260′ pass separating San Miguel from Peak 13,491′ and is the logical route to use if you plan on combining it with Lake Point (next entry). The pass is reached by leaving Lake Hope Trail at about 11,000′ and contouring into the drainage to the north of San Miguel. Once on the ridge, bypass the large rock face to the right (south). The final portion of the Class 3 west ridge is narrow and exposed in spots on loose rock.

Peak 13,506'—"Lake Point"

UNRANKED

Lake Point is located 0.5 mile northwest of San Miguel Peak and is the block-topped peak east of Sheep Mountain, which is clearly visible from the Trout Lake area and Colorado Highway 145. There is no easy way to get to Lake Point.

East Face

From Lake Hope TH at 10,740': 3.5 miles, 3,010′

The best approach for Lake Point is to leave Lake Hope Trail and contour into the drainage north of San Miguel Peak. The east face is a steady climb over small loose rock to reach the 30′ near-vertical summit block. The summit can be reached either from the east or the west sides of the summit block. The Class 5.2 route on the east is easier than it looks because of a ledge on the route that is out of view from the base.

Rolling Mountain

13,693′ RANK 150

The approach for Rolling Mountain takes the road to the south fork of Mineral Creek past the campground to the Rico-Silverton Trail and follows the trail to South Park. We recommend the east basin–east-southeast ridge route as an ascent route and the southeast basin–southwest face route as a descent route.

East Basin–East-Southeast Ridge

From South Park at 11,150′: 1.1 miles, 2,550′

From South Park, climb directly up into the large basin east of Rolling Mountain. In the lower basin, climb the talus and boulder field left (south) of the stream rather than bushwhack through brush right (north) of the stream. Once in the upper basin, bear to the left (south) to gain the Class 3 southeast ridge, which you follow to the summit.

Southeast Basin–Southwest Face

From South Park at 11,150′: 2 miles, 2,550′

This route is easier and more roundabout than the east basin route. To gain the southeast basin, follow the Rico-Silverton Trail for 0.5 mile after reaching South Park before leaving the trail and heading west. Once atop the basin, contour north to gain the Class 2 southwest face, which is composed of loose scree and talus.

Rolling Mountain from Peak 13,300′ to the north.

Peak 13,042′—"V-7"

RANK 612

V-7 is located 2 miles east of Twin Sisters and is best accessed via the Colorado Trail from Little Molas Lake Trailhead.

South Slopes

From Little Molas Lake–Colorado Trail TH at 10,940′: 6.2 miles, 2,650′

Ascend the pedestrian Colorado Trail from the trailhead for 5.1 miles at 11,550′. Leave the trail and head north on a faint trail (or bushwhack if you cannot locate it) toward the obvious gap between Peak 12,329′ and Peak 12,764′. Once through the gap, you'll gain views of U. S. Grant, Vermillion, and Golden Horn and continue northeast on a faint trail to 12,250′, where you will veer right (east) up the gentle grassy slopes until you reach the top of the ridge. Once on the ridge, turn left (north) and gain the summit of V-7. You can easily combine Peak 12,764′ and return via the same route. More adventurous travelers can combine V-7 with Bear Mountain (12,987′) located 1.3 miles northeast of V-7; however, it would be a very long day of hiking.

Ascending the gentle slopes of V-7.

Twin Sister West and Twin Sister East

13,374′ and 13,432′ **RANKS 341 AND 298**

The approach to Twin Sisters takes you to the South Mineral Campground with 2WD and to the Bandora Mine 2.3 miles beyond South Mineral Campground with 4WD. At 0.2 mile past the Bandora Mine, cross a stream, and 0.5 mile past Bandora Mine, you reach Rico-Silverton Trailhead. With 2WD, the approach to Twin Sisters begins on the road at South Mineral Campground and adds 2.5 miles on foot, one-way, to your approach.

West Flank

From South Park at 11,150′: 1.2 miles, 2,220′ (West Sister only)

From South Park at 11,150′: 1.7 miles, 2,670′ (both sisters)

To reach the west flank of the West Sister, leave the Rico-Silverton Trail in South Park and climb through oak brush and grassy slopes to reach the rocky talus slope ridge. Follow a ridge on the Class 2 west flank directly to the summit or do an ascending traverse to gain the ridge south-southwest of the summit on the West Sister on Class 2+ terrain. The west flank is neither exposed nor particularly difficult. The talus is tedious, but the views are great. The ridge between the sisters presents little difficulty, and it is about 0.5 mile from the West Sister to the East Sister, with 450′ of elevation gain from the saddle between the summits to the top of the East Sister. The Twin Sisters are the two easiest ranked mountains in the San Juans to combine in one climb.

Southeast Slopes

From Little Molas Lake–Colorado Trail TH at 10,940′: 8.2 miles, 3,900′ (both sisters)

This adventurous route follows the same route as V-7 described above. When you reach the gap between Peak 12,329′ and Peak 12,764′, follow a trail to the left (west), which contours gradually to the north to a saddle between Peak 12,601′ and the long ridge of Peak 12,579′ (both worthy as extra credit). From this saddle, continue on the trail, which descends into a spacious basin filled with small tarns and a larger lake to the southwest. In July, the flowers in this basin are incredible, and it makes for a wonderful backpacking destination. To here, everything is Class 2. From the large lake at 12,270′, begin an arduous and steep Class 2+ sufferfest up the southeast slope of East Sister. Pick out a zigzagging route, which utilizes dirt patches to avoid back-sliding talus until you reach the summit. Head down to the saddle between East Sister and West Sister and climb to the summit of East Sister for a quick combination. You can reclimb East Sister and return the way you came on poor dirt and scree (not advised) or descend from the saddle of East and West Sister to the

Left: Twin Sister West at sunrise with Engineer peeking out on the left. **Right:** East Sister and Rolling, from West Sister.

southeast to 12,250′, where you rejoin the trail that brought you to the large lake originally. From here, reclimb into the basin to the northeast and back the way you came, all the way to Little Molas Lake.

Grizzly Peak B

13,738′ RANK 130

Grizzly Peak B is connected via a long, rugged ridge 1.6 miles south of San Miguel Peak. When driving north from Durango on US 550, it is visible on your left after you pass Purgatory ski area. The approach to Grizzly Peak B is on a rough dirt road that we call the Grizzly Peak Road, accessed from the Purgatory ski area. Grizzly B is hard to combine with any other peaks.

Southwest Couloir and Southwest Ridge

From Cascade Divide Road at 11,170′: 3.6 miles, 2,600′

From the end of Cascade Divide Road, climb northwest on a trail for 0.25 mile to join the Colorado Trail and turn right (north). Contour on the Colorado Trail another 0.25 mile until you cross a stream. Continue on the trail another 0.25 mile looking for a climbers' trail that branches left from the Colorado Trail to make an ascending traverse of 400 vertical feet east and north to a flat level area southwest of Grizzly with two ponds at 11,400′. From the ponds, there are two visible, prominent couloirs on Grizzly. One couloir runs down the center of the southwest face and another couloir, to the left (west), intersects the southwest ridge of Grizzly below a rock buttress. Climb the couloir to the left to reach the Class 2+ southwest ridge of Grizzly, which takes you to the summit.

Peak 13,475′—"V-10"

RANK **271**

V-10, 0.5 mile northwest of Grizzly Peak B, is wild and remote, with no easy way to get to it. The most direct access route is to hike up the remains of the old road past the end of the South Mineral Campground Road. Hiking this abandoned road takes you to the saddle between Rolling Mountain and V-9 (13,290′). By this route, you hike 4.5 miles and gain almost 4,000′ one-way to climb V-10. Note that V-9 combines well with V-10 since it sits on the western end of the 12,800′ saddle that you reach early on your approach to V-10.

North Face

From Bandora Mine at 10,660′: 5 miles, 4,200′

From the saddle between Rolling Mountain and V-9, downclimb into the upper basin of Cascade Creek and then ascend into the basin north of V-10. The summit of V-10 is on the western end of the mountain's spine. Aim to gain the V-shaped notch on the western side of the summit ridge and after gaining the summit ridge, follow it west, on loose, exposed Class 3+ ground, to the top. Much of the approach and the climb of V-10 is made on rubble and dinner-plate talus.

Grizzly B and V-10, from the east.

Left: Engineer from below on the approach. **Right:** Engineer's terrain on the final section.

Engineer Mountain

12,968′ RANK **655**

Just shy of 13,000′, Engineer Mountain is close, convenient, and majestic. Located just west of Coal Bank Pass, on US 550 between Durango and Silverton, Engineer is one of the most frequently climbed peaks in the San Juans. The parking lot on the west end of Coal Bank Pass is usually jammed full of vehicles, and the trail buzzes with hikers, climbers, and mountain bikers.

Northeast Ridge

From Coal Bank Pass TH at 10,680′: 6.4 miles, 2,280′

It's almost impossible to get off-route on the hike up to the foot of the northeast ridge of Engineer Mountain; the trail is well worn, usually with throngs of other trail users. The northeast ridge is bounded to the north by sheer cliffs. To the east and south, the angle is not severe. The northeast ridge takes you directly to the summit. The crux of the route is a Class 3+ chimney that you have to stem at the top to reach easier ground above on the sloping east face that leads to the summit.

Grand Turk

13,180′ RANK **502**

Grand Turk is frequently approached from the Little Molas Lake and Colorado Trail Trailhead area just below Molas Pass on US 550 to the west. Grand Turk can be combined with Sultan Mountain and Spencer Peak.

Southwest Ridge

From Little Molas Lake at 10,890′: 3 miles, 2,400′ (Grand Turk only)

From Little Molas Lake at 10,890′: 3.75 miles, 2,840′ (Spencer, Grand Turk, and Sultan combo)

At 0.8 mile from US 550 on the gravel road to Little Molas Pass, a climbers' trail heads uphill to the north for 1.5 miles toward the saddle between points 12,849′ and 12,734′. The trail can be hard to find as it weaves through willows and corn lilies, but the canyon narrows as it gains elevation. The trail steepens and becomes well defined on the canyon's east side as it gets closer to the 12,300′ saddle. From the saddle, a well-defined climbers' trail makes an ascending traverse of a grass slope to the northeast and the saddle between points 12,899′ and 13,087′ (Spencer Peak). From the saddle, head north-northeast toward Spencer Peak by climbing a Class 3 40′ irregular block on the ridge or circumventing it by a short downclimb. The well-defined climbers' trail splits as you gain elevation on Spencer Peak, allowing you to either climb Spencer or traverse it on its northwest flank as you head toward the southwest ridge of Grand Turk. The trail leads you up the southwest ridge of Grand Turk to the three high points on Grand Turk's summit. The entire route is Class 2 with the exception of a steep Class 2+ section before you reach the initial 12,300′ saddle and the Class 3 block at the saddle between point 12,899′ and Spencer Peak, which can be easily circumvented by a short downclimb.

Grand Turk (right) and Sultan (left), from the approach via Spencer.

Sultan from the approach via Little Molas Lake.

Sultan Mountain

13,368′ RANK 346

Sultan Mountain is located 0.7 mile northwest of Grand Turk and just 2.3 miles southwest of Silverton. Sultan Mountain towers above the Mineral Creek Basin to the north and is prominently visible from Red Mountain Pass on US 550 coming south from Ouray.

South Ridge

From Little Molas Lake at 10,890′: 3.75 miles, 2,840′ (Spencer, Grand Turk, and Sultan combo)

The Class 2 climbers' trails on Grand Turk and Sultan are well defined, stable, and efficient. When combined with Grand Turk, the base of the south ridge on Sultan is reached by downclimbing the northeast ridge of Grand Turk from its western summit to the shared saddle between the two peaks. From afar, the south ridge on Sultan looks daunting but turns out to be a Class 2 climb on generally stable ground.

OFF THE BEATEN PATH

Beattie Peak

13,342′ RANK 359

0.65 mile south-southeast of Vermillion

Beattie can be approached from either Ice Lake Basin or from Lake Hope Trail.

From Ice Lake Basin TH at 9,820′: 4.3 miles, 3,520′

From Lake Hope TH at 10,740′: 3.75 miles, 2,600′

North Ridge: From the 13,020′ saddle connecting Beattie to Fuller Peak, Beattie's summit is reached by a Class 2 hike up scree.

Peak 13,300′

RANK 403

1.05 miles south of Vermillion

From Lake Hope TH at 10,740′: 3.5 miles, 3,010′

Southwest Flank: Peak 13,300′ (referred to as "V-8" by some) is climbed from Lake Hope Pass via its southwest flank and southwest ridge on Class 2+ terrain.

Peak 13,260′—"V-9"

RANK 435

1 mile northeast of Rolling Mountain

From Bandora Mine at 10,660′: 2.75 miles, 2,600′

Southeast Ridge: From the saddle between V-9 and Rolling Mountain, climb the southeast ridge of V-9, bypassing the cliffs on the ridge to the north (right) on Class 2+ terrain.

Peak 13,309′—"V-2"

RANK 387

0.75 mile east of U. S. Grant

From Ice Lake Basin TH at 9,820′: 3.5 miles, 3,490′

From Clear Lake at 11,940′: 1.5 miles, 1,370′

Western Ridge: From either basin, climb to the pass between U. S. Grant and V-2 (Clear Lake to the northeast and Island Lake to the south). V-2 is a Class 2 climb up its western ridge.

Peak 13,528′—"V-3"

RANK 238

0.5 mile northwest of U. S. Grant

From Swamp Canyon TH at 10,210′: 2.75 miles, 3,350′

Northwest Flank: An ascending traverse of the west side of Swamp Canyon gains the V-3 and point 12,348′ saddle. Above the saddle, a Class 4 scramble concludes with a traverse on the east side of the summit block.

At Island Lake, gazing up at V-4 and U. S. Grant at night.

Peak 13,540′—"V-4"

RANK 228

0.3 mile southwest of U. S. Grant

From Ice Lake Basin TH at 9,820′: 4 miles, 3,720′

Southwest Ridge: Some loose rock and difficult terrain low on the ridge is avoided by some Class 2+ moves, after which it becomes an easy climb.

Peak 13,156′—"V-5"

RANK 518

1.25 miles southwest of South Lookout Peak

From Clear Lake at 11,940′: 1 mile, 1,210′

Southeast Flank: An old mining road or grassy slopes lead to a prominent couloir that takes you to a Class 2+ route on the southeast ridge and to the summit.

Jura Knob

12,614′ RANK 925

2.65 miles north of Engineer Mountain

From Coal Bank Creek TH at 10,350′: 3.8 miles, 2,204′

Southeast Ridge: A Class 1 hike above tree line leading to a short Class 2+ ledge not far from the summit that presents the only difficulty.

SILVERTON EAST GROUP

7

Left to right: Half Peak, Kendall Mountain, Kendall Peak, Mountaineer, Rhoda, and Whitehead.

This smaller subset of mostly gentle mountains is located between Silverton and the Grenadiers and covers approximately 56 square miles of terrain, including Kendall Mountain, Kendall Peak, Little Giant Peak, King Solomon Mountain, Galena Mountain, Canby Mountain, "Stony Pass Peak," Sheep Mountain A, Greenhalgh Mountain, Peak 13,109′, Whitehead Peak, Mount Rhoda, and "Mountaineer Peak." The peaks offer fantastic views of the Grenadiers to the south and, thanks to various high-elevation access points and less technical terrain, make for easier climbs suited for beginners or those looking for a casual day in the mountains.

SILVERTON EAST

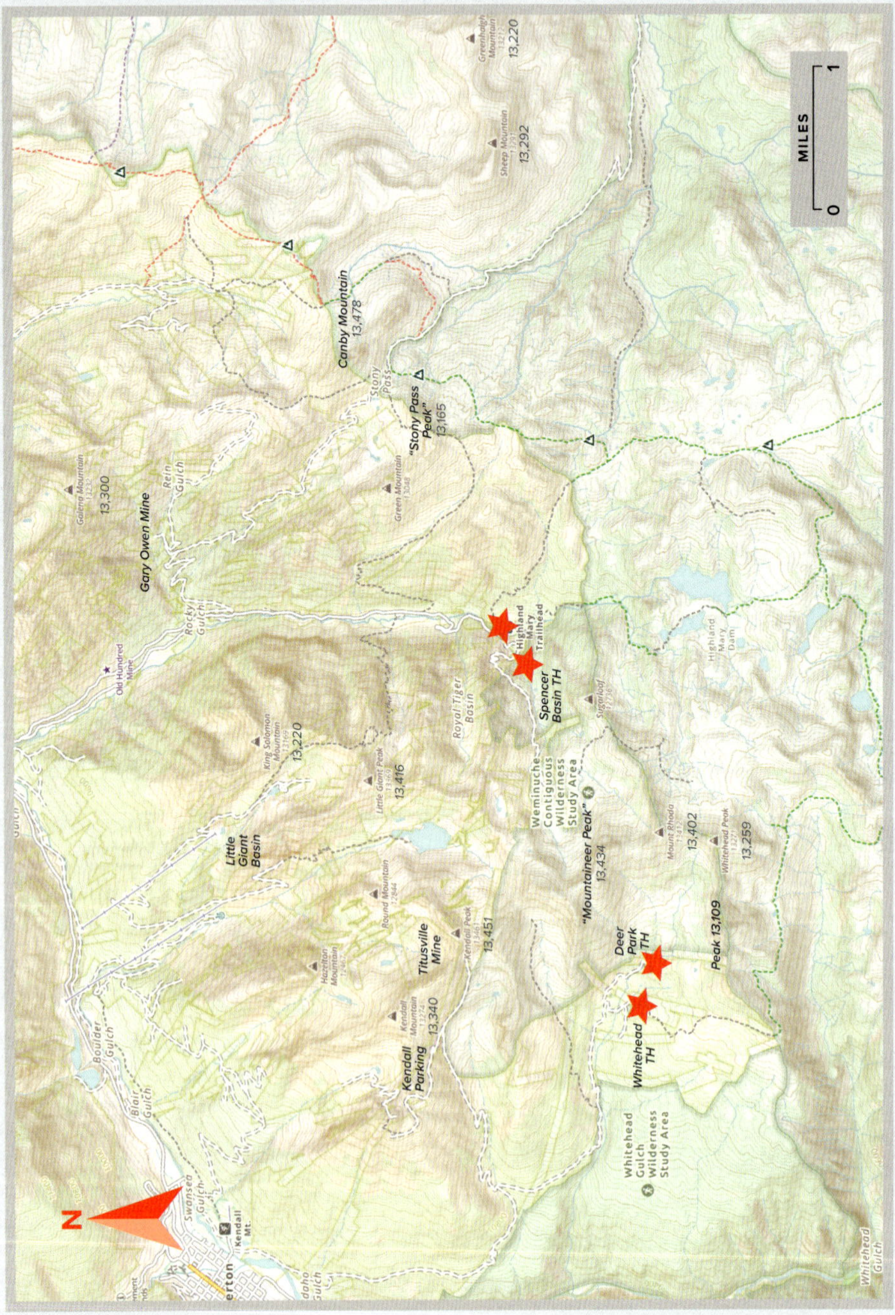

ACCESS AND HIKING

Kendall Gulch

Kendall Gulch is a 4WD road providing high-altitude access to Kendall Mountain, Kendall Peak, "Mountaineer Peak," Mount Rhoda, and Whitehead Peak. From Silverton, take Greene Street north to Fourteenth Street and turn right (east). Continue on Fourteenth Street for 0.25 mile, and turn right (south) on County Road 33 (Kendall Mountain Road). Continue up this high-clearance, bouldery road for 4.5 miles to a junction at 12,250′. Park here or continue 0.75 mile west to a small parking area at 12,720′ if you are looking to climb Kendall Mountain easily from the saddle between Kendall Mountain and Kendall No. 2 Benchmark. Alternatively, continue driving east up the road junction to the Titusville Mine if you are looking to climb Kendall Peak, Mountaineer Peak, Mount Rhoda, Whitehead Peak, and Peak 13,109′ from this access point.

Deer Park—Whitehead Trail/Deer Park Trail

Deer Park provides access from the west for Mountaineer Peak, Mount Rhoda, Whitehead Peak, and Peak 13,109′ and offers a way to combine peaks in a loop on the Whitehead Trail and Deer Park Trail. From Silverton, take Greene Street north to Fourteenth Street and turn right (east). Continue on Fourteenth Street for 0.25 mile and turn right (south) on County Road 33 (Kendall Mountain Road). Continue on this high-clearance, bouldery road to mile 3.6 and take the Deer Park junction on your right. Continue up the road until you locate a large meadow at mile 5.2, just below Montana Mine, where you'll find ample parking and camping. There is a road junction here, which splits the road, with one split going east and one going south. Deer Park Trail is located at the eastern end of the road, and Whitehead Trail is located at the south end of the road.

Little Giant Basin

For those with 4WD, Little Giant Basin offers quick access to Little Giant Peak and King Solomon Mountain, which can easily be climbed together from the road. From the end of Greene Street in Silverton, turn right (east) on CO Highway 110. Continue 2 miles east to County Road 52, turn right (south) and continue 1.1 miles before turning sharply to the left (north). Continue 2.6 miles to 11,930′ to the start of the trail, which ascends the Little Giant–King Solomon saddle.

Cunningham Gulch/Highland Mary Lakes Trailhead

Cunningham Gulch offers access to Highland Mary Lakes Trailhead, a popular backpacking destination. From Highland Mary Lakes, climbers can easily access Peak

13,109′, Whitehead Peak, Mount Rhoda, and Mountaineer Peak. This road is usually accessible by medium-clearance vehicles with 2WD, but the final 0.17 mile requires a creek crossing that is not generally advised without high clearance and 4WD. From the end of Greene Street in Silverton, turn right (east) on CO Highway 110 and continue 3.8 miles to a junction on your right for Stony Pass and Cunningham Gulch. Turn right (south) here and then south on the Cunningham Gulch Road #589. At mile 4.2, the road splits; either option is fine as they meet up at mile 5.7, where the road splits again, providing access to the left for Stony Pass and to the right for Highland Mary Lakes Trailhead. Stay right at the Stony Pass junction and continue south on the road to mile 8.4. The road will switchback a few times until you reach the turnoff on your left (east) for the Highland Mary Trailhead parking lot. Low-clearance vehicles may opt to park here as the creek crossing can be deep.

Spencer Basin

Spencer Basin is a suitable access point for Peak 13,109′, Whitehead Peak, Mount Rhoda, and Mountaineer Peak and is accessed the same way that Highland Mary Lakes Trailhead is via Cunningham Gulch from Silverton on the same roads, except instead of turning left near the end of the road to Highland Mary Lakes Trailhead, you'll either continue an additional 0.5 mile to a small parking lot suitable for two or three vehicles (4WD only) or park at the 2WD lot for Highland Mary Lakes.

Stony Pass

Stony Pass and the road leading up to Stony Pass provide access to Galena Mountain (prior to the summit of the pass) and Canby Mountain, "Stony Pass Peak," Sheep Mountain A, and Greenhalgh Mountain from the summit of the pass at 12,650′ and beyond to the southwest side of the pass. High clearance and 4WD is recommended, and consider airing down your tires as well due to the sharp rocks. From the end of Greene Street in Silverton, turn right (east) on CO Highway 110. Continue for 3.8 miles to a junction on your right for Stony Pass and Cunningham Gulch. Turn right (south) here and then south on the Cunningham Gulch Road #589. At mile 4.2, the road splits; either option is fine as they meet up at mile 5.7 where the road splits again, providing access to the left for Stony Pass and to the right for Highland Mary Lakes Trailhead. Stay left at the Stony Pass junction and continue to mile 7.3 to a junction at 11,150′. For Galena Mountain, go left (north) toward the Gary Owen Mine. All others continue right (south) to mile 10, where you will find ample parking at the Stony Pass summit. For Sheep Mountain A and Greenhalgh, descend southeast on the other side of the Stony Pass summit to mile 11.3 at 11,920′, near where the road first crosses the headwaters of the Rio Grande, and begin from here.

CLIMBING ROUTES

Kendall Mountain

13,340′ RANK 363

Kendall Mountain, located just 2 miles southeast of Silverton, is one of the most prominent peaks seen from town. There are two separate summits for Kendall Mountain, so don't be confused. The 13,066′ point farthest to the west is actually Kendall No. 2 Benchmark, connected via a ridge to the east with the true 13,340′ summit just 0.7 mile away.

Southwest Ridge

From Kendall No. 2 Benchmark–Kendall Mountain saddle parking at 12,720′: 0.65 mile, 630′

Park near the Kendall No. 2 Benchmark–Kendall Mountain saddle at 12,720′. From this spot off the road, simply climb east over the 12,860′ point and along the saddle to the southwest slopes of Kendall Mountain and up to the summit on Class 2 terrain.

Kendall Peak

13,451′ RANK 288

Kendall Peak is located 0.7 mile southeast of Kendall Mountain and, when looking at the topo map, seems to be an easy ridge walk from Kendall Mountain; however, there is a cliff between the two, making the combination via the ridge virtually unclimbable.

Left to right: Little Giant, Kendall Peak, and Kendall Mountain.

South Ridge

From Titusville Mine 4WD parking at 12,770′: 0.3 mile, 580′

From the end of the road below Kendall Peak at Titusville Mine, gain the saddle south of Kendall Peak by ascending a steep Class 2 scree gully. From the saddle, turn left (north) to a mellow walk-up to the summit. To combine Kendall Peak with Mountaineer Peak, Mount Rhoda, Whitehead Peak, and Peak 13,109′, continue south to the Kendall Peak–Peak 13,409′ (unranked) saddle where a trail traverses around the north side of Peak 13,409′ to grassy slopes on the northwest side of Mountaineer Peak.

"Mountaineer Peak"

13,434′ RANK 296

Mountaineer Peak is located 1.2 miles southeast of Kendall Peak at the southwestern end of Spencer Basin and above Mountaineer Creek.

West Ridge

From Titusville Mine 4WD parking at 12,770′ via Kendall Peak: 2 miles, 1,450′

After summiting Kendall Peak, continue south on a gentle Class 2 slope to the Kendall Peak–Peak 13,409′ saddle just south of Kendall Peak. From here, follow a trail that traverses east and south around Peak 13,409′ to grassy slopes and continue to ascend up the Peak 13,409′–Mountaineer Peak saddle and south (left) up the northwest side of Mountaineer Peak to the summit. Mount Rhoda can be combined from here by descending the south slopes on easy terrain.

South Ridge

From Spencer Basin TH at 10,820′: 2.8 miles, 2,760′

From Deer Park TH at 11,750′ via Mount Rhoda (see the next entry): 2.1 miles, 1,910′

Starting from the end of Cunningham Gulch Road and the start of Spencer Basin Trailhead, follow the road west into the basin to a mine at 12,420′. From the mine, continue south and west to the Mountaineer Peak–Mount Rhoda saddle at 13,090′, turn right (north) and head up steep Class 2+ terrain to the summit. Mount Rhoda can also be combined from here by descending the south slopes on easy terrain.

Mount Rhoda

13,402′ RANK 319

Mount Rhoda, located 0.4 mile south-southeast of Mountaineer Peak and 0.4 mile north of Whitehead Peak, is easy to recognize by its flat, blocky summit. It is named for Franklin Rhoda, a member of the Hayden Survey and a pioneer in early San Juan mountaineering.

The sun sets behind Rhoda and Mountaineer, as seen from high above Highland Mary Lakes.

Northwest Slopes

From Titusville Mine 4WD parking at 12,770′ via Kendall Peak and Mountaineer Peak: 2.5 miles, 1,720′

From Spencer Basin TH at 10,820′: 3 miles, 2,780′

From Deer Park TH at 11,750′ via Mount Rhoda: 1.6 miles, 1,620′

Follow the route for the south ridge of Mountaineer Peak in the previous entry. From the Mountaineer Peak–Mount Rhoda saddle at 13,090′, turn left (south) up a steep Class 2 slope, where you'll encounter a small 10′ cliff band near the summit, which can be easily negotiated on Class 2+ terrain.

South Slopes

From Deer Park TH at 11,750′: 1.6 miles, 1,620′

From Highland Mary Lakes TH at 10,810′: 4.6 miles, 2,470′

There are three approaches to gain the south slopes of Mount Rhoda, one of which is a four-peak combination from Deer Park, which is covered in the Peak 13,109′ entry (below). The best way to climb Mount Rhoda on its own is from Highland Mary Lakes Trailhead, as it offers opportunities for backpacking and other adven-

Whitehead (left) and Rhoda (right), from the east.

tures in the area. It can also be done by itself from Deer Park. From Highland Mary Lakes Trailhead, ascend the well-traveled trail south for 2.3 miles to 12,160′ at a point between the two largest lakes in the basin, where you can turn right (west) and follow a faint trail to the Whitehead Peak–Mount Rhoda saddle at 13,060′. From the saddle, it is an easy Class 2 climb to the summit to your right (north). From Deer Park, this saddle can be reached by following the Deer Park Trail via a southeast climb and up switchbacks on Class 2 terrain.

Whitehead Peak

13,259′ UNRANKED

Whitehead Peak is an unranked peak 0.4 mile south of Mount Rhoda and was the very first mountain that coauthor Matt Payne's son Quinn climbed in 2020 (followed by Mount Rhoda just an hour later).

North Slopes

From Deer Park TH at 11,750′ via Mount Rhoda: 1.6 miles, 1,620′

From Highland Mary Lakes TH at 10,810′: 4.3 miles, 2,330′

The objective for this route is to gain the saddle between Whitehead Peak and Mount Rhoda via Class 2 terrain and then continue south to the summit on a gentle slope. Follow the route for Mount Rhoda from either Deer Park or Highland Mary Lakes to the saddle. If coming from Highland Mary Lakes, skirt left of the saddle by ascending directly up the east face on Class 2 terrain.

Peak 13,109′

RANK 562

Peak 13,109′ is 0.6 mile west of Whitehead Peak and connected to it by a long ridge. Climb it by itself from Deer Park to the west via Whitehead Trail or from Whitehead Peak to the east. It is also a great starting peak for a loop combining it with Whitehead Peak, Mount Rhoda, and Mountaineer Peak from Deer Park. Those with more endurance could start or end on Peak 13,109′ on a huge loop that included Whitehead Peak, Mount Rhoda, Mountaineer Peak, Kendall Peak, and Kendall Mountain.

Southwest Ridge

From Whitehead Trail TH in Deer Park at 11,650′: 2.6 miles, 1,700′

Starting at Whitehead Trailhead, ascend south to the saddle between point 12,829′ and point 12,162′ located west of Peak 13,109′. Continue on the trail to the northeast and wrap around the south face of point 12,162′, and after 2 miles at 12,380′, turn left (northeast) and leave the trail, ascending the ridge to the summit. If heading to Whitehead Peak from here, note there is a narrow, exposed ridge close to the summit of Peak 13,109′ that must be negotiated on Class 2+ terrain.

Loops and combinations

Peak 13,109′, Whitehead Peak, Mount Rhoda, Mountaineer Peak, Kendall Peak, and Kendall Mountain

Start or end at the Deer Park–Kendall Mountain Road Junction at 10,850′: 13 miles, 5,570′

Peak 13,109′, Whitehead Peak, and Mount Rhoda

Start and end in Deer Park by connecting Deer Park Trail and Whitehead Trail: 5.9 miles, 2,510′

The views of the Grenadiers and Needles on the Whitehead/Rhoda ascent from Highland Mary Lakes are quite spectacular.

Peak 13,109' obscures the last light of sunset.

Little Giant Peak

13,416′ RANK 309

Little Giant Peak is located 0.8 mile south-southwest of King Solomon Mountain between Little Giant Basin and Arrastra Basin just 3.5 miles east-southeast of Silverton.

East Ridge

From Little Giant Basin at 11,930′: 1.3 miles, 1,540′

From Little Giant Basin, resist the temptation to drive to the end of County Road 52 and instead look for a trail that ascends southeast toward the saddle between Little Giant Peak and King Solomon Mountain on Class 2 terrain. From this saddle, continue west up a grassy slope for 100′ to more rugged terrain, which can be bypassed on the left (south) side. Continue ascending east up the ridge to the summit. From the saddle, you can also climb King Solomon Mountain.

OFF THE BEATEN PATH

King Solomon Mountain

13,220′ SOFT RANKED

0.8 mile north-northeast of Little Giant Peak

From Little Giant Basin at 11,930′: 1.3 miles, 1,540′

South Ridge: From the Little Giant–King Solomon saddle, climb northeast and bypass a cliff on the east side and regain the ridge and climb to the summit on grassy Class 2 terrain.

Galena Mountain

13,300′ RANK 401

1.8 miles east-southeast of the Howardsville townsite and 2.4 miles north-northeast of the summit of Stony Pass

From Stony Pass Road near Gary Owen Mine at 11,240′: 0.9 mile, 2,060′

South Slopes: Bushwhack 0.5 mile northeast up steep, unrelenting Class 2 terrain and turn left (north) toward the summit of Galena on Class 2 terrain.

Canby Mountain

13,478′ RANK 267

0.3 mile northeast of Stony Pass

From Stony Pass summit at 12,650′: 0.5 mile, 830′

West Slopes: From the parking area at the summit of Stony Pass, follow a trail northeast then north to 12,920′, then turn right, and climb northeast to the summit on Class 2 terrain.

"Stony Pass Peak"

13,165′ RANK 509

0.4 mile southwest of Stony Pass

From Stony Pass summit at 12,650′: 0.5 mile, 520′

Northeast Slopes: From the summit of Stony Pass, head southwest through a meadow and then south up a Class 2 climbers' trail to the summit.

Sheep Mountain A

13,292′ RANK 408

1.9 miles southeast of Stony Pass

From Stony Pass Road at 11,920′: 1.1 miles, 1,370′

Northwest Slopes: Climb to a broad flat shoulder at 12,590′, where you will turn right and continue east up the northwest slope to the summit on Class 2 talus.

Greenhalgh Mountain

13,220′ RANK 463

0.7 mile east of Sheep Mountain A

From Stony Pass Road at 11,920′ via Sheep Mountain A: 2 miles, 1,740′

West Ridge: From the summit of Sheep Mountain A, descend loose Class 2 talus to the Sheep–Greenhalgh saddle and up Class 2 talus to the summit.

WEST NEEDLE MOUNTAINS

8

Sunrise catches the West Needles, as seen from the slopes of Grand Turk.

This cluster of peaks is separated from the Needles and Grenadiers by a 4,000′- to 5,000′-deep gorge created by the Animas River. The group comprises Snowdon Peak to the north and North Twilight Peak, Twilight Peak, South Twilight Peak, and West Needle Mountain to the south. A day climb of Snowdon Peak is one of the more delightful climbs in the San Juan Range. The view from its large, roomy summit gives the full panorama of the Needle and Grenadier Ranges. The Twilights and West Needle Mountain are more remote and best climbed in conjunction with an overnight backpack into Crater Lake. All three of the Twilights and West Needle Mountain offer challenging and, at times, exposed climbing. While the Twilights

WEST NEEDLE MOUNTAINS

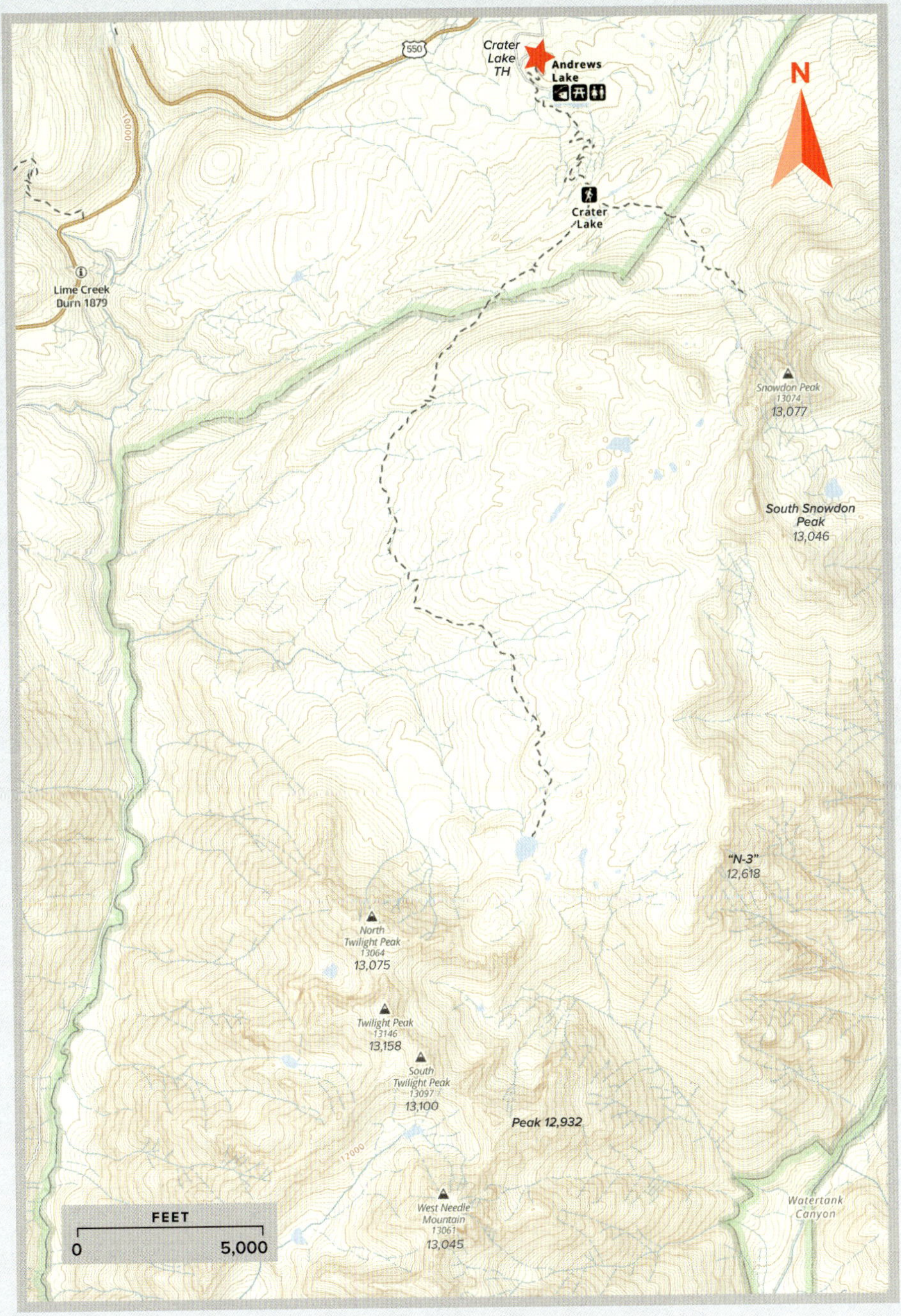

West Needles from Purgatory ski area.

can be reached after a pleasurable backpack, there is simply no reasonable way to get to West Needle Mountain. Climbing West Needle Mountain from Crater Lake makes for a long but rewarding day. The other options are far less pleasant. The long, steep bushwhacks west from Needleton or east from Lime Creek Road would be extremely difficult.

CLIMBING HISTORY

The first recorded ascent of Snowdon Peak was made by the Hayden Survey in September 1874. It is named for Francis M. Snowden (note different spelling) who built the first cabin in Silverton the same year that the Hayden party made the first ascent of the peak. Reports on other early climbs in the area are sparse. In *The San Juan Mountaineers Climber's Guide to Southwestern Colorado*, written in 1932, Carleton Long reported that "the West Needle Mountains are, even today, relatively unexplored. There are no recorded ascents of any of the peaks except Snowdon . . . and, while it is possible that most or all of the peaks have been climbed by prospectors or other peregrinating individuals, there still remains for the mountain climber a wealth of unexplored routes."

ACCESS AND HIKING

Crater Lake Trail

Crater Lake Trail starts at Andrews Lake, near Molas Pass. The turnoff to Andrews Lake is 8 miles south of Silverton and 42 miles north of Durango on US Highway 550. A well-maintained gravel road turns off US 550 0.75 mile south of Molas Pass. From US 550, it is 0.33 mile to Andrews Lake and ample parking. From Andrews Lake, the 5-mile trail starts at 10,744′ and ends at 11,600′. From Andrews Lake, the trail climbs just over 400 vertical feet to the south. After topping out, you lose, regain, and lose again 200′ of elevation before slowly gaining elevation to reach Crater Lake. There are several excellent camping spots here. From Crater Lake, a rounded saddle that overlooks Watertank Canyon and the Animas River lies several hundred yards and 150 vertical feet to the southwest. Don't be tempted to use Watertank Canyon as an access to the Animas River and Needleton. Those who have tried it do not recommend it.

CLIMBING ROUTES

Snowdon Peak

13,077′ RANK 588

Snowdon Peak is 2.75 miles south of Molas Lake and a 6+-mile round-trip climb from Andrews Lake with 2,300′ of elevation gain. When you look at Snowdon from Andrews Lake you see, from left to right, the Northeast Ridge, Northwest Couloir, West Buttress, and West Rib.

Left: Snowdon and South Snowdon, from the Colorado Trail. **Right:** Snowdon and South Snowdon at sunrise.

Northeast Ridge

From Andrews/Crater Lake TH at 10,750′: 3.3 miles, 2,330′

The northeast ridge is the standard route on Snowdon. Where Crater Lake Trail briefly tops out 0.5 mile south of Andrews Lake, leave the trail and head southeast for 0.75 mile. From here, aim to climb east to the 12,340′ saddle between Snowdon and Peak 12,628′, just north of Snowdon. Once on the ridge, follow it directly toward the summit. Near the top, it is best to leave the ridge where it narrows at the top of the northwest couloir and traverse left across the east face to gain the southeast ridge. The southeast ridge takes you to the summit. The traverse of the east face involves delicate and somewhat exposed Class 3 climbing.

West Rib

From Andrews/Crater Lake TH at 10,750′: 3.3 miles, 2,330′

The 800′ west buttress descends directly from the summit. To the right (south) of the buttress, there is a prominent dihedral and the west rib. When viewed from US 550, the dihedral and rib look severe, but they are a very enjoyable Class 3+ or Class 4 climb on exceptional quartzite rock. The climbing becomes more difficult and exposed as you get higher on the buttress. We recommend taking a rope and several pieces of protection in case of rain.

The Three Twilight Peaks

The three Twilights (North, Twilight, and South) are often climbed together from a camp at Crater Lake. Whether climbed clockwise or counterclockwise, the crux of the loop is the Class 3 north ridge of Twilight Peak.

Twilights in late May.

North Twilight Peak

13,075′ RANK 590

From Andrews/Crater Lake TH at 10,750′: 7.2 miles, 2,400′

From Crater Lake at 11,650′: 1.3 miles, 1,420′

Northeast Shoulder/East Ridge

A faint trail climbs the northeast shoulder above Crater Lake. The trail leads to the long, Class 2 east ridge, which runs out to the summit.

South Face

From the saddle between North Twilight and Twilight Peak, the south face is a walk-up if climbing North Twilight or an easy descent on your way to Twilight.

North Couloir

From Crater Lake, traverse west across the north face to gain the prominent snow chute. This classic snow climb, requiring an ice ax and crampons early in the climbing season, is a steep Class 3 climb on which care should be taken because of loose rock late in the year.

Twilight Peak

13,158′ RANK 515

From Andrews/Crater Lake TH at 10,750′ via North Twilight: 7.7 miles, 2,800′

From Crater Lake at 11,650′: 1.8 miles, 1,820′

Left: Twilight Peak in autumn. **Right:** Twilight Peak at night with Comet Wirtanen in 2018.

North Ridge

The summit is roughly 400 vertical feet above the saddle between North Twilight and Twilight. The north ridge connecting the saddle to Twilight's summit has a stretch of Class 3 climbing as you near the summit.

South Twilight

13,100′ **UNRANKED**

Northwest Ridge

From Andrews/Crater Lake TH at 10,750′ via North Twilight and Twilight: 8 miles, 2,910′

From Crater Lake at 11,650′ via North Twilight and Twilight: 2.1 miles, 1,930′

If you climb South Twilight in conjunction with Twilight Peak, downclimb the Class 2 south ridge of Twilight Peak, and from the saddle connecting the two peaks, the summit of South Twilight Peak is only 200 vertical feet above on Class 2 terrain.

East Face

From Andrews/Crater Lake TH at 10,750′: 7.4 miles, 3,360′

From Crater Lake at 11,650′: 1.5 miles, 1,700′

When climbing from Crater Lake by itself, head toward North Twilight Peak's east ridge and then contour around the large basin, which drains the eastern flanks of the Twilight Peaks. The east face of South Twilight Peak is a Class 3 scramble up the well-broken face. Those discouraged by the east face can continue the traverse south to gain the Class 3 southeast ridge, which leads to the summit.

West Needle Mountain

13,045′ RANK 600

West Needle Mountain can be combined with the Twilights in a long day from Crater Lake or saved for a second day that includes the hike back to Andrews Lake from Crater Lake. From the saddle between South Twilight and Peak 12,800′, you can either descend due south toward the prominent western couloir of West Needle or traverse southeast to the saddle between Peak 12,932′ and West Needle to the base of West Needle's northeast ridge on Class 3 and 4 terrain. The western couloir is the standard route on West Needle. West Needle has twin summits: north and south. The USGS map puts the south summit at 13,045′, but the north summit appears higher and has a large cairn and the register.

All three Twilights, Peak 12,932′, and West Needle

Since it is most typical to climb all three Twilights with West Needle, we are providing that mileage here.

From Andrews/Crater Lake TH: 9.1 miles, 4,050′

From Crater Lake at 11,650′: 3.25 miles, 3,070′

Western Couloir

This Class 2+ route follows the prominent couloir on the northwest face of West Needle and runs right to left (or west to east) from the base of the peak when viewed from the saddle between South Twilight and Peak 12,800′. The western couloir works as a snow climb early in the year and a talus climb later.

The Twilights from the west at sunset, left to right: Twilight, South Twilight, Peak 12,932′, and West Needle Mountain.

Northeast Ridge

From the notch between West Needle and 12,932′, climb the broken face to gain the northeast ridge, which leads to a broad, double-humped summit. This route involves some Class 3 climbing and a couple of Class 4 sections over broken-up but relatively solid rock.

OFF THE BEATEN PATH

South Snowdon Peak—"N-2"

13,046′ RANK 611

0.7 mile southwest of Snowdon Peak

From Andrews/Crater Lake TH at 10,750′ via Snowdon: 4.2 miles, 2,900′

Northwest Slopes: From Snowdon, descend west-southwest to 12,500′ and head south where you will find a mellow Class 2 slope all the way to the summit.

Peak 12,932′

RANK 693

0.5 mile southeast of South Twilight

From Crater Lake at 11,650′: 2.6 miles, 2,300′

Northeast Ridge: A Class 2 gully filled with talus leads to the summit.

Peak 12,618′—"N-3"

RANK 920

1 mile east of Crater Lake

From Andrews Lake/Crater Lake TH at 10,750′: 6.9 miles, 1,870′

From Crater Lake at 11,650′: 1 mile, 970′

West Slopes: From Crater Lake, make your way on untrailed terrain up the gentle slopes of the summit.

NEEDLE MOUNTAINS

9

The heart of the San Juans, as seen from the summit of Turret at sunrise. Left to right, far: Arrow, Vestal, the Trinities, Peak Six, Jagged, Knife Point, and Rio Grande Pyramid. Left to right, near: Index, Animas, Peak Thirteen, Monitor, Peak Fifteen, and Peak Sixteen.

The Needles, together with their northern counterparts, the Grenadiers, are the heart of the San Juans. They are a mountaineering paradise and an area with seemingly limitless climbing opportunities. The most frequently climbed peaks are the Chicago Basin 14ers, and although Eolus, Sunlight, and Windom are by no means the most difficult 14ers in Colorado, they tend to be underestimated. While the Chicago Basin area can be overcrowded at certain times of the year, other areas in the Needles are generally sparsely traveled. Pigeon Peak and Jagged Mountain are among Colorado's toughest Centennial peaks, requiring excellent routefinding skills and presenting a challenge to even experienced mountaineers. A wealth of other high 13ers, including Animas Mountain, Monitor Peak, Glacier Point, Jupiter Mountain, Turret Peak, and Peaks Fifteen and Thirteen, provide a wide variety of climbing opportunities and challenges. Technical climbers have been lured into the area by pinnacles, such as the Index, Gray Needle, Sunlight Spire, and Little Finger (Peak Seventeen), and large faces, such as Monitor's east face and the north face of North Eolus. In short, there is something for everybody in the Needles. It is a place you can look forward to coming back to year after year, and it will be a long time before you run out of things to climb.

CLIMBING HISTORY

The Needles is one of the few areas in the San Juans that was not explored by members of either the Hayden or Wheeler Surveys. Reports of early surveyors were, however, filled with descriptions of the "Quartzites," which was the term the surveyors used to describe an area encompassing both the Needles and Grenadiers. Franklin Rhoda of the Hayden Survey shared thoughts on the distinctive weather pattern in the area in his book *Summits to Reach*:

> *Early in the day we noticed clouds hovering about the quartzite peaks, as we had seen them so often before. They never completely veiled all the peaks in the group, but early each day began to circle about them in a restless sort of way, like so many mighty lions about their lair. To us this apparent restlessness suggested a consciousness of their terrific destructive power, which only awaited a mandate from the "God of Storms" to be set in motion. We even now held these peaks in awe, as there seemed to be established somewhere in their midst a regular "manufactory of storms."*

Given this description, it is not surprising that the highest peak in the range, Eolus, was given its name in honor of the Greek god of the winds.

Beginning in the late 1870s, Needle Creek and Chicago Basin were invaded by prospectors and miners. The high peaks that rim Chicago Basin, including the three 14ers—Eolus, Windom, and Sunlight—were all probably climbed during this period by miners. The first party to be lured into the Needles solely for its climbing possibilities was William S. Cooper and John Hubbard in 1908. Two years earlier, Cooper had visited Silverton and climbed Kendall Mountain. From the summit of Kendall, he reported in his book, *Mountains,* seeing "mountains that I must see again and at the earliest opportunity; the whole San Juan country, the Needle Mountains in particular, and, first of all, Pigeon Peak."

Cooper and Hubbard climbed Pigeon after a bushwhack up New York Basin and a gully on the south face of the peak. After sunbathing on the summit for two and a half hours, their "final deed was to look down the 1,500′ [actually 900′] 85-degree east face—almost as spectacular as the east face of Longs."

In 1920 and 1927, the summer outings of the Colorado Mountain Club were held in Chicago Basin. During these outings, mass ascents were made of the Chicago Basin peaks, including Eolus, North Eolus, Sunlight, Windom, Jupiter, and Aztec. In addition, a large party during the 1920 outing made a probable first ascent of Grizzly Peak to the southeast of Chicago Basin.

The 1930s were a period of intense activity in the Needles. More difficult routes were established on the 14ers, and several difficult traverses were made in the Chicago Basin area. In addition, climbers began making ascents of the rugged 13ers in the area, such as Jagged Mountain, Animas Mountain, and Monitor Peak.

The first ascents of Jagged Mountain and several other peaks in the area were made during the 1933 climbing expedition of the San Juan Mountaineers. On their first attempt at climbing Jagged, Dwight Lavender, Mel Griffiths, Lewis Giesecke, Henry McClintock, and Carleton Long climbed the western, or third-highest, summit. The party reached the third summit in wet weather and did not attempt the difficult traverse over to the highest summit. Two days later, the party returned to the south face of Jagged and climbed a route that started in a gully immediately west of the highest summit. This gully led the party to the summit just west of the true summit. From this intermediate summit, they rappelled down to the col and scrambled up 150′ to the final summit. In the 1934 issue of *American Alpine Journal,* Lavender reported that "Jagged Mountain is probably the most difficult peak yet ascended in the Colorado Rockies." During the 1933 expedition, the San Juan Mountaineers also climbed both summits of Twin Thumbs, Peak Eleven, Peak Twelve, and Peak Six. All were probably first ascents, except Peak Six, which had been climbed by at least one other party.

A small tram car crossing the Animas River near Noname Creek during the 1937 Colorado Mountain Club outing. Photo by Louise Roloff

Left: The first ascent route of the Index. **Right:** Frank McClintock rappelling on Peak Fifteen after its first ascent in August 1940. Photos by Joe Merher

The second ascent of Jagged Mountain was made in July 1934 by William P. House and Elizabeth Woolsey, who established a route farther east on the south face that climbed to a col near the east end of the main ridge of the mountain and then traversed along the north faces of the pinnacles until about 150′ below the true summit. In her book *Off the Beaten Track*, Woolsey reported a "rare fall while leading, when a chockstone rolled over as I tried to pull myself up and over it. Fortunately for me, I landed on Bill's head, and he fielded me very neatly." Their descent was down the north face that is now the standard route on Jagged. House and Woolsey also climbed Sunlight Peak's north face, reportedly traversing east to the ridge 100′ or so below the summit.

During the 1930s, there was interest in difficult traverses as well as first ascents. Mel Griffiths and Robert Ormes made the first traverse of Needle Ridge between Sunlight and Peak Eleven, in July 1937. They noted that the traverse required rappels at several points and a wide variety of rock technique. In August 1937, during a Colorado Mountain Club outing in the area, Bob Blair and Prather Ashe traversed the ridge from Jupiter to Windom. Later during the outing, a large party led by Jack Heeney extended the traverse from Jupiter over Windom to Sunlight.

The Index is a prominent pinnacle just west of Animas Mountain. In September 1934, a San Juan Mountaineers party consisting of Mel Griffiths, Henry McClintock, and Frank McClintock made a reconnaissance of the Index and reported in *Trail and Timberline* (February 1935) that a ridge leading to the "true summit is wild beyond description." On September 6, 1937, the same party returned to the Index and reached the summit by means of a difficult and complicated route.

During the 1930s, Pigeon Peak received renewed interest. In August 1935, Henry McClintock, Frank McClintock, and Lewis Giesecke discovered a route on the north

Left: Jack Fralick (left) and John Speck at daybreak after a rainy bivouac high on the east face of Monitor Peak, August 10, 1947. **Right:** Equipment used during a 1947 climb of Monitor's east face: army boots with steel spikes, 7/16 nylon rope, hammers, pitons, and carabiners. Photos by Joe Stettner

flank of Pigeon from a camp in Ruby Basin above Ruby Lake, reportedly making their way up on the grassy ledges on the west side of the north face. They made the first traverse of Pigeon by *descending* the southeast chimney. During the 1940s, few new routes were established in the area, but several climbs are noteworthy.

In August 1940, Frank and Henry McClintock, Joe Merhar, and Chris Schoredos made three probable first ascents of Peaks Fifteen, Sixteen, and Seventeen (Little Finger), which lie between Eolus and Turret Peak and are more commonly known as the Turret Needles. The most difficult of the Turret Needles to climb was Peak Seventeen.

Undoubtedly, the most difficult climb of this era, not only in the San Juans but in all of Colorado, was the August 1947 ascent of the east face of Monitor Peak by Joe Stettner, John Speck, and Jack Fralick. Stettner was a climber from Chicago who had previously gained a degree of fame by establishing the difficult Stettners Ledges route on the east face of Longs Peak with his brother Paul. The route on the 1,200′ east face of Monitor was accomplished only after the party was forced to bivouac high on the route. In a *Trail and Timberline* (December 1947) report, Joe Stettner called the climb the most difficult he had ever done, "even more severe than the north wall of the Grand Teton and the Stettners Ledges route on the east face of Longs Peak." While in the area, Stettner also made the first west-to-east traverse of Needle Ridge with Marguerette Sharp, Donald Gruber, and Edmund Lowe.

Interest in the Needles was renewed during the 1960s. In 1960, a party of eight led by Charles Walsmith opened a new route on the northeast corner of Pigeon Peak. The team reported ascending the first two small couloirs lying north of the east (or southeast) face of Pigeon, which faces Turret, and attaining the northwest ridge about 200′ below the summit. Several pitons were used for protection. George Bell Sr., David Michael, and John Marshall climbed the summit pinnacle on Sunlight Spire in July 1961 using direct aid to climb what was noted in *Trail and Timberline* (February 1962) as "a large vertical crack on the north side of the summit obelisk." During this trip, George Bell Sr. and Grant Mathews also climbed what they named "Ominous Pinnacle," which lies in the Noname Creek drainage midway between Animas Mountain and Peak Thirteen.

In September 1968, Joe Stettner's nephew, Paul Stettner Jr., and Larry Dalke established a more direct route on the east face of Monitor Peak. The 1968 route lies north of the 1947 route and joins the original route high on the face. A line between the 1947 and 1968 routes was established on July 4, 1976, by Gary Neptune, Rob Blair, Melisa Geise, and Tom Norton, who summited at 9:00 p.m. and ended a long day by making a moonlight downclimb and rappel into Ruby Basin. Another line on the lower two-thirds of the east face was established in July 1980, by Larry Coats, Tim Coats, and Jim Haisley. The 1980 route starts to the right of the 1968 route but converges with the other routes on the upper face.

Several climbs of note were made in the area during the late 1970s and 1980s. In June 1977, Alan Roberts and Ted Kerasote climbed the sheer northwest spur of Knife Point. The north face of North Eolus was climbed by Tony Meyer and Davis (first name unavailable) in 1978. The sheer east face of Pigeon Peak is probably the most prominent feature in the Needles. Steve Matous and Dave Maxwell made its first ascent in July 1977 by a ten-pitch, 5.9 route on the right (north) side of the face. Jeff Achey made the first free ascent of the spectacular Sunlight Spire in 1988 and rated the summit pitch 5.10c.

The inaccessibility of the Needles discouraged winter climbing until 1966. In that year, Sunlight and Windom were climbed on December 22 and 23 by Don Monk, Kermit Ross, and Phil Schmuck. This party hiked up the narrow gauge tracks from Rockwood. They reached the old miner's cabin at Twin Lakes after three days with the assistance of food caches placed earlier in the year. They also made an attempt on Eolus but were turned back high on the peak by "threatening weather and a precarious-looking snow-covered north ridge."

The first winter ascent of Eolus was left for Barry Nash, Rick Nolting, Steve Lewis, and Lloyd Frank, who started from the Purgatory ski area on US Highway 550 between Durango and Silverton. After their snowshoe approach down Cascade Creek and up the Animas River and Needle Creek, they too reached the miner's cabin after three days. On January 26, 1971, they climbed the north ridge of Eolus. Although being somewhat taken aback by their first view of the summit ridge, they reported that the route was "considerably easier than it had looked."

NEEDLE MOUNTAINS (NORTH)

NEEDLE MOUNTAINS (MIDDLE)

NEEDLE MOUNTAINS (SOUTH)

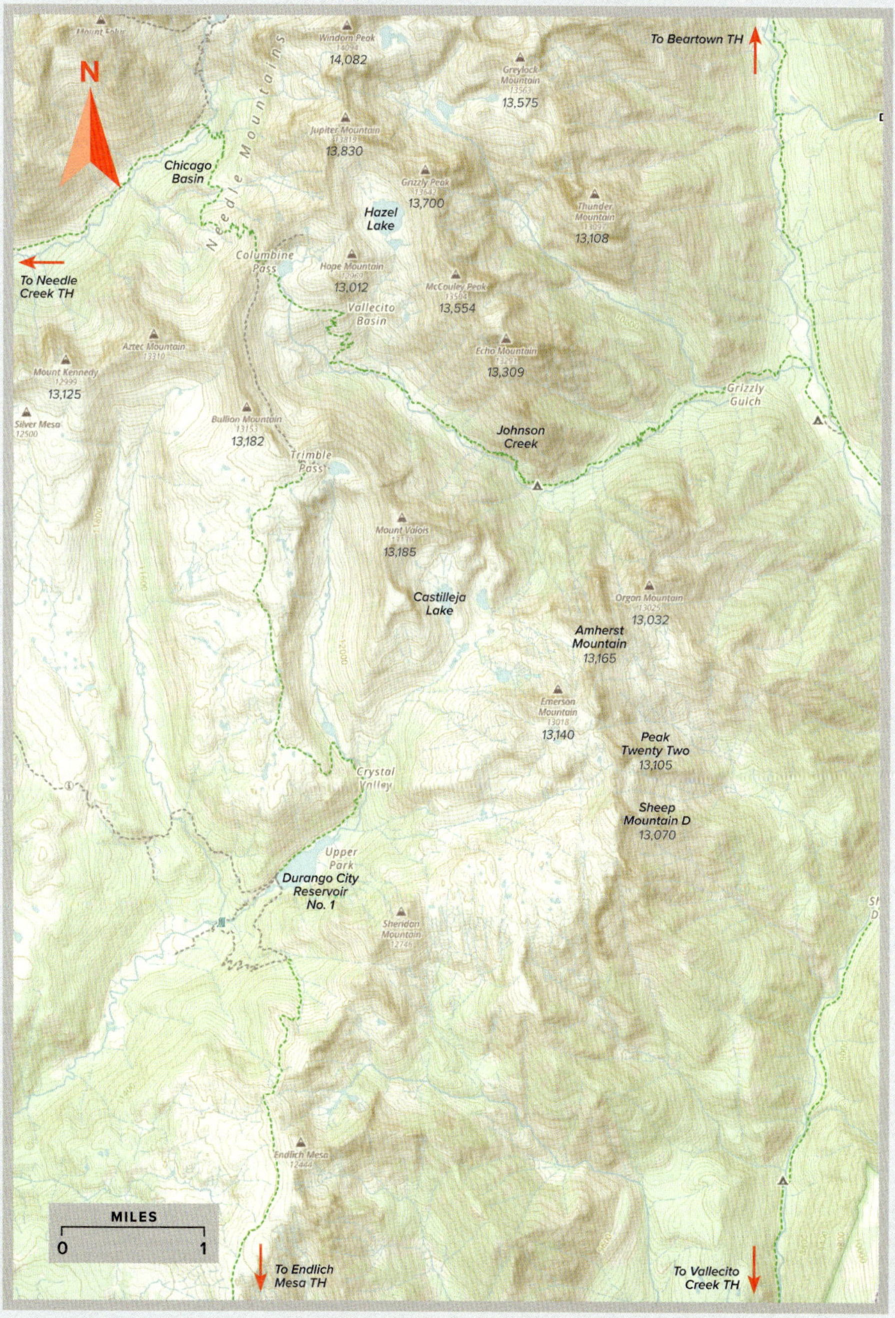

ACCESS AND HIKING

Durango and Silverton Narrow Gauge Railroad

The train is the most convenient way to start a trip into the Needles, saving you at least 9.5 miles of hiking. The train provides wilderness access with stops at Needleton (for the Needles) and Elk Park (for the Grenadiers) from May to October. It is also possible to ride from Silverton south on the train, but the only wilderness stop for southbound trains is at Elk Park. For information, check durangotrain.com or call 1-877-872-4607. Make reservations well in advance and always confirm boarding and departure times with the depot in Durango, located at 479 Main Avenue. Policies for backpackers vary depending on the time of year. Times and policies for return trips should be confirmed before departure. To stop a train, you need to flag it down by waving your arms in front of your knees (like you're doing the Charleston). Flag the train from the east side of the tracks at both Needleton and Elk Park.

Purgatory Flats Trail

Purgatory Flats Trail provides access to Needleton by foot rather than railroad. Twenty-seven miles north of Durango on US Highway 550 or 23 miles south of Silverton, turn east at Tacoma Village and look for a sign that says "Purgatory Flats Trail Access." The turn is across the road from Purgatory ski area, just south of milepost 40, and the trailhead and parking lot are 0.2 mile east of US 550 on the south side of the road. From the trailhead, the trail steeply descends 1.2 miles through the wooded Purgatory Creek drainage to Purgatory Flats. Once in Purgatory Flats, the trail turns

south and follows the Cascade Creek drainage for 2.9 miles down to the Animas River, which you cross on a bridge. The trail never crosses Cascade Creek. Once across the river, you will be south of the railroad bridge that crosses the Animas. The trail up to Needleton turns to the right just before the railroad bridge and follows the east bank of the Animas. From the railroad bridge, it is 5 more miles to Needle Creek Trail or 6 miles to Needleton. From Purgatory Campground, it is approximately 9.5 miles to the junction with Needle Creek Trail or 10.5 miles to Needleton. Because most of these distances are either downhill or flat, it is possible to reach Needle Creek or Needleton by lunchtime with a reasonably early start.

Needle Creek Trail

Needle Creek Trail starts at the footbridge across the Animas at Needleton. From the bridge, 1 mile of flat walking south brings you to the junction with Purgatory Creek Trail at Needle Creek, where the trail begins to gain elevation as it climbs southeast up the Needle Creek drainage. From the junction of the two trails, 1.6 miles of hiking brings you to a spot where the trail skirts the creek. If you want to hike up to Webb, Pear, or Emerald Lakes, cross the creek at this point and search for Webb Lake Trail. Needle Creek Trail stays on the north side of Needle Creek and continues to climb up the drainage for a total of 6 miles from Needleton to a trail junction at 11,000′. If you turn right at the junction and cross Needle Creek, you will continue for 2 miles and 1,700 vertical feet to the top of Columbine Pass, which connects with the Johnson Creek drainage. If you continue straight at the junction, you will climb

The Needles, as seen from the summit of Vestal.

into the upper Chicago Basin. From the junction, it is 1.5 miles and 1,500 vertical feet to Twin Lakes, but camping is not permitted at the lakes. You will need to find a campsite between the trail junction at 11,000′ and the lakes. If the basin is too crowded, you can take the right-hand fork at the 11,000′ junction, which leads up to Columbine Pass, and camp in the wooded area near the foot of Jupiter Mountain near where the trail turns south toward the pass. Beginning with Jupiter and continuing in a counterclockwise direction, the peaks that line Chicago Basin are Jupiter Mountain, Windom Peak, Sunlight Spire, Sunlight Peak, Peak Eleven, Twin Thumbs, Glacier Point, North Eolus, and Mount Eolus. Located within the basin, directly west of Windom Peak, is Peak Eighteen (13,472′). From the train drop-off to Twin Lakes requires 4,700′ of elevation gain over 8 miles.

Endlich Mesa Trail

Endlich Mesa Trail is the long way to access the Chicago Basin mountains, including Jupiter Mountain, Windom Peak, Sunlight Peak, and Mount Eolus. It can also be used to access Durango City Reservoir No. 1 and the peaks nearby, including Sheep Mountain D, Peak Twenty-Two, Emerson Mountain, Amherst Mountain, and Organ Mountain B east and north of Durango City Reservoir No. 1 as well as Grizzly Peak C, McCauley Peak, and Echo Mountain, all found east of Columbine Lake. The trail begins after a long, winding drive up a rough Forest Service road near Lemon Reservoir, northwest of Durango. You'll want a high-clearance vehicle. From downtown Durango, head north on East Third Avenue until it forks at Florida Road, where you turn right. Continue on Florida Road for 13.8 miles until you reach the junction for County Road 243 at Helen's Country Store and turn left toward Lemon Reservoir. This is a crucial junction for those coming from Bayfield to the southeast. Continue on this road for almost 5 miles to the end of the reservoir and continue north for 2.2 miles to reach a junction for Forest Service Road 597 on the right. Take this winding, ascending, rugged road 9.7 miles to another junction. Stay right, and Endlich Mesa Trailhead is 1.25 miles farther. The trail begins at 11,570′ and continues north for several miles with distant views of the Chicago Basin peaks ahead, all above tree line without shelter from weather. Continue on the mostly flat or descending trail for 6 miles to the northeast end of Durango City Reservoir No. 1. If heading to Chicago Basin, continue north on the trail, climb a steep hill and veer east (left) toward Lake Marie. The trail winds south (left) for 0.2 mile and then right (west) for 350′, and then right again (north) where it slowly climbs Silver Mesa. From here, it is 2.75 miles to Trimble Pass, which rests above Lillie Lake, a great location to camp for a night. This is also a great location to climb Florida Mountain or Mount Valois. From Trimble Pass, it is an additional 1.5 miles to Columbine Pass, where you can access

Chicago Basin as well as the easiest route up Jupiter Mountain. Twin Lakes, which sits at the high end of Chicago Basin, is 3.5 miles from Columbine Pass.

Webb Lake Trail

Webb Lake Trail starts 1.6 miles east of the junction between the Needle Creek and Purgatory Creek Trails, where Needle Creek Trail meets Needle Creek near an old water wheel. (The water wheel is surrounded by foliage and can be difficult to spot.) Here, cross south over Needle Creek and hike back through the woods to where the trail begins its climb up to Webb Lake. Mileage from Needle Creek to Webb Lake is about a mile as the crow flies, but the endless switchbacks make the trail closer to 2 miles. Although a relatively short distance, the 1,800′ vertical gain makes this as tough a trail as you will ever care to hike. The best campsites at Webb Lake are on the north end of the lake. From the lake, as you look south, you see two major drainages. Pear Lake is located in the left-hand drainage about 0.7 mile and 650 vertical feet away. From Pear Lake, you can continue 0.5 mile over a small rise to the east and join Emerald Lake. Although the USGS map indicates that there is a trail from Emerald Lake down to Needle Creek, don't be tempted to try it, as it may well result in a miserable bushwhack. From Pear Lake, a rough trail climbs to the pass southwest of the lake. From the pass, there is an easy climb up to Overlook Point that affords an excellent view of the main body of the Needles to the northwest.

A view of the Needles from the south, left to right: Pigeon Peak, Turret Peak, Peak Fifteen, Peak Thirteen, Monitor Peak, and Mount Eolus.

Vallecito Creek and Johnson Creek Trails

These two trails allow an approach to the Chicago Basin peaks from the east and are a great way to access Grizzly Peak C, McCauley Peak, or Echo Mountain, all east of Columbine Lake. This trail system is not used as often by climbers as the Needle Creek approach since it typically requires a two-day backpack. Vallecito Reservoir is 13 miles north of Bayfield on US Highway 160 or 20 miles east of Durango on Florida Road. Once at the reservoir, stay west (left) of the dam for 5 miles until you come to a well-marked junction that offers a choice between Vallecito Campground and Pine River Campground. Turn left at the junction and drive 3 miles to the Vallecito Campground and trailhead. At 7 miles up Vallecito Trail, you need to ford Vallecito Creek to reach the main trail at a spot where a bridge was washed out or continue north on the west side of the creek on an unmaintained user trail. Nine miles north of the trailhead, reach the turnoff to the Johnson Creek Trail, which is located where a well-constructed bridge crosses Vallecito Creek. There are many excellent campsites in this area. From the trail junction, hike 6 miles west and 3,500 vertical feet to the top of Columbine Pass at 12,700'.

Vallecito Creek and Sunlight Creek Trails from Vallecito Reservoir

The Sunlight Creek drainage joins Vallecito Creek 11.3 miles north of the trailhead. There is not a bridge across Vallecito Creek here, and it's necessary to wade the creek before you reach Sunlight Creek. Crossing Vallecito Creek is not as serious a proposition as crossing the Animas, but it is best to plan such a trip for late summer or fall when the stream is lower. The route up Sunlight Creek follows the north side of the drainage on a faint trail; it's important to cross Vallecito Creek south of the point where Sunlight Creek runs into the Vallecito. There is an excellent camping area on Sunlight Creek in the last stand of timber between 11,400' and 11,600'. It is possible to cross from the Sunlight Creek drainage into the Noname Creek drainage by using the pass between Knife Point and Peak Ten or the pass just north of Jagged Mountain. A campsite high in Sunlight Creek Basin is an excellent beginning point for climbs of Knife Point, Peak Ten, Jagged Mountain, Leviathan Peak, and Vallecito Mountain.

Vallecito Creek and Sunlight Creek Trails/Beartown Trailhead

This is the best way to access many of the mountains found in the Needles west of Vallecito Creek, including Knife Point, Jagged Mountain, Leviathan Peak, Vallecito Mountain, Peak Ten, Grizzly Peak C, McCauley Peak, Echo Mountain, and Greylock Mountain. It is also a great way to access many of the peaks on the west side of Vallecito Creek, covered in the Rio Grande Pyramid–Mount Oso Group section.

Getting to Beartown Trailhead requires a high-clearance 4WD vehicle and includes of several river crossings, making it tough until midsummer or later.

The road to Beartown is accessible either from Silverton or Lake City. The Silverton route is shorter and easier. From Silverton, drive northeast on Colorado Highway 110, toward Howardsville. At 4.2 miles, reach Howardsville, where you turn right on a well-signed road (FSR 589) going up Stony Pass. Shortly you come to an intersection; the road to the left is signed for Old Mine Tour, the other one close to the creek continues straight. It does not matter which one you choose; both reconnect, and neither is technically challenging. You have to leave Cunningham Gulch and start climbing on a narrow 4WD road toward the marked road for Stony Pass: FSR 737. Gain Stony Pass and take caution as the road is narrow, with sharp rocks and many off-highway vehicles. The road down from the pass all the way to Rio Grande Reservoir is FSR 520. Continue down this road, and at 11.6 miles to a key intersection. Take the well-signed Beartown/Kite Lake Road (FSR 506) to the right. The road straight ahead (left) goes to Creede.

From Lake City/Creed, take Colorado Highway 149 to FSR 520 and turn west toward Rio Grande Reservoir. There are several river crossings, deeply rutted sections, and narrow rocky sections. It is about 25 miles to the turnoff for Beartown. Once you reach FSR 506, the road to Beartown is another 6.1 miles. You must cross the Rio Grande River at the start of this road, and the water can be deep, even in late summer. The rest of the road also has some challenging 4WD sections. For context, we were barely able to get a stock 2000 Jeep Cherokee with all-terrain tires to the trailhead.

The trail start is signed, with room to park two or three cars, plus a few spaces nearby. Consider finding a way to repel rodents if you plan to leave your car for more than a day or two, as they have been known to chew through wires and hoses, leaving many climbers stranded!

From Beartown Trailhead, hike 1 mile south to Hunchback Pass at 12,493'. Continue south and descend 6.5 miles on Vallecito Creek Trail to a turn on the right for Sunlight Creek access at 9,650'. Note: If you are accessing Nebo Creek for mountains described in the Rio Grande Pyramid–Mount Oso Group section, the turnoff is 1.35 miles on the left from Hunchback Pass on Vallecito Creek Trail.

North Pigeon Creek

This is the shortest way to approach Pigeon Peak and Turret Peak, but the trail is poor and hard to follow and requires a steep bushwhack, so it is not the most desirable approach. North Pigeon Creek is not identified on most maps, but it is located between Pigeon Creek and Ruby Creek. It is important to study a map before you depart, as it can be a daunting wilderness adventure. None of the trails nor junctions on this approach are signed.

Assuming you took the train, get off at Needleton and cross the Needleton Bridge. From the bridge, walk north about a third of a mile along the trail on the east side of the Animas River past some cabins. You will soon reach Pigeon Creek. Cross the creek, where you'll encounter an old metal railroad car and the floor of an old cabin. Continue 0.2 mile north on the trail to a long meadow located at 8,260'. Continue north, and as the meadow narrows, you'll find a fallen tree. Bypass the tree to the east (right) and continue an additional 20' to find Ruby Lake Trail, climbing steeply north up the slope of the meadow and through dense woods. Ascend this trail for approximately 0.75 mile to a trail junction at 9,800'. Here Ruby Lake Trail and North Pigeon Creek Trail diverge. Ruby Lake Trail continues northeast, and North Pigeon Creek Trail goes east. If you reach an aspen tree with a columbine carved into it, you know you have taken the wrong trail. Continue up a small ridge from the 9,800' junction for 0.2 mile. This trail becomes faint, then nonexistent. Commence bushwhacking. At 10,200', bushwhack for 0.6 mile east-southeast across a steep slope to 11,000' in the North Pigeon Creek drainage, where the terrain is easier. Continue 0.5 mile east-southeast through trees in the drainage to the west end of a large meadow at 11,740', where camping is ample and the views are incredible. From here, Pigeon sits 0.7 mile to your east and awaits your climb. Turret is out of view and requires backtracking on the traditional route that combines Turret and Pigeon later in this book.

Ruby Lake Trail

Ruby Lake Trail provides excellent access to Pigeon Peak, Turret Peak, Monitor Peak, Animas Mountain, and other high 13ers. Ruby Lake's upper basin is one of the most stunning locations in Colorado. It also provides a good starting point for several days of climbing in the Needles, since access to Chicago Basin is available via Twin Thumbs Pass. This unmaintained, unsigned trail is difficult to locate, and it is easy to get lost. You won't regret time you spend studying maps that show ridges, slopes, and the three creeks (Pigeon Creek, Unnamed Creek, and Ruby Creek, south to north from Needleton) before setting out.

Assuming you took the train, get off at Needleton and cross the Needleton Bridge. From the bridge, walk north about one-third of a mile along the trail on the east side of the Animas River past some cabins. You will soon reach Pigeon Creek. After you cross the creek, you'll encounter an old metal railroad car and the floor of an old cabin. Continue 0.2 mile north on the trail to a long meadow located at 8,260'. Continue north, and where the meadow narrows, look for a trail that continues north up the steep slope east of the meadow. The trail climbs steeply through the woods and crosses the drainage between Pigeon Creek and Ruby Creek. Near this crossing, look for an aspen tree with a columbine carved into it, indicating you are on the correct trail. The trail is easy to lose here; if you do, simply continue northeast toward a hill at 10,300', where you'll find the trail again. Just past this hill, the trail splits left or right; both options lead to the same place, but the high road (right) is more adventurous. At about 10,300', Ruby Lake Trail crosses the ridge that forms the south side of the Ruby Creek drainage and, after losing some elevation, traverses the south side of the drainage until reaching Ruby Creek about 0.5 mile west of Ruby Lake. The trail then continues on the south side of the creek until you reach the lake. At Ruby Lake, the best campsites are on the west or north sides of the lake.

If you can't find Ruby Lake Trail, the next-best option is to hike back to the trail on the east side of the Animas and head north on the river trail until you reach the stream between Pigeon Creek and Ruby Creek. Turn right before crossing the unnamed stream and start climbing while heading east (south of the stream) and gaining elevation until you find Ruby Lake Trail, which you follow as it climbs to the ridge on the south side of the Ruby Creek drainage at 10,300'. Whatever you do, don't attempt to climb directly up the Ruby Creek drainage. The elevation gain from the Needleton bridge to Ruby Lake is roughly 2,600'.

To continue into the upper basin above Ruby Lake, stay on the north side of Ruby Creek to climb the steep bench west of the lake, following a faint, steep trail

Mountain goats in Ruby Basin.

full of fallen trees and other obstacles. After topping out on the bench, fight your way through chest-high willows until you reach easier walking higher in the drainage. A large meadow at 11,600′ makes a good base camp for climbs of Pigeon, Turret, the Index, Animas, Monitor, and Peak Thirteen. A 12,700′ pass just south of Monitor Peak connects the Ruby Creek drainage with the Noname Creek drainage. The high pass between Pigeon and Turret provides access to the upper reaches of New York Basin, which provides good campsites for climbs of Peaks Fifteen, Sixteen, and Seventeen (Little Finger).

Noname Creek Trail

This traditional approach to Jagged Mountain also provides good access to Peak Four, Peak Five, Peak Six, and the Heisspitz. It is less rugged than Ruby Lake Trail but still challenging and steep. None of the trails nor junctions on this approach have signage, so it is important to pay close attention. The mouth of Noname Creek is located 2 miles north of the Needleton Bridge. To avoid wading the Animas, cross to the east bank and head north on the trail on the east side of the Animas. The trail heading north from the Needleton Bridge can be difficult to follow. There is a campers' meadow 0.4 mile north of the bridge. Continue to the end of the meadow and look for the North Pigeon Creek and Ruby Creek approaches 20′ beyond the meadow. Continue about 20′ past them and turn left (west) on an unsigned trail junction in

From Knife Point, a view down into Noname basin and the heart of the Needles, including Sunlight Peak at far left.

the meadow. This trail is fainter than the trail that continues straight. Continue on the trail north-northwest down a hill and enter another meadow. Pass some cabins and continue on the trail located on the northwest corner of the meadow. Hike 100 yards northwest and join Animas River Trail. Continue north and cross North Pigeon Creek. There is difficult terrain as the trail passes through the cliffs on Watertank Hill just south of Ruby Creek. Descend the steep Watertank Hill and, once past the cliffs, enjoy smooth sailing to Noname Creek, where a well-defined trail starts out to the north of the creek. It's possible to walk the railroad tracks from Needleton and then wade the Animas, but this crossing can only be made in late summer or fall, and even then can be difficult. From the Animas River, 4 miles and 2,300 vertical feet up the Noname drainage brings you to a trail junction. Left takes you toward Peak Six and Jagged Mountain, and right leads you to Twin Thumbs Pass, then heads east to Noname Creek, and climbs 0.5 mile to a beautiful meadow with a great view of Knife Point. In the meadow, make another left and head north up a steep bench if you are interested in Peak Six and Jagged. There are several excellent campsites in the upper basin of the Noname drainage.

CLIMBING ROUTES

Mount Eolus

14,083′ RANK 33

From Needleton via Needle Creek TH at 8,200′: 9.08 miles, 6,300′

From Purgatory Flats TH at 8,800′: 16.8 miles, 7,900′

From Endlich Mesa TH at 11,570′: 16 miles, 6,600′

From Vallecito TH at 7,900′: 20.5 miles, 9,100′

Eolus, a monarch of the San Juans, is visible from many directions. It is approached from Chicago Basin and frequently combined with either North Eolus and Glacier Point or Sunlight and Windom on a long day.

Northeast Ridge

From Chicago Basin, contour to the left (west) into the large basin below Eolus's east face. Once high in the basin, traverse right (north) toward the plateau at 13,720′. Alternatively, from Twin Lakes, you can reach the 13,720′ plateau by a Class 3 scramble up the steep couloir west of the lakes. From the plateau, traverse left (southwest) toward the narrow "catwalk" ridge connecting Eolus and North Eolus. The ridge is exposed but not hard—Class 2+ with a few Class 3 moves. Once you reach the southern end of the catwalk, choose between a direct climb of the northeast ridge or traversing out onto the upper part of the east face. The northeast ridge, composed of highly fractured blocks, is Class 4 and exposed. Take time to test holds for firmness.

Left: Eolus from North Eolus at sunrise. **Right:** North Eolus sits in front of the Grenadiers, from the summit of Eolus.

Upper East Face

This is the standard route on Eolus. From the southern end of the catwalk ridge connecting Eolus and North Eolus, the route weaves its way up the upper east face on Class 3 terrain. Although well-traveled and usually marked with cairns, the route can be difficult to follow. Watch for loose rock—what appear to be stable boulders can come loose with a slight touch.

North Eolus

14,039′ UNRANKED

North Eolus, an unranked 14er located just 0.3 mile northeast of Mount Eolus, offers perhaps the single most stunning view from any mountain in Colorado.

South Ridge

This is the standard route up North Eolus. From the ridge between Eolus and North Eolus, it's a short Class 3 scramble north to the summit of North Eolus.

A majestic sunrise from the summit of North Eolus.

North Face

This challenging route is accessed from the Ruby Lake basin. A report in the January–February 1979 issue of *Climbing* rated the north face of North Eolus Class 5.7.

Windom Peak

14,082′ **RANK 32**

Windom is approached from Needle Creek (Twin Lakes) and Chicago Basin and combines well with Jupiter and Sunlight.

West Ridge

From Needleton via Needle Creek TH at 8,200′: 8.8 miles, 5,940′

From Purgatory Flats TH at 8,800′: 17.4 miles, 8,650′

From Endlich Mesa TH at 11,570′: 15.7 miles, 6,600′

From Vallecito TH at 7,900′: 20.2 miles, 9,190′

Approach this moderate Class 2+ climb from either lower Chicago Basin or Twin Lakes. From Chicago Basin, traverse northeast (right) into the basin between Windom and Jupiter. From the basin, the easiest way to gain the ridge is to aim for the low point (13,260′). It is also possible to gain the ridge at the 13,400′ saddle by a more difficult scramble. From Twin Lakes, head east in the drainage between Sunlight and Windom and then traverse southeast to gain the ridge.

Sunlight Peak

14,059′ **RANK 39**

Sunlight, another Chicago Basin 14er approached from Needle Creek, combines well with Jupiter and Windom.

South Face

From Needleton via Needle Creek TH at 8,200′: 8.7 miles, 5,910′

From Purgatory Flats TH at 8,800′: 17.3 miles, 8,620′

From Endlich Mesa TH at 11,570′: 15.6 miles, 6,580′

From Vallecito TH at 7,900′: 20.1 miles, 9,160′

Sunlight and Windom are frequently climbed together. When this is done, it is best to climb Windom first and then downclimb a steep gully on the north side of Windom's west ridge. At the bottom of the gully, traverse across the drainage at about 13,600′ to the south face. If you are climbing only Sunlight from Twin Lakes, simply climb up the drainage on the north (left) side of the stream. From the upper parts of the south face, several variations lead to the summit, each requiring Class 3 scrambling. Sunlight's true summit is a large block that requires a short, exposed Class 4 move.

From the summit of Windom gazing into Sunlight Creek drainage, left to right: Sunlight, Sunlight Spire, Arrow, Vestal, Trinities, and the rest of the Grenadiers, all behind Jagged.

Sunlight Spire

13,995′ UNRANKED

From Needleton via Needle Creek TH at 8,200′: 8.7 miles, 5,910′

From Purgatory Flats TH at 8,800′: 17.3 miles, 8,620′

From Endlich Mesa TH at 11,570′: 15.6 miles, 6,580′

From Vallecito TH at 7,900′: 20.1 miles, 9,160′

Sunlight Spire is on the high rugged divide between Sunlight Peak and Windom Peak. The summit pinnacle of the spire is a slightly overhanging "obelisk" that is split by a 40′ leaning irregular finger crack, which varies in width from 1 to 2 inches. Forty feet of lower Class 5 climbing precede setting up a belay at the base of the finger crack. Jeff Achey made the first free ascent of the spire and rated it 5.10c. For most mountaineers, a free climb of Sunlight Spire is unthinkable and unnerving. The high altitude, difficulty, and awkwardness (left leaning, slightly overhanging, and irregular crack) are just too much. It is a test piece for a select few.

Jupiter Mountain

13,830′ RANK 92

Jupiter, one of the one hundred highest peaks in Colorado, is frequently combined with 14ers Eolus, Windom, and Sunlight after an approach from Needle Creek; however, it can be climbed on its own from Columbine Pass via Johnson Creek and Vallecito Creek.

Southwest Face

From Needleton via Needle Creek TH at 8,200′: 8.0 miles, 5,910′

From Purgatory Flats TH at 8,800′: 16.1 miles, 8,620′

From Endlich Mesa TH at 11,570′: 14.3 miles, 6,080′

From Vallecito TH at 7,900′: 17.1 miles, 9,160′

The best way to approach Jupiter is to take the trail from Chicago Basin toward Columbine Pass. At tree line (11,640′), leave the trail where it turns right (south) and head directly up the grassy slopes of the southwest face. Stay left (north) on the face to eventually gain the Class 2+ west ridge. If you plan on climbing Windom also, it is possible to save time by downclimbing the steep couloir on the north side of the west ridge (or you can ascend this route as well from Windom or Sunlight via the notch between Peak Eighteen and Windom).

South Ridge

From Needleton via Needle Creek TH at 8,200′: 10.4 miles, 6,250′

From Purgatory Flats TH at 8,800′: 18.7 miles, 7,650′

From Endlich Mesa TH at 11,570′: 13.4 miles, 5,230′

From Vallecito TH at 7,900′: 17.1 miles, 6,890′

From Columbine Pass, follow a trail northeast toward Hazel Lake and climb up to the 13,155′ point just south of Jupiter. From here, it's a Class 2+ scramble up the ridge on loose talus, scree, and dirt.

From Peak 13,190′, looking north, left to right: Sunlight, Windom, Jupiter, and Grizzly C.

Greylock and Thunder Mountain from the summit of Windom.

Greylock Mountain

13,575′ RANK 207

Greylock Mountain is 1 mile northeast of Grizzly Peak C and 1.2 miles southeast of Sunlight Lake high above Sunlight Creek, from where it is accessed.

West Ridge

From Beartown TH at 11,700′ via Sunlight Creek: 15.4 miles, 6,900′

From Vallecito TH at 7,900′ via Sunlight Creek: 18.4 miles, 7,140′

From the north side of Sunlight Lake, hike east across the lake outlet. Contour south and west on a ridge that leads south-southwest toward another lake at 12,545′. Before reaching the lake, head southeast at 12,500′, go around the 12,620′ point on the east side, and drop down to the flat basin at 12,400′. From here, ascend south, heading for a saddle just west of point 13,229′. Climb east to the summit of this minor point and follow the ridge southeast to a notch on Class 2+ terrain and continue west to the summit. To climb Grizzly Peak C and McCauley as well from here, descend as you came and head southwest to a lake at 12,235′ to gain the Jupiter–Grizzly saddle where the route for those two peaks begins.

Grizzly Peak C

13,700′ RANK 145

Grizzly Peak C is 0.65 mile southeast of Jupiter Mountain and can be approached from many locations. Every approach requires a great deal of mileage and elevation gain. Grizzly is often combined with McCauley Peak and Greylock Mountain.

Northwest Ridge

From Beartown TH at 11,700′ via Sunlight Creek: 14.4 miles, 6,250′

From Needleton via Needle Creek TH at 8,200′: 10.5 miles, 6,530′

From Purgatory Flats TH at 8,800′: 19 miles, 7,880′

From Endlich Mesa TH at 11,570′: 13.5 miles, 5,480′

From Vallecito TH at 7,900′ via Sunlight Creek: 17.4 miles, 7,140′

Regardless of your starting point, the goal is to gain the ridge between Jupiter and Grizzly. This can either be done from Columbine Pass or Sunlight Creek. If coming from the north (Sunlight Creek) via Greylock Mountain, stop 100′ before the saddle. If coming from the south (Columbine Pass), descend 100′ to the north from the saddle. From here, turn eastward by climbing out of the couloir and contouring upward, following a wide band of pink granite. This leads to another break in the ridge at 13,600′, where you contour below the summit and continue up solid Class 3 blocks of rock toward the summit. Note: If coming from the north (Sunlight Creek), it is easy to climb Greylock Mountain first.

From left to right, as seen from Knife Point: Echo, McCauley, Grizzly C, Sunlight Spire, and Sunlight.

McCauley Peak

13,554′ RANK 216

McCauley Peak is located 0.75 mile south-southeast of Grizzly Peak C directly east of Columbine Pass and is often climbed in conjunction with Grizzly Peak C and Greylock Mountain.

Northwest Ridge

From Beartown TH at 11,700′ via Sunlight Creek: 15.4 miles, 6,900′

From Needleton via Needle Creek TH at 8,200′: 11.5 miles, 6,530′

From Purgatory Flats TH at 8,800′: 20 miles, 7,880′

From Endlich Mesa TH at 11,570′: 14.5 miles, 5,480′

From Vallecito TH at 7,900′ via Sunlight Creek: 18.4 miles, 7,140′

The route for McCauley begins at Hazel Lake at 12,435′ and can be accessed from Columbine Pass to the west or Sunlight Creek to the north. If coming from the north, you can combine this climb with Grizzly Peak C by descending southeast from the saddle between Grizzly Peak C and Jupiter to 12,620′. From Columbine Pass, hike northeast on a trail, split the notch between Hope Mountain and point 13,155′, and descend to Hazel Lake. From either route, aim to contour southeast to the farthest south part of the saddle between Grizzly Peak and McCauley on Class 2 terrain. At the saddle, continue up the northwest ridge. The final 0.25 mile is Class 3 rock scrambling until you reach a steep couloir that takes you to the summit.

Pigeon Peak

13,972′ RANK 57

One of the most recognizable peaks in the San Juans due to its sheer eastern face, Pigeon sits as the westernmost peak on the divide between the Ruby Creek drainage and New York Basin and is frequently combined with Turret to the east.

Northwest Basin

From Purgatory Flats TH at 8,800′ via North Pigeon Creek: 13 miles, 7,370′

From Purgatory Flats TH at 8,800′ via Ruby Creek: 15.6 miles, 8,970′

From Needleton TH at 8,200′ via North Pigeon Creek: 3.5 miles, 5,760′

From Needleton TH at 8,200′ via Ruby Creek: 6 miles, 7,360′

From North Pigeon Creek at 11,740′: 1 mile, 2,230′

From Ruby Creek Basin at 11,620′: 2 miles, 3,750′

Pigeon's northwest basin is difficult to reach, but once there, it's the easiest and standard route on Pigeon. From Needleton, ascend into Ruby Basin via the Ruby Creek approach, and if you are backpacking, there is ample camping at 11,620′ in a large

Left: Spencer Swanger on the summit of Pigeon. Swanger was the first person of climb the one hundred highest peaks in Colorado. Photo courtesy of Spencer Swanger **Right:** Pigeon from the Pigeon-Turret saddle.

meadow. From the meadow, gain the northwest basin of Pigeon from Ruby Creek by climbing up to the 13,100′ saddle between Pigeon and Turret and then losing elevation as you circle around the south and west flanks of Pigeon. Once in the northwest basin, climb grassy slopes up toward the ridge northwest of Pigeon's summit. As you approach the ridge, there are several options. One that works well is to ascend a narrow Class 4 slot that angles left to right and then look for a grassy ramp above that ascends right to left. Alternatively, bypass the Class 4 slot by continuing south and west for 20′ to 30′ where you will find a Class 3 ramp heading up. On the final ridge, stay right (west) on Class 3+ terrain to gain the summit.

North Face

Mileage and elevation are same as above.

For years, the north face was regarded as the "easy" way up Pigeon; however, it can be a challenge to find and in bad weather is slick and difficult. To gain the route, contour west below the north face from the basin above Ruby Lake and then climb the grassy ledges that lead to the Class 4 northwest ridge.

The Needles, as seen from Peak 13,300' in the West Silverton group at sunset, right to left: Pigeon, Eolus, Glacier Point, Animas, Windom, Sunlight, Knife Point, and Jagged.

East Face

Mileage and elevation are the same as for Ruby Creek approaches, minus 1,500′ of elevation gain and 1.5 miles.

A ten-pitch route (five pitches involving 5.9 climbing) was reported in the January/February 1978 issue of *Climbing* and follows a prominent dihedral crack system on the right (north) side of the face. One pendulum was used to switch cracks, but otherwise the route was all free. The rock is reported to have been "extremely rotten."

Southeast Chimney

Mileage and elevation are the same as for Ruby Creek approaches, minus 1,500′ of elevation gain and 1.5 miles.

This is a rappel route for parties climbing both Pigeon and Turret in a day from Ruby Creek. It is located to the left (east) about 400′ down the couloir on the south face between the twin summits. A double rope rappel is required. The first rappel anchor is a small chockstone, with multiple old slings around it. From the chockstone, rappel 70′ to a ledge on the wall about 8′ left (west) of the chimney. The ledge can only hold two people comfortably. The second rappel is about 120′ long. Have cams and nuts on hand to protect against the possibility that the second rappel anchor no longer exists. You can't see the second rappel anchor from the top of the first rappel.

Turret Peak

13,835′ RANK 89

Turret is 0.5 mile southeast of Pigeon and separated by a 13,100′ pass. It is usually approached from a high camp in Ruby Creek. Turret has one of the best views from any mountain in Colorado due to its position deep within the Needles and also happens to be where the cover photo of this book was photographed.

Northwest Slopes

From Purgatory Flats TH at 8,800′ via North Pigeon Creek: 14.25 miles, 7,370′

From Purgatory Flats TH at 8,800′ via Ruby Creek: 14.5 miles, 7,470′

From Needleton TH at 8,200′ via North Pigeon Creek: 4.75 miles, 5,760′

From Needleton TH at 8,200′ via Ruby Creek: 4.9 miles, 5,860′

From North Pigeon Creek at 11,740′: 2.25 miles, 2,100′

From Ruby Creek Basin at 11,620′: 1 mile, 2,220′

Via the northwest slopes, Turret is one of the easiest climbs in the Needles. From Ruby Creek basin or North Pigeon Creek, climb up toward the 13,100′ saddle between Turret and Pigeon before turning east toward Turret. Given the moderate nature of the northwest face, there are several variations you can take, but a Class 2+ route on scree to the right (south) side of the face works well. Enjoy spectacular views of the San Juans in all directions.

Peak Fifteen

13,700′ RANK 146

Peak Fifteen is due east of Turret but not easily combined with it. Peak Fifteen combines well with Sixteen, and they are both approached by the same couloir from New York Basin.

Left: Pigeon and Turret from Ruby Lake. **Right:** Peak Fifteen from Ruby Basin.

New York Basin Approach

From Purgatory Flats TH at 8,800′ via North Pigeon Creek: 15.75 miles, 8,630′

From Purgatory Flats TH at 8,800′ via Ruby Creek: 16 miles, 8,720′

From Needleton TH at 8,200′ via North Pigeon Creek: 6.25 miles, 5,760′

From Needleton TH at 8,200′ via Ruby Creek: 6.4 miles, 7,010′

From North Pigeon Creek at 11,740′: 3.75 miles, 3,360′

From Ruby Creek Basin at 11,620′: 2.5 miles, 3,480′

From the 13,100′ saddle between Turret and Pigeon or the 12,820′ saddle south of Pigeon, make a descending eastward traverse into New York Basin, dropping to 12,200′. The initial objective is to reach the saddle between Peaks Fifteen and Sixteen. To do so, climb the steep couloir between the peaks. Early in the year, the couloir is filled with snow. Later, it can be slick and wet. Near the top of the couloir, exit left (west) to bypass an overhang. From the small, airy saddle between the peaks, there are several Class 5.2 variations that afford few opportunities to place protection. Keep an eye out for cairns. Most of the problems are on the lower half of the route above the saddle where loose scree makes for difficult footing.

Peak Sixteen

13,500′ UNRANKED

Peak Sixteen is due east of Fifteen and west of Little Finger (Peak Seventeen) and is best approached from a camp high in New York Basin after an initial approach via the Ruby Creek drainage.

New York Basin Approach

From Purgatory Flats TH at 8,800′ via North Pigeon Creek: 15.75 miles, 8,430′

From Purgatory Flats TH at 8,800′ via Ruby Creek: 16 miles, 8,520′

From Needleton TH at 8,200′ via North Pigeon Creek: 6.25 miles, 5,560′

From Needleton TH at 8,200′ via Ruby Creek: 6.4 miles, 6,810′

From North Pigeon Creek at 11,740′: 3.75 miles, 3,160′

From Ruby Creek Basin at 11,620′: 2.5 miles, 3,280′

Peak Sixteen is usually combined with a climb of Fifteen. From the saddle between the peaks, climb to the right to gain a steep gully on the south side of the summit block. Take a rope to belay the Class 5.2 pitch above the saddle that is hard to protect on the ascent. If you are climbing both peaks, climb Sixteen first to get a good view of the route on Fifteen.

Little Finger—"Peak Seventeen"

13,220′ UNRANKED

Little Finger sits due east of Peak Sixteen and northwest of North Eolus and, because of its difficulty, is usually not climbed with other peaks.

South Face Chimneys

From Purgatory Flats TH at 8,800′ via North Pigeon Creek: 15.75 miles, 8,150′

From Purgatory Flats TH at 8,800′ via Ruby Creek: 16 miles, 8,240′

From Needleton TH at 8,200′ via North Pigeon Creek: 6.25 miles, 5,280′

From Needleton TH at 8,200′ via Ruby Creek: 6.4 miles, 6,530′

From North Pigeon Creek at 11,740′: 3.75 miles, 2,880′

From Ruby Creek Basin at 11,620′: 2.5 miles, 3,000′

The south face on this spectacular granite spire is split by two chimneys. The climbing route starts just right of the west (left) chimney, gains the west chimney after 40′, and continues up the west chimney almost to halfway. Here, it traverses right to gain the east chimney, which leads to the top. The crux is a 5.8 stemming move just above the large sandy alcove, 50′ up in the west chimney. The rest of the route is 5.4 to 5.5. The descent is made by rappelling down the western chimney.

Monitor Peak

13,695′ RANK 148

Monitor lies just north of the pass that separates the Ruby Creek drainage from the Noname drainage and 1.2 miles east-northeast of Pigeon Peak. It is frequently combined with Peak Thirteen and Animas Mountain.

South Basin—North Ridge

From Purgatory Flats TH at 8,800′ via Ruby Creek: 15 miles, 7,560′

From Needleton TH at 8,200′ via Ruby Creek: 5 miles, 5,880′

From Ruby Creek Basin at 11,625′: 0.5 mile, 2,080′

This is the standard and easiest route up Monitor. From Ruby Basin, the initial objective is to climb into the south basin below Monitor, Peak Thirteen, and Animas. As you reach the basin, you will see two ramps slanting left to right (west to east) below the face of Peak Thirteen. The lower ramp is a Class 3 scramble on generally solid rock. From the top of the ramp, climb over to a point about 50′ below the Thirteen-Monitor saddle and begin climbing on the right (west) side of the north ridge on Class 3+ terrain until you have circumvented spires and blocks. Once reaching higher ground, you can climb the ridge directly.

Left: From Ruby Basin at sunset, left to right: the Index, Animas, Peak Thirteen, and Monitor. **Right:** The east face of Monitor Peak, from left: the 1947, 1976, 1968, and 1980 routes. The black cross marks the site of the 1947 bivouac. Photo by Joe Stettner

East Face

The intimidating 1,200′ east face of Monitor has several difficult technical routes. Although the four routes established to date cover different portions of the lower two-thirds of the face, they all converge high on the face below a delicate pitch known as the "140′ lead." The four routes are named according to the year of their first-known ascent:

1. **1947 Route.** This route starts in a "very steep gully marking the left-hand margin" of the central face and works up to a junction with a long chimney on the left, at least 450′ above the face. From the junction, the route follows the chimney to an overhang at about two-thirds the height of the gully with two traverses to the right. A delicate traverse below the overhang leads to a lieback crack that puts you on the central face where a succession of cracks and ledges lead alternately upward and to the right into the central face About 300′ below the top, you reach the 140′ lead, which is difficult, hard to protect face-climbing rated at least 5.8. Above the 140′ lead, the route follows a V-shaped chimney for 15′ before gaining the edge of the rib forming the left side of

the chimney by a difficult move and then follows the steep wall to the left of the chimney. The first ascent party placed a total of nineteen pitons. The pitons were used for protection only and not aid. The ascent was free except for a couple of shoulder stands. They noted that although the rock on the upper face was generally good, they encountered much loose rock in the lower face. A detailed account of this route can be found in the December 1947 issue of *Trail and Timberline.*

2. **1968 Route.** This route starts just to the right of the center of the face and works slightly to the right to meet the 1947 Route high on the face below the 140′ lead. A section about halfway up the sheer east face requires direct aid. Approximately fifteen pitons and two nuts were placed by the 1968 party, which also encountered much loose rock on the lower half of the face. A short account of this climb was published in the July 1969 issue of *Trail and Timberline.*

3. **1976 Route.** This route starts up a chimney on the central face between the 1947 and 1968 Routes. Tom Norton describes the first pitch as being 5.5 climbing on loose, rotten rock with poor protection. From a chimney belay, the second pitch goes 15′ up a corner across the face (5.5) into a left-sloping 5.7 jam crack, and then left to a ledge below a 75′ corner. The third pitch climbs the 75′, left-facing corner via a 5.8 off-width crack. The whole thing turns into a chimney at the top. It is best to exit as high as possible to the left onto a ledge and continue up two more ledges. Near the top of the pitch, move left up a crack on two points of aid and then traverse right to a fixed pin and free climb up a difficult (5.9+) section to a belay ledge. The fourth pitch lets up in difficulty (5.5 to 5.6) and ends with some scrambling to the belay. The fifth pitch follows a 75′ chimney, which is also 5.5 to 5.6. The sixth pitch is the 140′ lead, which Norton describes as being "tricky face climbing" (5.8). The seventh pitch, which follows the chimney initially before moving out onto the steep face, is rated 5.7. The eighth, and last pitch, is easy but loose and should be climbed carefully.

4. **1980 Route.** This route starts in the deep chimney at the junction between the center and right sides of the wall to the pitch past a chockstone and then exits onto the face following a faint, left-leaning groove and crack system before traversing left to the large ledge system that connects with the 1947 Route just below its junction with the 1968 Route. The maximum difficulty of the route has been rated 5.9, with a scarcity of good protection noted.

Peak Thirteen—"Sceptor"

13,705′ UNRANKED

Peak Thirteen is located on the divide between the Noname and Ruby drainages and is frequently combined with Monitor and Animas.

South Basin—Upper East Face

From Purgatory Flats TH at 8,800′ via Ruby Creek: 15.25 miles, 7,570′

From Needleton TH at 8,200′ via Ruby Creek: 5.25 miles, 5,890′

From Ruby Creek Basin at 11,620′: 0.75 mile, 2,090′

This is the standard route up Peak Thirteen. The initial approach for Peak Thirteen from Ruby Basin is the same as that for Monitor Peak. Once in the basin, take the left-to-right slanting ramp toward the base of the south cliffs of Peak Thirteen and then contour below them to the upper east face. Before reaching the east face, you lose about 50′ of elevation in one spot. The east face is a Class 3+ scramble over ledges with crumbling rock.

South Basin—Northwest Ridge

An alternate route to climbing Thirteen, or a descent route if you are on your way to Animas, is the northwest face. If ascending from a start at the saddle between Animas and point 13,620′, climb up the northwest face, with a few Class 3 moves, toward a notch about 100 vertical feet below the summit, which allows you to cross over onto the north face. You can scramble up the north face to the summit.

Animas Mountain

13,786′ RANK 112

Animas is located on the divide between the Noname and Ruby drainages and is frequently combined with Monitor and Thirteen.

South Basin—Upper Southeast Face

From Purgatory Flats TH at 8,800′ via Ruby Creek: 15.25 miles, 7,650′

From Needleton TH at 8,200′ via Ruby Creek: 5.25 miles, 5,970′

From Ruby Creek Basin at 11,620′: 0.75 mile, 2,170′

From Ruby Creek basin, the easiest way up is to scramble through the rock band at 13,000′ to the right of the prominent chimney. Once you reach the saddle between Animas and point 13,620′, start up the upper southwest face. It is Class 2 until the last 100′, which is Class 3+ in the broad gully just east of the summit.

Turret, Pigeon, Monitor, and Peak Thirteen, from Knife Point.

The Index

13,420′ UNRANKED

From Purgatory Flats TH at 8,800′ via Ruby Creek: 15.25 miles, 7,290′

From Needleton TH at 8,200′ via Ruby Creek: 5.25 miles, 5,610′

From Ruby Creek Basin at 11,620′: 0.75 mile, 1,810′

This prominent point juts south from the west ridge of Animas Mountain. The summit of the Index is the southernmost point on the ridge. The route is complex, and climbers attempting it should consider spending a day scouting the route before making a push for the summit. The climb leading to the summit block involves Class 5.7 climbing on near-vertical off-width cracks. The route used by the first ascent party starts on the northwest corner of the ridge and climbs over the middle summit. From the middle summit, it's necessary to rappel to the col between the middle and main summits before facing the crux on the summit block that requires climbing a 12′ vertical 5.9 crack that is too wide for a fist jam. The first ascent party used a shoulder stand on the summit block.

Jagged Mountain

13,824′ RANK 94

Jagged Mountain, which adorns this book's cover, is a stunning peak in a surreal and remote setting. Located in the center of Needles, it is usually the exclusive focus of any climber on the day it is climbed. The mountain is composed of fractured granite blocks, and ascending this peak requires nerves, patience, and grit as you snake your way up and around the mountain to gain the summit. With three cruxes and

Left: Jagged Mountain from Knife Point, a jumble of broken rock blocks. **Right:** The first crux of Jagged.

a tremendous amount of exposure on solid rock, this is arguably the most exciting climb in the San Juans.

North Face

From Beartown TH at 11,700′ via Sunlight Creek: 11.7 miles, 7,870′

From Purgatory Flats TH at 8,800′ via Noname Creek: 18.9 miles, 7,660′

From Needleton TH at 8,200′ via Noname Creek: 9.4 miles, 6,050′

From Vallecito TH at 7,900′ via Sunlight Creek: 15.5 miles, 7,870′

From 13,020′ on Jagged pass: 0.8 mile, 840′

The initial objective when climbing Jagged is to reach Jagged pass at 13,020′ just north of the peak, which separates the Noname and Sunlight drainages. This area can be reached either from the west via Noname drainage or from the southeast via Sunlight Creek. From the pass, pick out the prominent snow couloir and make a mental note that the true summit is just right (west) of the couloir. There is a notch to the right (west) of the true summit that you must gain, but from the pass, it is partially obscured. When viewed from the pass, the Class 5.2 route you will follow looks very improbable. From the pass, traverse to the north face and begin climbing 100′ to the right (west) of the snow couloir. Climb the Class 2+ base of the face to a small Class 4 vertical crack/gully that angles up and then left for 80′. This is the first crux. A cam can be placed about halfway up for protection. From here, zigzag up steep Class 2+–3 terrain, using grassy ramps and ledges, always staying right of the couloir. Continue to the top of the highest grass ramp and turn right (west). Zigzag to ascend to a saddle and then cross a gully below a large chimney. After crossing the gully, continue west up more ledges to a Class 4 chute filled with big rocks and grass.

The heart of the Needles, as seen from Jagged.

To the left of this chute is a large vertical wall. Ascend this chute, which terminates on a rounded ledge. The first couple of moves are the hardest. This is the second crux.

After the second crux, zigzag west for 120′ on Class 2+–3 ledges. Turn left (south) for the third crux, arguably the hardest. There are two ways up: one to the east and one to the west. The western route contains a crack and is shorter and more difficult, but it's easier to find protection. The final move to ascend the third crux is a challenge; take your time and use leverage on the right boulder to gain the top. Above the third crux, continue southwest into a notch west of the summit. From the notch, contour out onto the south face on solid but very exposed terrain. Two routes go on the upper south face: One is strenuous with good handholds and goes straight up Class 4 terrain after contouring for about 50′. The other is easier but more exposed, traversing across the south face to a 30′ Class 3 chimney that leads to easy Class 3 scrambling. The summit is flat, roomy, and awe-inspiring.

Knife Point

13,265′ RANK 428

Knife Point is located on the ridge due north of Sunlight and southwest of Jagged Mountain and overlooks the upper basin of Noname Creek.

East Face

From Noname Creek, climb the steep slopes to the 12,860′ pass between Knife Point and Peak Ten. From the pass, the summit via the east face is a pleasant Class 2 walk-up on sandy scree. Alternatively, the east face can be approached from a high camp in Sunlight Basin, and this route is often combined with Jagged Mountain.

Left: Knife Point from Noname basin. **Right:** From Jagged, right to left: Peak Ten and Knife Point.

Northwest Spur

A technical route rated 5.7 A2 has been established on the northwest spur. An account of the climb is found in *Trail and Timberline* (May 1978), which indicated that the route was protected with nuts and a couple of knife blades. Aid was used on a roof and a crack that would probably go free at around 5.9 to 5.10.

Peak Ten

13,420′ **SOFT RANKED**

Peak Ten is located between Knife Point and Jagged but does not combine well with either peak. Peak Ten does combine well with a climb of Noname Needle.

Gray Needle, Peak Ten, and Jagged, from Knife Point.

Southeast Face

From the Sunlight drainage, climb toward the pass just north of Peak Ten before traversing out onto the southeast face. Once on the face, you are confronted by a labyrinth of sandy gullies, clumps of grass, and granite boulders. There are dozens of Class 3 variations on the face. Near the top, you will be on an exposed Class 4 ridge that warrants use of a short rope. On the summit, enjoy an otherworldly view of the south flank of Jagged.

Peak 13,620′—"Noname Needle"

UNRANKED

Noname Needle is located 0.25 mile north of Peak Ten and 0.25 mile west of Jagged Mountain. It is the apex of the ridge that extends north of Peak Ten. It has been confused by some for Gray Needle, which is due west and lower at 13,430′. From the Noname drainage, approach by hiking toward the pass just north of Peak Ten. Just below the pass, climb north to the base of Noname Needle. Once at the base, an 80′ pitch of 5.7 on the southwest side of the tower leads to a col between the twin summits. The western summit is higher and capped by an overhanging slab on a pedestal which, from the col, is best climbed in a clockwise manner.

Rappelling Noname Needle. Photo by Bob Rosebrough

Leviathan Peak

13,528′ RANK 237

Leviathan is located 1 mile east-northeast of Jagged above a basin that drains into the Sunlight Creek.

Southwest Ridge

From Beartown TH at 11,700′ via Sunlight Creek: 11.7 miles, 7,570′

From Purgatory Flats TH at 8,800′ via Noname Creek: 18.8 miles, 7,360′

From Needleton TH at 8,200′ via Noname Creek: 9.3 miles, 5,650′

From Vallecito TH at 7,900′ via Sunlight Creek: 15.4 miles, 7,570′

From 13,020′ on Jagged Pass: 1 mile, 800′

The southwest ridge is a rocky Class 3 climb on quartzite rock with great views of Jagged Mountain. The one thing to remember is to bypass the 13,420′ false summit to the left (west).

South Couloir

The south couloir tops out between the 13,420′ false summit and the true summit. The couloir is filled with talus, and this Class 2+ route can be used as either a descent or ascent route to also climb Vallecito.

Leviathan (left) and Vallecito (right), from the base of Jagged.

Vallecito Mountain

13,428′ **RANK 301**

Vallecito is located east of Leviathan, and the two are commonly climbed on the same day.

West Ridge

From Beartown TH at 11,700′ via Sunlight Creek: 11.7 miles, 7,470′

From Purgatory Flats TH at 8,800′ via Noname Creek: 18.9 miles, 7,260′

From Needleton TH at 8,200′ via Noname Creek: 9.4 miles, 5,550′

From Vallecito TH at 7,900′ via Sunlight Creek: 15.5 miles, 7,470′

From 13,020′ on Jagged Pass: 0.5 mile, 600′

On the lower portion of the west ridge, accessed the same way that you gain Jagged pass (see the descriptions for Jagged Mountain above, p. 191), scramble left (north) of the ridge before gaining the top of the ridge. Follow the Class 2+ ridge directly to the top thereafter, except to skirt a couple of small ridge humps to the left (north). A few spots of moderate scrambling break up what is otherwise a walk-up.

Peak Four

13,410′ **RANK 312**

Peak Four sits on the divide between the Noname and Tenmile drainages and combines well with The Heisspitz, which sits west of Peak Four on the same divide.

Gray Needle from Knife Point with Peaks Four, Five, and the Heisspitz, including Arrow, Vestal, and West Trinity.

South Flank

From the old cabin in the Noname drainage or farther east up the drainage in the meadows at 10,800′, bushwhack and switchback up the steep, forested south flank of Peak Four. Above tree line, a ridge extending due south from point 13,206′ becomes more pronounced, indicating that it's time to stay east of the ridge and shoot for the saddle between point 13,206′ and Peak Four. From the saddle, climb the Class 2+ route on the western ridge of Peak Four to the summit.

The Heisspitz

13,262′ RANK 429

The Heisspitz is the westernmost peak on the north side of Noname Creek located 1.5 miles north-northeast of Animas Mountain and 0.85 mile west-northwest of Peak Four.

Noname Approach

From Needleton TH at 8,200′ via Noname Creek: 7 miles, 5,300′

From Purgatory Flats TH at 8,800′ via Noname Creek: 17.1 miles, 7,080′

A prominent drainage near the old cabin in Noname Creek extends north toward Peak Four. The best approach for the Heisspitz climbs to the right (east) of the drainage. Near tree line, contour into the drainage and climb left (west) to gain the Noname-Tenmile divide between Heisspitz and Peak Four. Follow the ridge northwest on Class 2+ terrain with a few Class 3 moves. There are twin summits on Heisspitz—east and west—with the eastern summit generally considered to be the high point. The summit block requires Class 3 scrambling and routefinding to negotiate a gap between the summits.

Sheep Mountain D—"Peak Twenty-Three"

13,070′ RANK 595

Sheep Mountain D is located approximately 2 miles east of Durango City Reservoir No. 1 and is best accessed via Endlich Mesa Trailhead. From the reservoir, it is best to combine Sheep Mountain D with Peak Twenty-Two, Emerson Mountain, Organ Mountain, and Amherst Mountain in a long day. From the trailhead to the campsites at the northeast part of the reservoir, you will gain 1,340′ of elevation over 6.1 miles.

South Slopes

From Endlich Mesa TH at 11,570′: 8 miles, 3,500′

From Durango City Reservoir No. 1 at 10,980′: 2 miles, 2,100′

Sheep Mountain D, as seen below Peak Twenty-Two.

From the reservoir, follow the drainage coming from the east below Sheep Mountain D, aiming for a small tarn at 11,860′. Continue to ascend east toward the summit up a tundra-covered slope, where you will find granite ledges, rock outcroppings, and large slabs that you must negotiate until you reach the summit on this pedestrian but fun Class 2 climb.

Peak 13,105′—"Peak Twenty-Two"

RANK **566**

Peak Twenty-Two is located along a ridge between Sheep Mountain D and Emerson Mountain.

Northwest Ridge

From Endlich Mesa TH at 11,570′: 8.3 miles, 3,540′

From Durango City Reservoir No. 1 at 10,980′: 2.3 miles, 2,140′

From Sheep Mountain D, descend on Class 2+ grass and rock. Routefinding is critical here due to sections where it simply cliffs out. If you cliff out, scan the area for another way up and down to an easier section. Make your way to the saddle between Sheep and Peak Twenty-Two and skirt left (west) of two rock spires. Continue north toward the base of Peak Twenty-Two until you reach a steep grassy slope leading north and east at 12,750′. Climb this steep slope to the ridge of Peak Twenty-Two and then turn right (south) to encounter a bombproof but challenging Class 3 block to the summit.

Sheep D, Peak Twenty-Two, Emerson, and Amherst from Organ B.

Emerson Mountain

13,140′ SOFT RANKED

Emerson Mountain shares a ridge with Amherst Mountain to the north and Peak Twenty-Two to the south.

South Slopes

From Endlich Mesa TH at 11,570′: 8.8 miles, 3,580′

From Durango City Reservoir No. 1 at 10,980′: 2.8 miles, 2,180′

From the summit of Peak Twenty-Two, scramble northwest to the saddle between Peak Twenty-Two and Emerson. Mark this location, as it is where you will return if you are going to climb Organ and Amherst. From here, climb north up a gentle slope to reach the summit on Class 2 terrain. To climb Amherst and Organ, return to the saddle between Peak Twenty-Two and Emerson and descend on a well-established game trail to the northeast and follow it north for 1 mile to the saddle between Amherst and Organ.

Amherst Mountain

13,165′ RANK 508

Amherst Mountain sits 0.36 mile southwest of Organ Mountain B and towers 1 mile south of the Johnson Creek drainage.

From Peak Twenty-Two, right to left: Organ B, Amherst, and Emerson.

East Slopes

From Endlich Mesa TH at 11,570′: 9.5 miles, 4,500′

From Durango City Reservoir No. 1 at 10,980′: 3.5 miles, 3,100′

From the saddle between Amherst and Organ, climb the east ridge on gravelly Class 2 terrain to 12,850′, where you will turn left (south) and work your way up the east slope of the peak to the ridge. Resist the temptation to ascend a nasty couloir as you wrap around to the south as it can be bypassed by continuing south and west. From the ridge, the summit is a short walk to the north.

Organ Mountain B—"Peak Twenty"

13,032′ RANK 620

Organ Mountain shares a ridge with Amherst Mountain and is impressive from every angle. From below in Johnson Creek, it looks virtually unclimbable next to Amherst. From Peak Twenty-Two to the south, the mountain looks like a castle minaret rising above Sheep Draw valley to the south.

Southwest Ridge

From Endlich Mesa TH at 11,570′: 9.5 miles, 3,400′

From Durango City Reservoir No. 1 at 10,980′: 3.5 miles, 3,000′

The Needles at sunset from Tower Mountain.

From the saddle between Amherst and Organ, climb northwest up loose scree to the base of the summit block and wrap around the block to your right (east) and then north until you locate a cairn leading left on the north side of the block. Follow this cairn to the right (north) to reach the base of the very top of the summit block where you'll enjoy a Class 3 move to reach the airy summit, which has just enough room for one person.

Note: These five peaks are an excellent combination on a long day: Sheep D, Peak Twenty-Two, Emerson, Organ, and then Amherst.

From Endlich Mesa TH at 11,570′: 12.1 miles, 6,200′

From Durango City Reservoir No. 1 at 10,980′: 6 miles, 4,500′

OFF THE BEATEN PATH

Peak Six

13,705′ RANK 144

1 mile north of Jagged Mountain

From Needleton TH at 8,200′ via Noname Creek: 8.2 miles, 5,760′

Southwest Ridge: From the 12,900′ pass between Peaks Five and Six, the southwest ridge is a Class 2 walk-up over large talus.

Peak Five

13,283′ RANK 412

1 mile northwest of Jagged Mountain

From Needleton TH at 8,200′ via Noname Creek: 8.2 miles, 5,330′

Northeast Ridge: From lake 12,552′, climb due north to gain the northeast ridge, which is largely Class 2+ with a few Class 3 moves including a nice friction slab near the summit.

Peak Twelve

13,140′ RANK 536

0.5 mile southeast of Monitor Peak

From Ruby Creek Basin at 11,620′: 0.8 mile, 1,400′

West Ridge: From the pass between Ruby and Noname Creeks, the west ridge on Peak Twelve is a rare Class 2 walk-up amidst a sea of giants. The last false summit is passed by a slight downclimb to the right (south).

Glacier Point

13,704′ SOFT RANKED

0.4 mile east of North Eolus

From Twin Lakes at 12,550′: 0.5 mile, 1,020′

East Face—Southeast Ridge: Frequently climbed with North Eolus and Eolus. From Twin Lakes, climb up the east face to gain the Class 2+ southeast ridge, which takes you to the summit.

A view from above Twin Lakes of Eolus, Glacier Point, and Twin Thumbs.

Twin Thumbs

13,420′ UNRANKED

0.1 mile northeast of the 13,060′ Twin Thumbs pass that separates the Noname drainage from Chicago Basin

From Twin Lakes at 12,550′: 0.3 mile, 870′

Chicago Basin Approach: From Twin Lakes high in Chicago Basin, head north toward the col between the Twin Thumbs and point 13,460′. The South Thumb is a Class 3 scramble up its northeast face. The North Thumb is climbed from the southeast. A short Class 4 section near the summit of the North Thumb is exposed and difficult enough to warrant the use of a rope. The Thumbs can be easily combined in one climb. It works well to climb the South Thumb first.

Peak Eleven

13,540′ RANK 227

0.5 mile east-northeast of Glacier Point

From Twin Lakes at 12,550′: 0.3 mile, 830′

Chicago Basin Approach: Peak Eleven can be climbed by skirting point 13,460′ to the north from the col just east of Twin Thumbs on Class 3 terrain.

Peak 13,472′—"Peak Eighteen"

UNRANKED

0.5 mile west of Windom and southwest of Twin Lakes

From Twin Lakes at 12,550′: 0.7 mile, 720′

Northeast Ridge: From the 13,260′ saddle connecting Peak Eighteen with Windom, the summit is a Class 3 scramble up this ridge.

Top: From the summit of Sunlight, left to right: Eolus, Glacier Point, Turret, Pigeon, Monitor, and Animas, with Peak Eleven closest at center. **Bottom:** Peak Eighteen at center, in front of Eolus and North Eolus.

Valois (top left) towers above Castilleja Lake before the Needles to the north.

Mount Valois

13,185′ **RANK 496**

2.2 miles north of Durango City Reservoir No. 1

From Endlich Mesa TH at 11,570′: 9.4 miles, 3,880′

From Durango City Reservoir No. 1 at 10,980′: 2.7 miles, 2,210′

Southwest Slopes: Ascend to your right (east) up steep tundra toward a break in the cliffs on Valois's southern ridge. Gain the ridge and ascend north up Class 2 tundra to the summit.

Aztec Mountain

13,310′ **RANK 385**

2.1 miles northwest of Mount Valois

From Durango City Reservoir No. 1 at 10,980′: 5.3 miles, 3,050′

West Ridge: A Class 2+ scramble on blocks and talus from Silver Mesa and Trimble Pass to the south.

GRENADIER RANGE 10

Remote, rugged, and beautiful, the Grenadiers exemplify the best the San Juans have to offer. Steep faces and hard quartzite make for the highest concentration of quality rock climbs in the San Juans. The main spine of the Grenadiers runs west to east from Electric Peak, Arrow, Vestal, the Trinities, Storm King Peak, and Mount Silex to the Guardian. Arrow and Vestal are the most celebrated of the Grenadiers. Arrow had for some time been reputed to be the most difficult major mountain in Colorado to climb, a reputation created by its rugged south face, which early climbers felt was the easiest route on the peak. A less-demanding route on the northeast rib has since been established. Vestal's reputation is largely based upon its eye-catching beauty. Vestal's north face, Wham Ridge, has to be seen to be believed. Electric Peak, Graystone Peak, Point Pun, and Mount Garfield are some of the least frequently climbed peaks in Colorado. Located on the west end of the Grenadiers, they are the most inaccessible peaks in a remote range. The east end of the main spine is formed by three high 13,000′ peaks that sport steep north faces: Storm King Peak, Mount Silex,

The Grenadiers, as seen from the summit of Peak Three, from left to right: Silex, Storm King, East Trinity, Trinity, West Trinity, Vestal, and Arrow.

and the Guardian. To the south of Storm King Peak, Peaks Seven, Eight, and Nine connect the Grenadiers to the Needle Mountains. To the north, Peaks One, Two, and Three and White Dome separate the Grenadiers from the Continental Divide.

CLIMBING HISTORY

The combined inaccessibility and ruggedness of the Grenadiers prevented incursions for many years, and it is one of the few areas in the San Juans not climbed by the Wheeler or Hayden Survey teams. Although the surveyors did not climb in the Grenadiers, the range occupied their thoughts. They generally referred to the Grenadiers and neighboring Needles as the "Quartzites." Comments by early surveyors were filled with feelings of fear, foreboding, and respect. Marshall's 1876 report for the Wheeler Survey noted:

> *The hard metamorphic rocks are shivered along their cleavage planes for hundreds of feet, leaving their odd pinnacles, there the likeness of the shattered outspread wings of some gigantic bird, and again of the grim grinning teeth of death.*

Marshall admitted that his "condemnation" of the Quartzites stemmed from the fact that he was "deeply prejudiced against them" because of a "disagreeable experience." In October 1874, Marshall's party was attempting to establish a triangulation

The mighty Grenadiers from high above Highland Mary Lakes.

station on the fringes of the range when they were trapped above tree line for three days by an early-season snowstorm, which left between "18 inches to 4 and 5 feet" of snow.

Although the Hayden team did not go so far as to "condemn" the range, they shared similar feelings. From the summit of Mount Sneffels, Franklin Rhoda of the Hayden Survey reported:

> *The group of quartzite peaks stood out as boldly as ever about 30 miles to the southeast. In fact, I may state here that we have never yet seen a group from any station (and we have viewed it from all sides) without feeling both deep respect and awe for their terrible ruggedness. The fact already stated, that the storm clouds seem to hover about them before starting on their meandering ways, only served to add to our other feelings of uneasiness.*

The closest that either team came to climbing the main peaks here was the Hayden Survey's climb of White Dome, where Wilson and Rhoda reported that the Grenadiers formed a "row of ten distinct peaks stretching in a nearly east-and-west line before our eyes."

The first climbers to reach the Grenadiers were William S. Cooper and John Hubbard in 1908, who camped at Balsam Lake and climbed to the saddle between Vestal and Arrow Peaks. They climbed Vestal by a rock gully on the south face, which Cooper described in his book *Mountains* as "interesting, but fairly easy." The south face of Arrow was an entirely different matter. Cooper noted that "Arrow Peak proved to be really difficult. Several times our holds depended on the strength of our fingers. I rather think, too, that we found the easiest route."

Cooper and Hubbard did not write an account of their climbs, and hence, when Carleton Long and John E. Nelson climbed Arrow Peak twenty-four years later in 1932, they thought that they had made a first ascent. In *Trail and Timberline* (November 1932), they described precarious climbing that eventually led them to a "perfectly delicious overhang." Appropriately, this obstacle has since been given the name "Long's Overhang." Long and Nelson are also credited with naming Vestal's north face "Wham Ridge." After studying Wham Ridge for several minutes from the top of Arrow, Nelson muttered, "I still don't believe it!"

In 1941, the Colorado Mountain Club held its twenty-eighth annual summer outing in the Grenadiers. During the outing, first ascents were made of West and Middle Trinity Peaks and Storm King Peak. The biggest climb of the outing,

Left: John E. Nelson and the rugged south face of Arrow Peak, just before the peak's second ascent in 1932. Photo courtesy of John E. Nelson **Right:** Wham Ridge on Vestal Peak four days before its first ascent during the 1941 Colorado Mountain Club outing. Photo by Werner Schnackenberg

Looking up Wham Ridge during the first ascent in 1941. Photo by Warner Schnackenberg

however, was the first ascent of Wham Ridge by Rit Burrows, Werner Schnackenberg, and Jim Patterson. After a warm-up climb of Arrow by the south face, they glissaded down the snowfield on the north face of Arrow and walked over to the base of Wham Ridge. The first several hundred feet went easily until the gradient increased and they were forced to rope up. In spite of fog and light rain, the party reached the summit of Vestal, using only one piton for protection, in three hours of actual climbing time.

John C. Ohrenschall and Doug Ward were lured to the area in 1962 by Burrow's report of the first ascent of Wham Ridge. Ohrenschall and Ward made several technical climbs during their stay in the Grenadiers, including the northeast face of Vestal, the east face of Arrow Peak, and the north face of West Trinity Peak. They also made what was probably the first winter ascent of Electric Peak by a technical route on the east face.

Winter climbing was the next challenge to lure climbers into the Grenadiers. A team of Harvard Mountaineers consisting of David Roberts, Matt Hale, Larry Muir, Steve Pomerance, Burt Redmayne, and Don Jensen spent their 1963 Christmas vacation in the Grenadiers. After two days of snowshoeing, the party reached Vestal Lake. The group split up into pairs and made ascents of the southwest ridge of West Trinity, the southeast ridge of Vestal, the west ridge of Vestal, the south face of Arrow, the south ridge of Storm King, the southwest ridge of Peak Eight, and the south face of East Trinity Peak. Roberts and Jensen's climb of Peak Eight is noteworthy for the fact that it may have been a first ascent for any season. Roberts noted in *Trail and Timberline* (July 1964) that there "was not the slightest pile of rocks on either summit, and after searching through the snow meticulously, we could find no trace of visitation."

One route that the Harvard Mountaineers did not touch was Wham Ridge. The first winter ascent of Wham Ridge was left to Arthur Mears, Don Vasicek, Steve Tandy, John Pinamont, and Tom Ruwitch in January of 1968. This strong party was slowed by the steepness of the upper ridge and did not reach the summit until sunset. Forced to bivouac high on the south ridge, they made it down without trouble the next day.

During the late 1960s and 1970s, many multiple-pitch technical routes were established on the steep faces of the Grenadiers. In August 1968, Martin Etter and Sam Casey climbed the northwest face of Arrow Peak via the Arrowhead pinnacle on Arrow's west shoulder. In August 1969, Etter teamed with Bo Shelby to climb a direct route on the east face of Vestal Peak. In July 1971, Henry Barber and Tom Stimson climbed the north saddle between West and Middle Trinity.

The first ascent of the 1,500' north face of Storm King was made in August 1974 by Bob Bliss and Don Jones. Bliss had climbed five pitches on the northeast shoulder in late August 1966 with Andy Lichtman, only to be forced to retreat by a hailstorm. Although warned by Larry Dalke that "those faces are to be looked at, not climbed," Bliss returned and was surprised to find what he described as a "path of ledges, short cracks, and chimneys, leading up and right for hundreds of feet, all hidden before by a plate of rock."

These long, hard routes exemplify the current trend of climbing in the Grenadiers. More than any other area in the San Juans, the Grenadiers offer an abundance of high-quality, multiple-pitch climbs.

ACCESS AND HIKING

Molas Trail—Lower Creek Trail—Vestal Creek

This is the most popular means of access to the Grenadiers, and its initial aim is to reach Elk Park on the Animas River. Elk Park is a stop for the Durango and Silverton Narrow Gauge Railroad. Call the railroad at 877-872-4607 or check durangotrain.com for current information. For those not interested in riding the train, the best way to reach Elk Park is from Molas Pass between Durango and Silverton on US Highway 550 (6 miles south of Silverton).

GRENADIER RANGE (WEST)

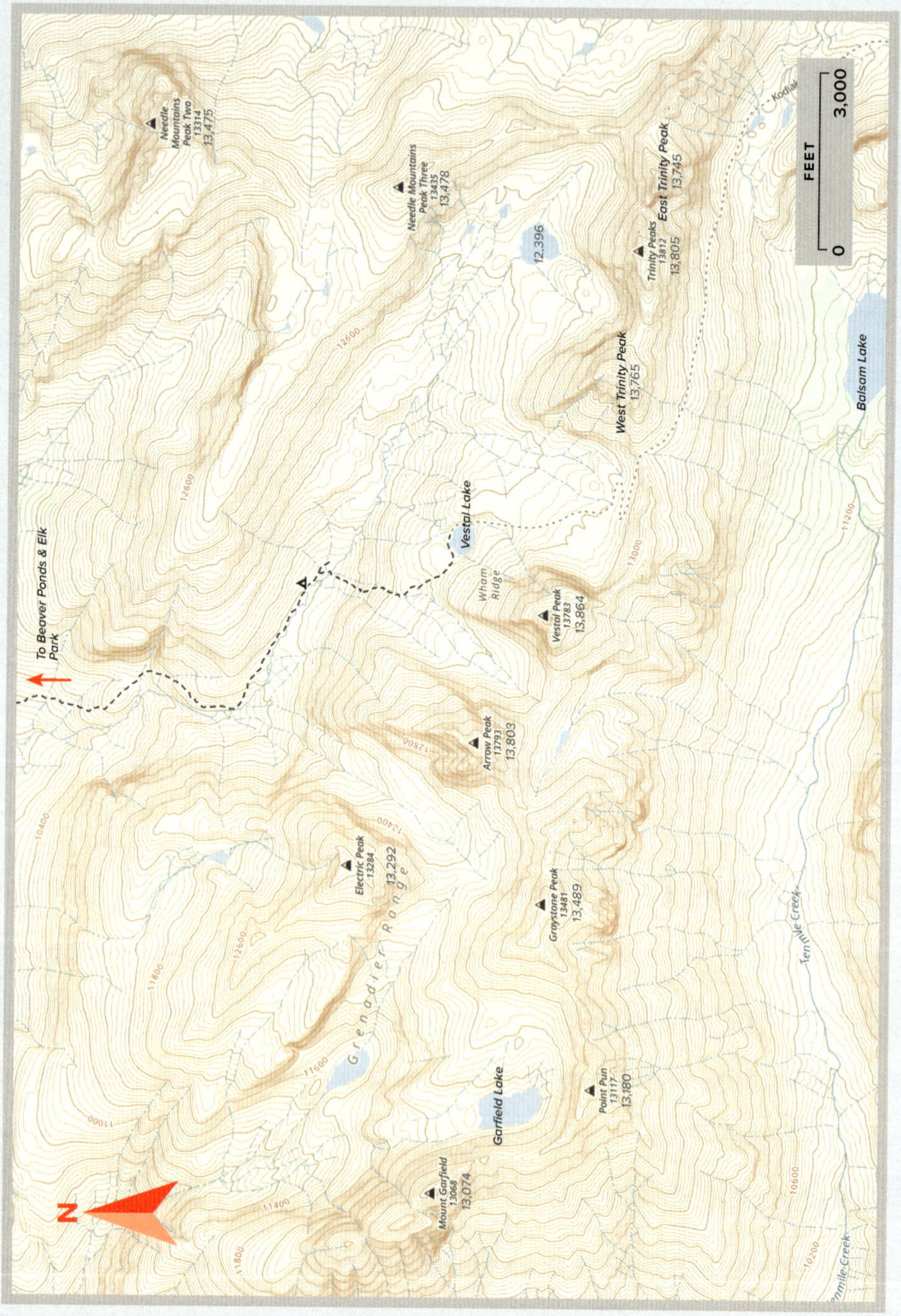

GRENADIER RANGE (EAST)

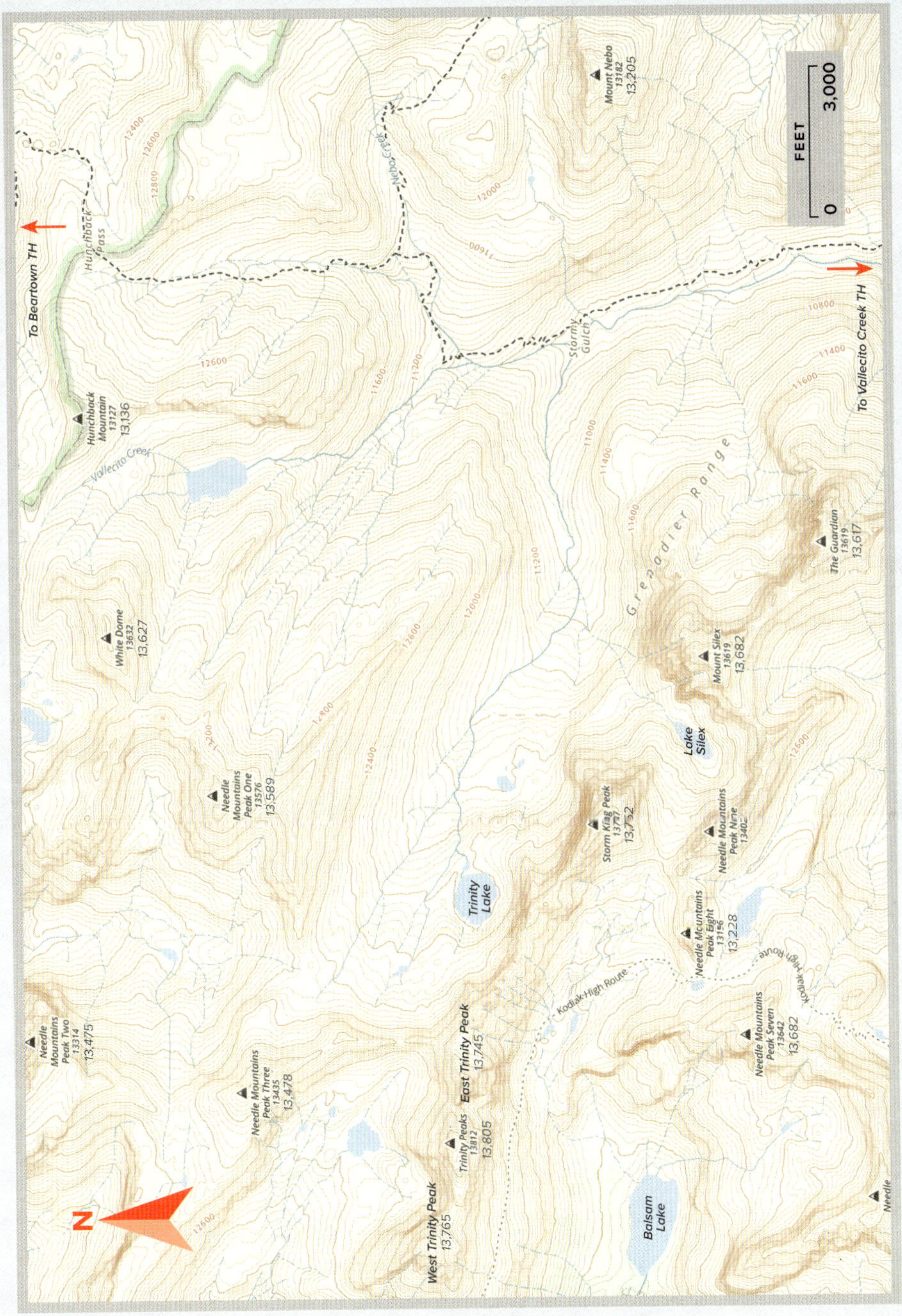

Elk Park Trailhead starts from a gravel road just south of Molas Lake (44 miles north of Durango and 5 miles south of Silverton). From the trailhead, the trail (which at first is a dirt road) takes off south and then traverses east through several large meadows as you begin the descent to the Animas River. Although only a few miles as the crow flies, there are over thirty switchbacks in the trail, which make the total walking distance almost 4 miles. After you cross the bridge over the Animas and the railroad track, the signed Colorado Trail angles off to the left. This is your route. After 0.75 mile, it meets Elk Creek Trail coming up from Elk Park. Follow the Colorado Trail east for 3 miles to some beaver ponds. After passing the ponds, turn right and follow a faint trail that makes a U-turn around the ponds and heads south to cross Elk Creek and leads to the Vestal Creek drainage. Cross Elk Creek by downclimbing into the steep gorge and walking across some logs at the bottom. This unmaintained, unsigned trail climbs left (east) of Vestal Creek before meeting it about a mile up the drainage. It's worthwhile to find the trail because a climb up Vestal Creek without it is miserable. From here, the trail is steep and unrelenting for 1.3 miles. About a mile and a half up Vestal Creek, arrive at marshy meadows below Arrow Peak at 11,400'. A wooded bench on the northern fringe of the meadows offers camping as do woods on the east end of the meadows at the foot of the steep bench. A campsite here is a great starting point for Arrow and Vestal Peaks, or continue on the trail for another 0.25 mile, up a steep bench to some wooded campsites below Vestal at 11,600'.

The approach by Vestal Creek is the best access for Arrow Peak and Vestal Peak and a good means of access for the Trinity Peaks. Graystone Peak, Electric Peak, Point Pun, and Mount Garfield can be reached from Vestal Creek by climbing up into the drainage between Arrow and Electric Peaks. Peaks Two and Three, to the north, can also be climbed from a campsite in Vestal Creek. From Vestal Creek, it's possible to reach the Tenmile Creek drainage and Balsam Lake by the 12,860' pass between Vestal and West Trinity. It's also possible to connect with Trinity Creek and Stormy Gulch by continuing east up Vestal Creek to the 12,980' pass at the head of the drainage. This pass looks very difficult from low in the drainage but is actually not that bad. When coming up from Vestal Creek, it's best to climb the pass from the left.

Vallecito Creek Trail

Vallecito Creek Trail is a very popular trail, providing access for peaks on the eastern end of the Grenadier Range. Vallecito Reservoir is 13 miles north of Bayfield on US Highway 160 and 20 miles east of Durango on Florida Road. Once past the dam, stay west (left) of the lake for 5 miles, where you will come to a well-marked road

Left: Vestal Peak, Pigeon Peak, and Arrow Peak, as seen from above Highland Mary Lakes. **Right:** Vestal Peak and Arrow Peak with the Milky Way above.

junction offering a choice between Vallecito and Pine River Campgrounds. Turn left at the junction and drive another 3 miles to the trailhead at Vallecito Campground.

The trail starts on the west side of Vallecito Creek and crosses to the east on a bridge at 3 miles and then back to the west at about 5 miles. At 6.5 miles, it's necessary to wade the creek at a spot where a third bridge was wiped out in an avalanche. At 9 miles, a marked trail takes off to the left and heads up Johnson Creek to Columbine Pass and Chicago Basin. For the Grenadiers, stay on the main Vallecito Creek Trail, which continues north on the east side of the creek. After a total of 15.5 miles, reach Stormy Gulch and Trinity Creek. Trinity Creek drains the north sides of Storm King Peak, Mount Silex, the Guardian, and Peak Nine. From Vallecito Creek, it's 3 miles up to the 12,980′ pass at the head of Trinity Creek Basin, which connects with Vestal Creek. After hiking about a mile up Stormy Gulch, it's possible to climb to Lake Silex, which is located in a semicircle formed by Storm King Peak, Peak Nine, and Mount Silex. The total distance from Vallecito Creek to Lake Silex is 1.8 miles. From Lake Silex, it is another steep 0.3 mile to the northwest to a 12,820′ pass between Storm King Peak and Peak Eight that connects you with the upper end of the Tenmile Creek drainage and Balsam Lake.

Although it is a day and a half or two days of hiking, the Vallecito Creek Trail is the best means of access for Mount Silex and the Guardian. It is also good for Storm King Peak, Peak Eight, and Peak Nine. Vallecito Creek Trail can also be used to access White Dome and Peak One. Rather than turning west at Stormy Gulch, continue up Vallecito Creek drainage for another 0.75 mile and then turn left and follow the trail up the Vallecito Creek drainage, which turns off the main trail. The main trail turns right near the junction between Nebo Creek and Vallecito Creek and continues north to Hunchback Pass. Instead of following the main trail, turn left and hike up the steep Vallecito Creek drainage to Vallecito Lake at 12,010′.

Upper Elk Creek Trail

From the beaver ponds 3 miles east of Elk Park, the trail continues up the north side of Elk Creek for a total of 7.5 miles from the Animas, where it levels out at 12,100′ near an old mining cabin above tree line. Here the trail turns north toward the Continental Divide. For access to the peaks north of the Grenadiers, leave the trail and turn right (southeast) at the old mining cabin, head southeast, and contour east to Eldorado Lake or continue south to the 12,780′ pass between White Dome and Hunchback Mountain. From the pass, you can drop down into Vallecito Lake. The pass also provides a convenient point from which to climb White Dome, Peak One, and Hunchback Mountain.

Cunningham Gulch and the Continental Divide Trail

The combination of these two trails provides an alternate means of access to White Dome and Peak One. Drive 4 miles northeast from Silverton to Howardsville. From Howardsville, turn right and drive 3.6 miles up Cunningham Gulch to the remains of the Highland Mary Mill. Near the mill, the road crosses a stream and should only be driven by 4WD vehicles. After about a third of a mile, the road crosses Cunningham Gulch to the left. Cunningham Gulch Trail takes off to the left near the crossing and climbs for 2 miles from 10,800′ to 12,200′ where it intersects the Continental Divide Trail. Don't follow the road (which turns into a trail) or you will end up at Highland Mary Lakes. From the junction with the Continental Divide Trail, hike 4.6 miles south, above tree line to a point where you can drop west to Eldorado Lake or continue south between Hunchback Mountain and White Dome to Vallecito Lake.

Beartown Trailhead

The rugged two-track road to the Beartown Trailhead requires a high-clearance, 4WD vehicle. If you are able to reach the trailhead, it provides access to Storm King Peak, Mount Silex, the Guardian, Peak Eight, Peak Nine, Peak One, and White Dome. Directions to this trailhead are provided in the Needle Mountains section (p. 170).

Noname Creek

The trail up Noname Creek is described in the Needle Mountains section (p. 174). From Noname Creek, the 12,900′ pass between Peak Five and Peak Six offers access to Tenmile Creek and Balsam Lake.

CLIMBING ROUTES

Mount Garfield

13,074′ RANK 592

Garfield is the westernmost peak in the Grenadiers and overlooks the Animas drainage. It's frequently combined with Point Pun. On a long day with good weather, it's possible to combine Garfield with Electric and Graystone as well.

Southeast Ridge

From Molas Lake TH at 10,620′: 11.3 miles, 5,580′

From Elk Park at 8,860′: 6.8 miles, 5,360′

From Vestal Creek, the best approach for Garfield is to climb into the drainage between Electric and Arrow Peaks. From the 12,460′ saddle between Electric and Graystone Peaks, take a high traverse around the northern face of Graystone over steeply angled, smooth slabs. When dry, the slabs make for a fast traverse. When wet or blocked by snow, the traverse can be difficult. After finishing the traverse and reaching Garfield Lake, climb steeply up to the saddle between Mount Garfield and Point Pun. Garfield's southeast ridge is a long ridge climb with Class 3 scrambling that is not very exposed. Stay directly on the ridge with only very slight deviations.

Point Pun

13,180′ UNRANKED

Point Pun is one of the western, lesser Grenadiers. It's frequently combined with Garfield or Graystone or both from a camp in the Garfield Lake basin.

North Face

From Molas Lake TH at 10,620′: 11.1 miles, 5,680′

From Elk Park at 8,860′: 6.6 miles, 5,460′

The initial approach for Point Pun is the same as for Mount Garfield, except that after finishing smooth slabs on the traverse, turn south and climb a bit to gain a 12,640′ bench on the west flank of Graystone Peak. Point Pun has two summits. The eastern summit is higher, although inexplicably, USGS gives an exact elevation for the western summit but not the eastern summit. The north face of the eastern summit is a Class 3+ scramble over lichen-covered rock. Steep foot- and handholds are plentiful, although a few are a little loose. To combine Mount Garfield with Point Pun, traverse the western summit to the north on a talus-covered ledge system. The western summit of Point Pun is best climbed by its northwest ridge—a Class 4 climb. It's difficult to combine both summits of Point Pun because of the cliffs on the eastern side of the western summit. The ridge connecting Mount Garfield to Point Pun is a cakewalk.

Graystone Peak

13,489′ **RANK 263**

Graystone is on the divide separating the Vestal and Tenmile drainages southwest of Arrow. It is commonly combined with Point Pun and Garfield from a camp in the Garfield Lake basin or with Arrow from a camp in Vestal Creek.

Northeast Ridge

From Molas Lake TH at 10,620′: 10.7 miles, 5,990′

From Elk Park at 8,860′: 6.6 miles, 5,770′

This route starts at the 12,980′ pass between Arrow and Graystone. The pass can be gained from either side but is steeper from the west. From the pass, walk up the ridge to the northwest end of point 13,404′ and then turn right (west) and scramble along the ridge toward Graystone's east face. Head directly up the face on Class 2+ terrain toward the false summit and then traverse right onto the north face before climbing to the true summit.

North Couloir

From Molas Lake TH at 10,620′: 10.5 miles, 5,970′

From Elk Park at 8,860′: 6.4 miles, 5,750′

This couloir runs directly up the north face of Graystone between the two rounded summits. The couloir makes for a steep snow climb requiring an ice ax and crampons.

Left to right: Electric, Graystone, and Garfield, as seen from Molas Lake.

Later in the year, when the couloir becomes discontinuous at several points, it's necessary to climb right (west) to regain the snow. The couloir is usually not worth messing with after early August. From the top of the couloir, the summit is a walk-up.

Electric Peak

13,292′ RANK 407

Electric is a western, lesser Grenadier that combines well with Garfield and Point Pun.

South Face

From Molas Lake TH at 10,620′: 10.4 miles, 5,790′

From Elk Park at 8,860′: 6.3 miles, 5,570′

The route on the south face of Electric starts from the 12,460′ saddle between Electric and Graystone and climbs up to the left-hand (west) couloir. Scramble up the couloir, traverse to the right (east), and then climb directly up the talus field to the rounded summit on Class 3 terrain. Take care while in the couloir to avoid setting off any of the loose rock.

East Face

From Molas Lake TH at 10,620′: 9.6 miles, 5,790′

From Elk Park at 8,860′: 5.5 miles, 5,570′

A fourteen-pitch route of lower fifth-class climbing was reported in the June 1963 *Trail and Timberline*. The east face is a narrow face between the "tree-studded northeast face" and the "sheer southeast face." Begin the climb from the left-hand (south) end of the large grass patch, which is uphill from the base of the northeast face. You will pass a chimney on the lower face to the right. From the chimney, traverse right to a gully system, climbing to a platform overlooking the sheer southeast face. From the platform, climb to the right to a ramp leading up and to the left. Continue up the ramp to the talus field leading to the summit.

Arrow Peak

13,803′ RANK 104

Arrow is one of the best climbs in the San Juans due to the solid Class 4 rock on the standard route and incredible views of neighboring Vestal Peak, with which it is often combined. Arrow is commonly climbed from a camp in Vestal Creek.

Northeast Rib

From Molas Lake TH at 10,620′: 10.2 miles, 5,790′

From Elk Park at 8,860′: 6.1 miles, 5,570′

Left: Arrow Peak at sunrise from the slopes of Vestal's Wham Ridge. **Right:** Climbing Arrow's excellent Class 4 standard route high above Vestal Lake.

Although no walk-up, this is the easiest route on Arrow. The route follows either of two prominent ribs (the larger eastern rib is frequently blocked by a large snowbank early in the season) to within 400′ of the summit. From this point, you can either climb right (west) and reach the summit by skirting the north ridge to the east or climb the final portion of the northeast face directly. Both routes are Class 4. The direct ascent of the upper northeast face is the more difficult variation.

South Face

From Molas Lake TH at 10,620′: 10.8 miles, 5,790′

From Elk Park at 8,860′: 6.7 miles, 5,570′

This is the first-ascent route for Arrow and a much less attractive route than the northeast rib. From the west end of Arrow Lake, go north and a little west to the parallel gullies on the west side of the south face. Take the right-hand (east) gully, which leads to a right-slanting ramp ending in a chimney with a short, slightly overhung move. After climbing the chimney, you find yourself on the knife-blade southeast ridge. The crux move is Class 5.3 or 5.4, and a rope and protection are recommended.

Northwest Face

From Molas Lake TH at 10,620′: 10 miles, 5,790′

From Elk Park at 8,860′: 5.9 miles, 5,570′

The October 1969 *Trail and Timberline* reports a climb of the northwest face via the Arrowhead pinnacle on Arrow's west shoulder. The route starts at the lowest point at the base of the west face and climbs eleven or twelve pitches to the top of the pinnacle. From the pinnacle a "60′ rappel into the notch is followed by 150′ of scrambling to the main summit." The route is rated 5.7.

Vestal Peak

13,864′ **RANK 77**

Vestal, with Jagged and Arrow, is one of the three best peaks in the San Juans, and its unearthly north face—Wham Ridge—is the most iconic climbing route in the range. In good weather, Vestal is frequently combined with Arrow from a camp in Vestal Creek.

Southeast Couloir

From Molas Lake TH at 10,620′: 10.3 miles, 5,830′

From Elk Park at 8,860′: 6.2 miles, 5,570′

The easiest route on Vestal ascends the large couloir on the eastern side of the south face. From the saddle between Arrow and Vestal, the couloir is out of view behind the rock rib that runs directly down the south face from the summit. From the saddle, traverse upward across the lower face to the couloir and climb to the summit on Class 3+ terrain over large boulders and some loose rock. Routefinding on the south side of Vestal is challenging and can be wrought with frustration.

Wham Ridge

From Molas Lake TH at 10,620′: 10.2 miles, 5,830′

From Elk Park at 8,860′: 6 miles, 5,570′

Perhaps the most classic climb in the San Juans, Wham Ridge is not a ridge but rather a huge triangular buttress. Although it appears as smooth as glass from a distance,

Left: Vestal Peak and Arrow Peak at sunset from halfway up West Trinity. **Right:** The rugged downclimb on Vestal Peak. Photo by Bob Rosebrough

the rock is highly fissured. While some parties climb Wham Ridge third-class, a rope and several pieces of protection are recommended, particularly in poor weather. The rock on the lower portion of the route is excellent. Higher up, the rock is broken up and a little loose in spots. There are countless variations you can take, but a route that starts just to the right of the prominent dihedral in the center of the face and then heads slightly to the right (west) works well. Regardless of which variation you take, you can, by judicious routefinding, avoid anything over 5.3 or 5.4 in difficulty.

East Face

From Molas Lake TH at 10,620′: 10.2 miles, 5,830′

From Elk Park at 8,860′: 6 miles, 5,570′

This route starts at the base of a dihedral in orange rock just left of the low point of the face. The first two lead pitches are the most difficult. The first is sustained 5.8 up the dihedral to a small ledge on the right wall above the prominent overhang. The second lead involves aid for a short distance and then several difficult moves to the large, left-slanting ledge that dissects the entire face. From the top of this 200′-long ledge, climb right on a second steep ledge to a sharp corner. One and a half easy pitches lead to the east summit, which is only a scramble away from the true summit. The direct route is rated 5.8, A-1. There are also several variations on the east face that are much easier than this direct line.

Left: Vestal Peak's Wham Ridge at the first pitch. **Right:** Looking down from halfway up Vestal's Wham Ridge.

West Trinity and Balsam Lake, from Vestal Peak.

West Trinity Peak

13,765′ RANK 120

The Trinities, alongside Arrow and Vestal, complete the core of the Grenadiers. From a camp in Vestal Creek, they combine with each other to offer a classic traverse that, for mere mortals, is enough for one day.

Southwest Ridge

From Molas Lake TH at 10,620′: 11.2 miles, 5,730′

From Elk Park at 8,860′: 7 miles, 5,470′

This is the standard route on West Trinity when approached from Vestal Creek and begins in earnest from the saddle between Vestal and West Trinity. It's also the beginning for a traverse of the Trinities, which is best attempted from west to east. A cairned Class 3 route generally follows the ridge or stays just to the right (south) of the ridge crest.

Traversing the ridge between West Trinity and Middle Trinity during the 1941 Colorado Mountain Club outing. Photo by Werner Schnackenberg

Southeast Face

From Molas Lake TH at 10,620′: 13.1 miles, 5,640′

From Elk Park at 8,860′: 8.9 miles, 5,340′

The upper southeast face is the most direct route on West Trinity when approached from Balsam Lake. A Class 3 scramble to the left (south) of the southeast ridge brings you to the summit.

North Face

From Molas Lake TH at 10,620′: 11 miles, 5,730′

From Elk Park at 8,860′: 6.8 miles, 5,470′

The lower portion of the north face is made up of short, broken cliffs and overhangs that look terrible. With a little patience, you can work your way through the obstacles without too much difficulty. Above the cliffs, you can go virtually anywhere on the face. Most of the climbing is Class 4. A rope and a few pieces of protection are prudent, particularly in threatening weather.

Trinity Peak

13,805′ RANK 103

West Ridge

From Molas Lake TH at 10,620′: 11.6 miles, 6,140′

From Elk Park at 8,860′: 7.4 miles, 5,880′

This route, the most difficult section of a traverse of the Trinities, will test your route-finding abilities and involves challenging climbing. When traversing over from West Trinity, stay as high as possible below the cliffs on the south side of the sharp ridge between the peaks. As you pass the saddle between the two peaks, begin an upward traverse staying as high as possible below the cliffs of the west ridge. Keep an eye out for cairns, which will lead you to a broken-up Class 4 chimney that tops out on ledges and allows you to either scramble over or traverse to the south of the 13,700′ false summit (called "the Fourth Trinity" by some). Once past the false summit, the last section to the true summit is easy.

The Trinities from across the valley high above Vestal Creek.

East Couloir

The east couloir is a Class 3 scramble that is accessed from the saddle between East Trinity and Trinity. Take caution with loose rock—once a rock is set loose, it tends to fall the full length of the couloir. For that reason, helmets and small parties, closely grouped, are preferable on the Trinities. When descending, as part of a traverse, stay left (north) when the couloir branches halfway down.

East Trinity Peak

13,745′ RANK 128

West Couloir

From Molas Lake TH at 10,620′: 12 miles, 5,710′

From Elk Park at 8,860′: 7.8 miles, 5,450′

The west couloir is a broad gully covering the entire west face of the East Trinity. As is the case with almost every Trinity route, the west couloir involves Class 3 scrambling over loose rock. The easiest variation is to stay to the right (south) to gain the final ridge, which takes you to the top. Early in the year, snow will likely force you to the middle of the couloir.

East Trinity at sunrise from an unnamed lake below the Trinities.

Northeast Ridge

From Molas Lake TH at 10,620′: 11.9 miles, 5,710′

From Elk Park at 8,860′: 7.8 miles, 5,450′

This is a good descent route for a west-to-east traverse. When East Trinity is climbed alone, this is the best route from Vestal Creek. The climb starts at the 13,060′ notch on the ridge between Vestal Creek and Trinity Creek. Easy to moderate scrambling (Class 2+ and 3) leads you to the summit.

South Face

A difficult fifth-class route that offers "perfect clean ledges for holds" was reported in the July 1964 *Trail and Timberline*. The first ascent party was "in love with rock," which was "as firm as Peak Eight's had been rotten." The route meets the southeast ridge 400′ below the summit.

Storm King Peak

13,752′ **RANK 125**

Storm King, Silex, and the Guardian comprise the eastern core of the Grenadiers and are generally accessed from the Beartown Trailhead, Tenmile Creek, or Elk Park via Vestal Creek. In good weather, Storm King can be combined with Silex and the Guardian in a long day from a camp in the Trinity Creek drainage or a camp located near tarns northeast of Balsam Lake at 12,200′.

Silex, Storm King, Peak Eight, and Peak Seven, from Peak Three.

Southwest Ridge

From Molas Lake TH at 10,620′ via Vestal Creek: 15.5 miles, 7,110′

From Elk Park at 8,860′ via Vestal Creek: 11.3 miles, 6,910′

From Molas Lake TH at 10,620′ via Tenmile Creek: 14.5 miles, 6,010′

From Elk Park at 8,860′ via Tenmile Creek: 11.3 miles, 5,250′

From Beartown TH at 11,700′ via Trinity Creek: 6.9 miles, 3,930′

This is the standard route for Storm King. From the 12,820′ pass that connects Tenmile Creek to the Lake Silex drainage, scramble directly up the southwest ridge over large boulders and loose rock on Class 3+ terrain.

North Face

From Molas Lake TH at 10,620′ via Vestal Creek: 14.5 miles, 7,110′

From Elk Park at 8,860′ via Vestal Creek: 10.3 miles, 6,910′

From Molas Lake TH at 10,620′ via Tenmile Creek: 15.5 miles, 6,010′

From Elk Park at 8,860′ via Tenmile Creek: 12.3 miles, 5,250′

From Beartown TH at 11,700′ via Trinity Creek: 5.9 miles, 3,930′

Storm King's north face is a dark, intimidating 1,500′ wall. Given its appearance, Bob Bliss was surprised to find what he describes as a "gentle flower-strewn-path-of-a-climb." His route starts below a central black streak of rocks and climbs 40′ to a ramp. From the ramp, climb right (west) up third- and fourth-class ledges and short chimneys and then 70′ up broken, wet rock to a formation that Bliss describes as a "bowl of tears." From here, climb up a steep, left-facing slab or dihedral and then four pitches up a chimney crack behind a great plate. Traverse 60′ right (west) below the smooth slabs and then up 90′ via a crack in a left-facing dihedral with a small wet overhang at the top (5.7). Three long pitches of third- and fourth-class climbing lead to snow and then up left (east) to a "pass" climbing on mud. From there, a pitch of poorly protected shattered quartzite and two more easy pitches up broken blocks lead to the summit ridge. There are a total of fifteen pitches.

Mount Silex

13,628′ **RANK 181**

Silex and the Guardian are often climbed together if weather permits. They are frequently photographed together hovering over the Vallecito drainage.

South Face

From Molas Lake TH at 10,620′ via Vestal Creek: 15.5 miles, 6,990′

From Elk Park at 8,860′ via Vestal Creek: 11.3 miles, 6,790′

From Molas Lake TH at 10,620′ via Tenmile Creek: 14.5 miles, 5,890′

Guardian, Silex, and Storm King, from the hike down the Vallecito Trail from Beartown.

From Elk Park at 8,860′ via Tenmile Creek: 11.3 miles, 5,130′

From Beartown TH at 11,700′ via Trinity Creek: 6.9 miles, 3,810′

The starting point for this climb—the easiest route on Silex—is the 12,820′ pass between Mount Silex and point 13,176′ just south of Lake Silex. When approached from Tenmile Creek, it's possible either to make a rugged traverse toward the saddle several hundred vertical feet above Lake Silex to the south or to stop struggling with the traverse and drop down almost to the lake. On the climb to the pass, avoid some of the scree and talus by kicking steps up the snowbank, early in the climbing season, and scrambling on the rock above. To gain the south face from the pass, it's necessary to lose some elevation before you can traverse through the cliff band on the lower portion of the face. After clearing the cliffs, the south face is a Class 2 talus climb. If you are interested in climbing the Guardian on the same day, it's best to downclimb this route before starting the rugged traverse east.

Southwest Ridge

From Molas Lake TH at 10,620′ via Vestal Creek: 15.4 miles, 6,990′

From Elk Park at 8,860′ via Vestal Creek: 11.2 miles, 6,790′

From Molas Lake TH at 10,620′ via Tenmile Creek: 14.4 miles, 5,890′

From Elk Park at 8,860′ via Tenmile Creek: 11.2 miles, 5,130′

From Beartown TH at 11,700′ via Trinity Creek: 6.8 miles, 3,810′

From the 12,820′ pass, the southwest ridge leads directly to the summit. The lower portion of the ridge consists of rugged Class 4 climbing over steep rock with good holds. There is also a rough section about halfway up that can be easily avoided by making a detour onto the south face.

Southeast Ridge

From Molas Lake TH at 10,620′ via Vestal Creek: 15.6 miles, 6,990′

From Elk Park at 8,860′ via Vestal Creek: 11.4 miles, 6,790′

From Molas Lake TH at 10,620′ via Tenmile Creek: 14.6 miles, 5,890′

From Elk Park at 8,860′ via Tenmile Creek: 11.4 miles, 5,130′

From Beartown TH at 11,700′ via Trinity Creek: 7 miles, 3,810′

The lower two-thirds of the southeast ridge are cliffs that force you into some fourth-class climbing just to the south. For the last few hundred yards, you can gain and keep the ridge to the summit.

The Guardian

13,617′ **RANK 185**

The Guardian, which presides over the upper reaches of the Vallecito drainage, is well named. Climbers usually approach it from a camp in the Trinity Creek drainage or from a campsite northeast of Balsam Lake at 12,200′.

Southwest Couloir–Northwest Ridge

From Molas Lake TH at 10,620′ via Vestal Creek: 16.3 miles, 7,640′

From Elk Park at 8,860′ via Vestal Creek: 12.1 miles, 7,440′

From Molas Lake TH at 10,620′ via Tenmile Creek: 15.3 miles, 5,540′

From Elk Park at 8,860′ via Tenmile Creek: 12.1 miles, 5,780′

From Beartown TH at 11,700′ via Trinity Creek: 7.7 miles, 4,460′

Assuming you have first climbed Silex, descend 400′ south from Silex to get below the cliffs and aim for the saddle between the Guardian and point 13,220′, then make an ascending traverse, and look for cairns below the cliffs of the Guardian's northwest ridge. At 13,350′, you will spot a talus-filled couloir running straight up to the northwest ridge. Follow the couloir to the ridge. At the top of the couloir, make a Class 3 scramble through some broken rock to reach the easier ridge above and walk to the summit. The summit affords an excellent view of the Vallecito Creek drainage.

Peak Seven

13,682′ **RANK 158**

Peak Seven is south of East Trinity Peak and east of Balsam Lake. It can be climbed from a camp at Balsam Lake or from a camp farther up (east) the Tenmile Creek drainage. It is sometimes combined with Storm King to the northeast or Peak Six to the southwest.

North Ridge

From Elk Park at 8,860′ via Vestal Creek: 11.3 miles, 6,810′

From Molas Lake TH at 10,620′ via Tenmile Creek: 14.5 miles, 5,910′

From Elk Park at 8,860′ via Tenmile Creek: 11.3 miles, 5,150′

From Beartown TH at 11,700′ via Trinity Creek: 7.9 miles, 4,330′

The north ridge is best approached by hiking up the Tenmile Creek drainage above Balsam Lake. Climb to the small lake between Peaks Eight and Seven. From there, climb up the talus field due west of the lake to gain the north ridge of Peak Seven at a high 13,020′ saddle. From the saddle, stay on the Class 3 ridge, which is somewhat exposed and loose, until you reach a gap in the ridge at 13,400′ that requires a tricky Class 3+ downclimb to the right (west). Once over the gap, it's an easy scramble to the top.

OFF THE BEATEN PATH

Peak Three

13,478′ RANK 268

0.8 mile north-northeast of Trinity Peak

From Elk Park at 8,860′ via Vestal Creek: 7.4 miles, 5,440′

Northwest Face: From Vestal Creek drainage, bushwhack up a steep slope to a ridge opposite of Vestal Lake to 12,800′. The northwest face of Peak Three is a Class 2 talus field.

East Face: From Trinity Creek drainage, hike up to the base of the east face, climb the talus field to a false summit, and then walk the ridge to the true summit on Class 2+ terrain.

Peak Two

13,475′ RANK 270

2 miles northeast of Vestal Peak

From Elk Park at 8,860′ via Vestal Creek and Peak Three: 6.5 miles, 4,950′

Southwest Ridge: From the 12,940′ saddle between Peaks Two and Three, the southwest ridge is a rarity in the Grenadiers: a Class 2 walk-up.

Peak One

13,589′ RANK 194

1.5 miles north of Storm King Peak

From Beartown TH at 11,700′: 3.2 miles, 2,230′

Northeast Ridge: From the 13,180′ saddle between White Dome and Peak One, climb the Class 2+ northeast ridge.

Peak Three and East Trinity, as seen from halfway over to Peak Two.

White Dome

13,627′ RANK 182

0.75 mile northeast of Peak One

From Beartown TH at 11,700′: 3 miles, 2,270′

Southwest Ridge: From the Peak One–White Dome saddle, the southwest ridge is a Class 3 or 2+ scramble.

Peak Eight

13,228′ SOFT RANKED

0.5 mile southwest of Storm King Peak

From Elk Park at 8,860′ via Tenmile Creek: 11.3 miles, 4,920′

West Ridge: A six-pitch, Class 5 route over loose rock on the west ridge was reported in the July 1964 *Trail and Timberline*.

North Face—East Ridge: Via the north face, gain the notch east of the summit and follow the narrow, exposed Class 4 east ridge to the summit on loose, lichen-covered rock.

Peak Nine

13,402′ RANK 317

0.5 mile south of Storm King Peak

From Elk Park at 8,860′ via Tenmile Creek: 11.3 miles, 5,090′

South Face and Southeast Ridge: On Class 3 and 4 terrain, make an ascending traverse of the south face to reach the southeast ridge, reverse your direction, and climb northwest up the southeast ridge on narrow, exposed ground.

RIO GRANDE PYRAMID–MOUNT OSO GROUP

11

Oso group from the summit of Nebo. Photo by Mason Cummings

The mountains between Vallecito Creek and the Pine River north of Vallecito Reservoir are popular with hikers, backpackers, and fishermen. There are several peaks of interest to climbers and a slew of ranked 13ers. Peaks in this group are frequently approached by backpack from the north, via trails from Thirty Mile Campground or Hunchback Trailhead. When approached from the south by either the Pine Trail or Vallecito Creek Trail, a two-day backpack is generally required to get into the heart of the area around Moon, Rock, and Flint Lakes.

Rio Grande Pyramid (RGP), on the Continental Divide, is the highest peak in the area, with four more ranked 13ers nearby. The highest peak in the main cluster of peaks is Mount Oso, which is centrally located among a group of high mountain lakes, including Emerald Lake, the second largest natural lake in Colorado. Irving

Peak, located in the southwest area of the group near Mount Oso, is a rugged pyramid that has caught the attention of many climbers due to its prominent position at the head of Vallecito Creek. There are eight ranked 13ers near Mount Oso and Irving. Finally, Mount Nebo and Ute Ridge lie in the northwest section of the group, each with ranked 13ers in their shadow: three near Nebo and two near Ute Ridge.

CLIMBING HISTORY

The first recorded ascent of a peak in the area was the Wheeler Survey's climb of the Rio Grande Pyramid in 1874, with the Hayden Survey team arriving in the area shortly after. Both teams were impressed by the beauty of Rio Grande Pyramid, with Franklin Rhoda reporting that "its pyramidal form is almost perfect." Upon reaching the summit, the Hayden team found a "nicely built monument of stones" and speculated that "its builder was something other than a common miner." They were right. In fact, the monument they found was a cairn left by the Wheeler Survey. After climbing Rio Grande Pyramid, the Hayden team turned its attention to Mount Oso, which they reportedly found to be steep and difficult to climb. Just below the summit, the party was startled by a grizzly bear that jumped up a few yards in front of them. The encounter prompted the Hayden team to name the peak "Mount Oso," which is the Spanish word for bear.

ACCESS AND HIKING

Vallecito Creek—Rock Creek

Vallecito Creek Trail is one of the most popular and well-traveled trails in the San Juans. Vallecito Reservoir is located 13 miles north of Bayfield (on US Highway 160) or 20 miles east of Durango on Florida Road. Once at the dam, stay west (left) of the dam for 5 miles until you come to a well-marked road junction that offers a choice between Vallecito Campground and Pine River Campground. Turn left at the junction and drive 3 miles to Vallecito Campground and the Vallecito Creek Trailhead. The first mile of the trail climbs steeply and affords fine views of the spectacular Vallecito Creek gorge. The trail, which starts on the west side of Vallecito Creek, crosses to the east on a bridge at 3 miles and then back to the west at slightly over 3 miles. At the time of this writing, the second bridge is still washed out; however, you can continue north on a faint trail on the west side of the river to the next bridge, where ample campsites are available. At mile 14, Rock Creek Trail takes off to the east. From the junction of the Vallecito Creek and Rock Creek Trails, it is 4 miles up to Rock Lake and 5.5 miles to Flint Lakes. Flint Lakes is a more popular camping area since

RIO GRANDE PYRAMID–MOUNT OSO (WEST)

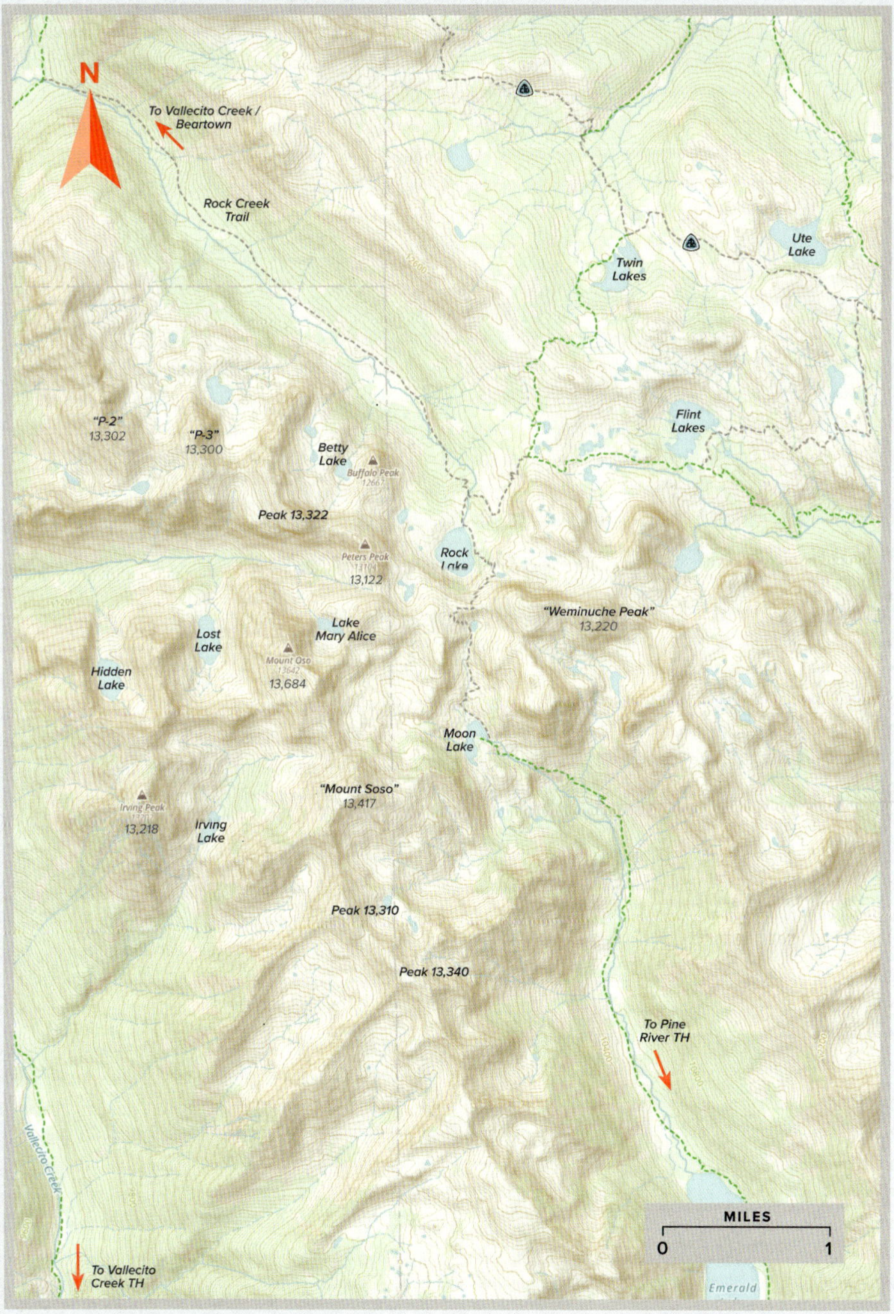

RIO GRANDE PYRAMID–MOUNT OSO (EAST)

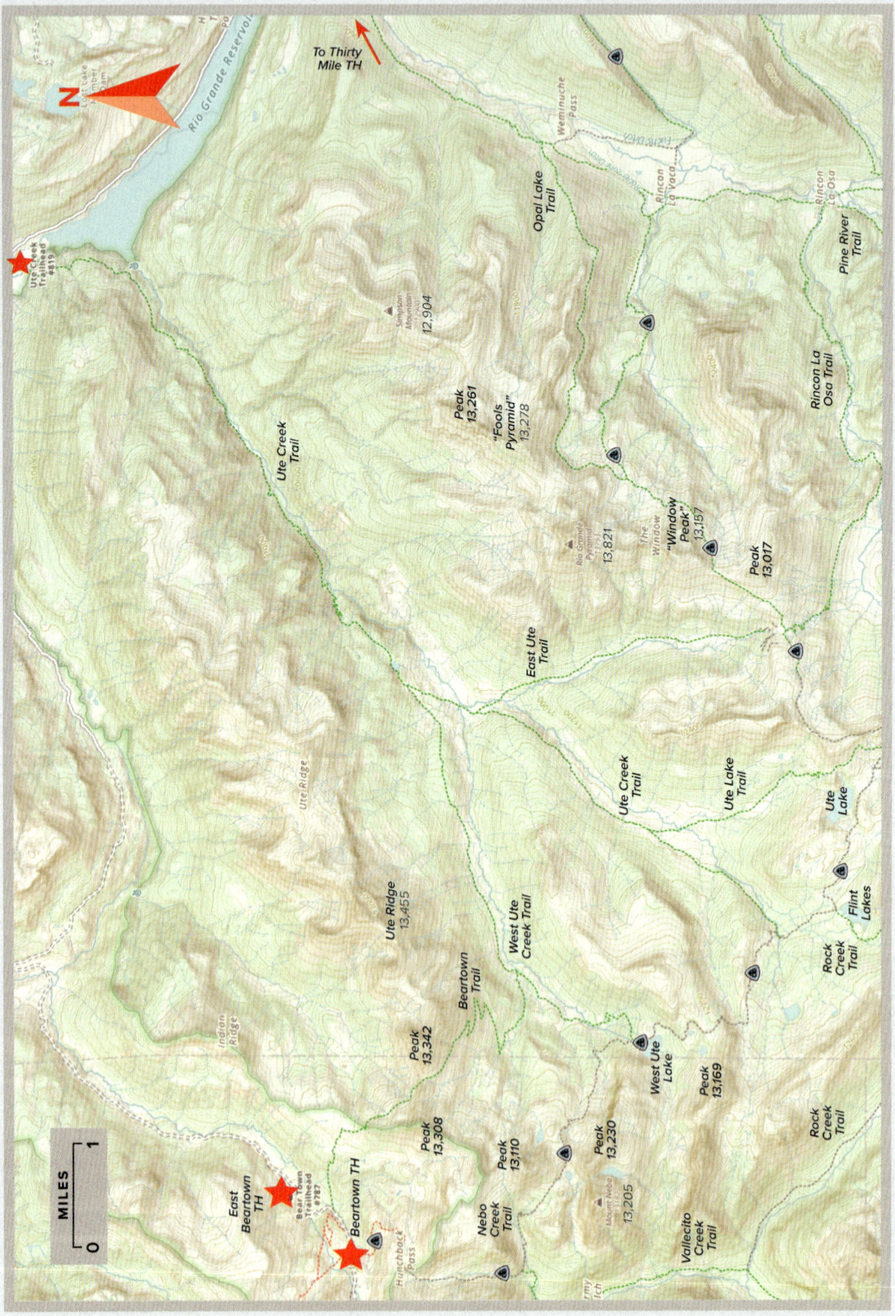

Oso (left middle), Organ (lower middle), and Irving (right middle), from Amherst.

Rock Lake is above tree line. There are also good campsites in the Rock Creek drainage before reaching tree line.

A good way to break up this two-day hike is to camp about 9 miles up Vallecito Creek Trail in the area where Johnson Creek Trail heads west. From this area, it is also possible to climb Irving Peak, which lies just to the east, 4,000 vertical feet above. Mount Oso can also be climbed from Vallecito Creek in a long day. Rock Creek is the best camping area if you are interested in climbing Mount Oso. A campsite at Flint Lakes provides a good base of operation for several day hikes of the unnamed peaks to the south or Ute Benchmark to the north. In addition, Rio Grande Pyramid can be climbed from a camp at Flint Lakes in a very long day.

Beartown Trailhead

This trailhead is a rugged access point for virtually every peak in this group from the north via Hunchback Pass to Nebo Creek or Rock Creek. Directions to the trailhead are provided in the Needle Mountains section (p. 170).

Pine River, Lake Creek, Flint Creek Trail

To reach the trailhead for Pine River Trail, proceed to the road junction north of Vallecito Reservoir, described above. From the junction, stay right and travel just over 7 miles to the trailhead. The first 6 miles of the trail are relatively flat. After

Mount Oso and Peters Peak, from above Flint Lakes. Photo by Mason Cummings

6 miles, you reach the trail that goes up Lake Creek, which turns to the left (northwest) and climbs 1,600 vertical feet in 4 miles to Little Emerald Lake and Emerald Lake. Once at the lakes, the trail stays on the right side of Emerald Lake and continues to Moon Lake at 11,620′. The total distance from Pine River Trail to Moon Lake is a little over 9 miles. From Moon Lake, a rugged trail climbs to the 12,420′ pass connecting the Rock Creek and Lake Creek drainage.

The best way to reach Flint Lakes is to stay on Pine River Trail rather than turning off on Emerald Lake Trail. The turnoff to Flint Creek Trail is located at mile 12 on Pine River Trail. From there, 7 miles and a 2,400′ elevation gain bring you to Flint Lakes.

Thirty Mile Campground (Rio Grande Reservoir)

The trail from Thirty Mile Campground provides the most direct access for a climb of Rio Grande Pyramid. The turnoff to Thirty Mile Campground is on Colorado Highway 149, 24 miles south of Lake City or 19 miles west of Creede. From the turnoff, Thirty Mile Campground is 11 miles southwest, just below Rio Grande Reservoir. From the campground, the trail heads west for 1.5 miles along Rio Grande Reservoir and then turns southwest and follows Weminuche Creek to the top of Weminuche Pass 4.7 miles from the trailhead and 3.2 miles from the footbridge that crosses Weminuche Pass. Weminuche Pass connects the Rio Grande drainage with the Pine River drainage to the south. From the pass, you can turn left (west) and head directly toward Rio Grande Pyramid on the Opal Lake Trail or continue another 1.2 miles south before heading left (west) on the Rincon de la Vaca Trail. A little over

2 miles up the Rincon de la Vaca Trail takes you to tree line and a good position to climb the eastern flank of Rio Grande Pyramid.

Ute Creek Trailhead

This trailhead offers access to Rio Grande Pyramid's western side as well as Mount Nebo, Flint Lakes, Rock Lake, Ute Lake, and virtually all the peaks in this area from a northern approach, which avoids the challenging 4WD approach from Beartown. From the turnoff for Thirty Mile Campground on Colorado Highway 149, continue west for 5.9 miles to a turnoff on your left for Ute Creek Trailhead.

CLIMBING ROUTES

Rio Grande Pyramid

13,821′ RANK 97

Rio Grande Pyramid is easy to spot from a distance. It's a monarch that towers above its surroundings and features a distinctive square gap known as "the Window" in the ridge that extends south of the pyramid. A climb of Rio Grande Pyramid usually involves a backpack or marathon hike from Thirty Mile Campground. It's also possible to approach it as part of a multiday backpack from the Pine River, Vallecito Creek, or Ute Creek Trails.

East Slopes

From Rio Grande Reservoir TH at 9,340′: 9.6 miles, 4,480′

Start from Rio Grande Reservoir Trailhead and follow "Weminuche Trail" for 5 miles to a marked sign for the "Skyline Trail" (now officially called Opal Lake Trail and marked as such on the Weminuche Wilderness Trails Illustrated map #140). Follow

Left: Rio Grand Pyramid and the Window, as seen from high above Highland Mary Lakes to the west. **Right:** Rio Grande Pyramid and the Window, as seen from the standard east slopes approach.

The Wheeler Survey team. A division of the Wheeler Survey made the first recorded ascent of Rio Grande Pyramid in 1874. Photo courtesy of USGS

this trail for approximately 3.5 miles to an unmarked trail junction at 12,200′. Follow this spur trail up to the 12,600′ saddle of Rio Grande Pyramid and Peak 13,278′. From here, the ascent is straightforward on Class 2 scree on a climbers' trail. The summit ridge is steep and broken but consists of generally stable volcanic rock.

Southwest Couloir/West Slopes

From Ute Creek TH at 9,460′: 12.6 miles, 4,820′

From Pine River TH at 8,250′: 27.2 miles, 9,940′

From Beartown TH at 11,700′ via Beartown Trail, West Ute Trail, and East Ute Trail: 12.5 miles, 5,210′

There are two routes on the western side of Rio Grande Pyramid worth exploring. Neither are for the faint of heart. One uses the southwest couloir and is the most direct route when approaching Rio Grande Pyramid from the Ute Creek Trailhead or from the south via Flint Lakes or Ute Lake. The couloir is filled with talus and scree that will tempt you to exit the couloir to the right and try one of the Class 3 scrambles on the south buttress. The other is a direct approach straight up the west slope from East Ute Creek on loose, unstable Class 3 talus.

Mount Oso

13,684′ RANK 157

Mount Oso can be climbed with Irving Peak in a long day from a camp in the Vallecito Creek drainage or from a high camp near either Rock Lake or Moon Lake. A high camp opens the option to climb one of the many 13ers within Oso's orbit.

Left: Mount Oso from Peak 13,417' (to the south). **Right:** Looking down at Moon Lake. Photos by Mason Cummings

Southwest Ridge

From Vallecito Creek TH at 7,900′ via Irving Peak: 20.5 miles, 7,280′

From the saddle north of Irving, drop into the drainage north of Irving Lake and then climb to the saddle between Peak 12,884′ and Mount Oso. The Class 3 southwest ridge looks difficult but is entirely negotiable. The most difficult portion of the climb is near the summit where it's necessary to climb over large, unstable rocks. The best descent route to a camp in Vallecito Creek follows the southeast ridge down to the Irving Creek drainage, which lands you back in the floor of the Vallecito drainage. On your way down in the lower portion of the Irving creek drainage, it's best to stay on the north side of the creek.

Southeast Ridge

From Beartown TH at 11,700′ via Rock Creek Trail: 12.2 miles, 4,920′

From Pine River TH at 8,250′ via Emerald Lake Trail: 17.4 miles, 7,440′

From Ute Creek TH at 9,460′ via Rock Creek Trail: 27.1 miles, 8,820′

From Vallecito Creek TH at 7,900′ via Rock Creek Trail: 20.5 miles, 7,280′

Mount Oso can be approached from Rock Lake or Moon Lake. The initial objective is to reach the basin east of the false summit southeast of Oso's true summit. From the basin, a route starts at the bottom of the main couloir coming down from the left (south) side of the false summit. After climbing 200′ northwest up a gentle scree slope, a series of grass ledges appear on the left side of the slope. Follow the grass as it bends left up a gully to the ridge. Once you gain the ridge at 13,000′, it's an easy scramble over or around the false summit to the top.

Irving Peak

13,218′ RANK 468

Western Face—North Ridge

From Vallecito Creek TH at 7,900′: 10.2 miles, 5,860′

From Beartown TH at 11,700′: 13.9 miles, 5,550′

From a campsite 0.25 mile south of Johnson Creek on Vallecito Creek Trail, aim for the talus slope that leads up to a saddle on the ridge north of Irving. From the saddle, there is easy access along the Class 2+ ridge to Irving's summit. From the campsite, you'll gain just over 4,000 vertical feet to reach the summit.

Eastern Basin—North Ridge

From Pine River TH at 8,250′ via Emerald Lake Trail: 18.1 miles, 8,280′

From Beartown TH at 11,700′ via Rock Creek Trail: 14.8 miles, 6,570′

From a campsite at Moon Lake, head west, climbing to the pass between Mount Oso and Peak 13,417′ ("Mount Soso") and then descend into the basin above Irving Lake as you aim for the col between Irving and point 13,006′ to the north. The Class 3 crux is the final move below the col. Once you are on the Class 2+ ridge, follow it south to the summit.

Mount Nebo

13,205′ RANK 483

Location, location, location. From the summit of Nebo, enjoy views of the Vallecito drainage, the Rock Creek drainage, the Grenadiers, and the Needles. It doesn't get much better than that. The closest trailhead to Nebo is Beartown Trailhead, which is 5 miles north and provides an approach to Nebo and several nearby 13ers.

Southeast Ridge

From Beartown TH at 11,700′ via Nebo Creek Trail: 5.1 miles, 2,670′

Coming from Beartown and over Hunchback Pass, hike 2.7 miles south to the marked Nebo Creek Trail (which is also the Continental Divide Trail) on the left. This trail ascends east to a 12,500′ saddle just 0.5 mile northeast of Mount Nebo, where your adventure begins. Nebo is frequently climbed with Peak 13,110′, Peak 13,230′, and sometimes Peak 13,169′. We recommend that you plan the sequence of climbs of Nebo's satellite peaks to put yourself in position to climb Nebo's Class 2 southeast ridge. Grassy slopes on this wide ridge give way to small rock flakes that make footing loose as you climb higher—a tiny price to pay for the view that is unfolding around you.

Ute Ridge

13,455′ RANK 285

Ute Ridge can be climbed as a day hike by itself or as part of a loop with two ranked 13ers: Peak 13,308′ and Peak 13,342′. When all three peaks are climbed together, they are best approached in this order: 13,306′, 13,342′, and Ute Ridge.

Southwest Ridge

From East Beartown TH at 11,420′: 4.2 miles, 3,540′ (loop including Peak 13,308′, Peak 13,342′, and Ute Ridge)

From East Beartown Trailhead (*not* Hunchback Pass and the nearby Continental Divide Trail), hike east toward Indian Ridge gaining elevation. After 1.25 miles, you can bypass Peaks 13,308′ and 13,342′ by leaving Beartown Trail and continuing east cross-country toward Ute Ridge or stay on the trail, which heads southeast and climbs to gain the 12,792′ saddle between Peaks 13,308′ and 13,342′. Either way, you want to end up at the base of the southwest ridge of Ute Ridge. Once on the southwest ridge, follow game trails, find a break in the cliff band that encircles the summit, and wind your way through large blocks to reach the top on Class 2 terrain.

OFF THE BEATEN PATH

Peak 13,417′—"Mount Soso"

RANK 308

0.9 mile southeast of Mount Oso

From Beartown TH at 11,700′: 34 miles, 10,075′

From Moon Lake at 11,600′ with Irving Peak: 5.1 miles, 3,775′

West Flank and Southwest Ridge: A stiff Class 2 climb that can be combined with Mount Oso and Irving Peak in a long day.

Peak 13,340′

RANK 362

2 miles south-southeast of Mount Oso

From Beartown TH at 11,700′: 28.2 miles, 8,020′

From Moon Lake at 11,600′: 4.5 miles round-trip, 1,720′

Northwest Ridge: A Class 2 stroll over tundra, rubble, and talus.

Peak 13,310′

RANK 386

1.54 miles south-southeast of Mount Oso

From Beartown TH at 11,700′: 27.55 miles round-trip, 8,350′

From Moon Lake at 11,600′ with Peak 13,340′: 3.75 miles round-trip, 2,050′

Southwest Ridge: A pleasant Class 2 stroll on tundra.

Peak 13,302′—"P-2"

RANK 390

1.75 miles northwest of Mount Oso

From Beartown TH at 11,700′: 19.2 miles round-trip, 7,475′

From Vallecito Creek Trail near Sunlight Creek Crossing: 3.5 miles round-trip: 3,675′

West Couloir to North Ridge: A stiff Class 3 climb with short sections of exposure.

Peak 13,300′—"P-3"

RANK 397

1.4 miles north-northwest of Mount Oso

From Beartown TH at 11,700′: 26.8 miles round-trip, 8,075′

From Rock Lake at 11,841′: 7 miles round-trip, 3,275′

South Ridge: A challenging Class 4 climb over steep loose boulders and a knife-edge ridge.

Peak 13,222′

RANK 459

0.8 mile north of Mount Oso

From Beartown TH at 11,700′: 27.05 miles round-trip, 6,750′

From Rock Lake at 11,841′ with Peters Peak: 7.25 miles round-trip, 1,950′

East Ridge: The east ridge is a steep, rocky Class 2+ climb with interspersed talus.

Left: Buffalo Peak and Weminuche Peak, from Rock Creek. **Right:** Peters Peak.
Photos by Mason Cummings

Weminuche Peak

13,220′ RANK 461

1.88 miles east of Mount Oso

From Beartown TH at 11,700′: 23 miles round-trip, 6,300′

From Rock Lake at 11,841′: 4 miles round-trip, 1,600′

West Ridge: A Class 2 ridge on broken, endless quartzite rock leads to the summit.

Peters Peak

13,122′ RANK 550

0.8 mile northeast of Mount Oso

From Beartown TH at 11,700′: 22.3 miles round-trip, 6,300′

From Rock Lake at 11,841′: 1.25 miles round-trip, 1,500′

North Slope: A Class 2 route; the easiest climb among the peaks in the Rock Lake vicinity.

Peak 13,157′—"Window Peak"

RANK 517

0.95 mile south of RGP

From Thirty Mile Campground at 9,330′: 21 miles round-trip, 4,125′ with Peak 13,017′

From Weminuche Pass campsite at 10,650′: 10.8 miles round-trip, 2,600′ with Peak 13,017′

East Flank: A pleasant Class 1 tundra stroll that combines well with Peak 13,017′.

Peak 13,017′

RANK 678

1.92 miles south of RGP

From Thirty Mile Campground at 9,330′: 23.35 miles round-trip, 4,925′ with Peak 13,278′

From Weminuche Pass campsite at 10,650′: 13.15 miles round-trip, 3,600′ with Peak 13,278′

Southeast Ridge: The final 200′ of this climb is an exposed, complicated Class 4 scramble on teetering blocks.

Peak 13,278′—"Fools Pyramid"

RANK 417

1.1 miles northwest of RGP

From Thirty Mile Campground at 9,330′: 21 miles round-trip with RGP and Peak 13,261′, 5,700′

From Weminuche Pass camp at 10,650′: 10.8 miles round-trip with RGP and Peak 13,261′, 4,395′

Southwest Ridge: The southwest ridge is a straightforward Class 1 climb along the crest of the ridge on tundra and embedded rocks.

Peak 13,261′

RANK 430

1.81 miles northwest of RGP

From Thirty Mile Campground at 9,330′: 21 miles round-trip with RGP and Peak 13,278′, 5,700′

From Weminuche Pass camp at 10,650′: 10.8 miles round-trip with RGP and Peak 13,278′, 4,395′

South-Southwest Ridge: From the shared saddle with Fools Pyramid, contour on the east side of the south-southwest ridge to gain the rocky summit.

Peak 13,110′

RANK 561

0.84 mile north-northwest of Mount Nebo

From Beartown TH at 11,700′: 9.5 miles round-trip, 3,560′

From Nebo Creek campsite: 7 miles round-trip, 1,660′

South Ridge: An easy Class 2 tundra basin leads to the south ridge, which is composed of tundra and interspersed rubble.

Peak 13,230′

RANK 454

0.63 mile west of Mount Nebo

From Beartown TH at 11,700′: 9.7 miles round-trip, 4,335′

From Nebo Creek campsite: 4.2 miles round-trip, 2,435′

Northwest Ridge: Stay on the south side of the ridge on Class 2 rock rubble that increases in size as you near the summit.

Peak 13,169′

RANK 506

1.56 miles southwest of Mount Nebo

From Beartown TH at 11,700′: 16 miles round-trip with Peak 13,110′, Nebo, and Peak 13,230′, 6,735′

From Nebo Creek campsite: 10.5 miles round-trip with Peak 13,110′, Nebo, and Peak 13,230′, 4,835′

Northwest Ridge: Tundra benches lead to a plateau at 12,800′. Above the plateau is Class 2 climbing on medium-sized rocks.

Peak 13,308′

RANK 388

2.09 miles west-southwest of Ute Ridge

From Beartown TH at 11,700′: 5 miles round-trip, 1,900′

East Ridge: From the pass between Peaks 13,308′ and 13,342′, follow the Class 2 east ridge that takes you onto some large rock blocks.

Peak 13,342′

RANK 357

1.42 miles southwest of Ute Ridge

From Beartown TH at 11,700′: 4.1 miles round-trip, 2,540′

West Ridge: From the saddle with Peak 13,308′, follow the west ridge over rocky terrain midway on the ridge and large rock blocks near the summit. Easy Class 2.

LAKE CITY WEST GROUP 12

From left to right: Handies, American, Jones, Niagara, and North Crown.

The Lake City West Group comprises the high, rounded summits between Lake City and Silverton. The area is best known for its three 14ers: Redcloud Peak, Sunshine Peak, and Handies Peak, which, together with San Luis Peak, are the easiest 14ers in the San Juans to climb. Redcloud and Sunshine lie just north of the Lake Fork of the Gunnison River and are usually climbed together. Handies Peak is located just east of American Basin. Six other peaks in the area exceed 13,800′. Niagara Peak, Jones Mountain, and American Peak lie south of American Basin and east of Burns Gulch and can be climbed in a day from either approach. Peaks 13,832′ and 13,811′ lie northeast of Redcloud Peak and are usually climbed in tandem from the trail up Silver Creek. Half Peak lies to the south of the other peaks in the group and requires a long hiking approach. Finally, there are interesting high peaks just north of Cinnamon Pass of interest: Wood Mountain, Peak 13,708′, and "Animas Forks Mountain" (Peak 13,722′).

CLIMBING HISTORY

Lake City West was an area of the San Juans in which miners likely preceded surveyors to the top of several summits. The Hayden and Wheeler Surveys sent parties into the area after the Brunot Agreement of September 13, 1873, when the United States Government forcibly took most of the San Juan Mountains, land that had been previously occupied by the Ute Indians. Even though the San Juans officially belonged to the Ute Indians, some miners had been prospecting in the area since the 1860s.

One of the peaks that was almost certainly climbed by miners was Handies. The Hayden Survey team climbed it in 1874, with Franklin Rhoda reporting in *Summits to Climb* that it was a "very easy matter." On the way up, they found shallow prospect holes sunk in a vein at about 13,500′. Just before climbing Handies, Rhoda and A. D. Wilson of the Hayden team climbed Sunshine Peak, surviving a near miss with lightning. Rhoda reported a "tickling sensation along the roots of our hair" at the summit, and a noise that increased until it sounded like that "produced by the frying of bacon." After rapidly concluding their work on the summit, the two "had scarcely got more than 30 feet from the top when it was struck. We had only just missed it, and we felt thankful for our narrow escape."

The first reported ascent of Redcloud Peak was made by J. C. Spiller of the Wheeler Survey. Spiller gave the peak its name, noting in the 1876 survey of the peak's "brilliant red color, which continues nearly to its base."

An editorial note in *Trail and Timberline* (November 1935) gives an interesting insight into the frequency with which peaks in this region were climbed in the early days. In 1921, William F. Ervin, Carl Blaurock, and Dudley T. Smith left a CMC register on the summit of Handies. Fourteen years later in 1935, Kenneth Segerstrom of the USGS climbed Handies and reported that forty-one climbers in fifteen different parties had climbed Handies during the intervening years. It is safe to say that at least that many climbers now climb Handies on an average August weekend.

The rounded summits in this region do not afford climbers many opportunities for technical climbing, with the exception of the rugged 800′ north face of Half Peak, which was climbed in May 1973 by Larry Derby and Jeff Lowe.

ACCESS AND HIKING

Silver Creek Trail

Silver Creek Trail is the best means of access for Sunshine Peak, Redcloud Peak, Peak 13,832′, and Peak 13,822′, with alternate access to "Cooper Creek Peak." To reach the trailhead, turn west off Colorado Highway 149, 2.5 miles south of Lake City on

LAKE CITY WEST (WEST)

LAKE CITY WEST (EAST)

LAKE CITY WEST (SOUTH)

Hinsdale County Road 30, and drive past Lake San Cristobal. Follow the Lake Fork of the Gunnison River on a well-maintained gravel road for a total of 19 miles from Lake City where you reach the trailhead at 10,400′ elevation. From the trailhead, hike 3.5 miles to the 13,020′ pass northeast of Redcloud. From the pass, Redcloud and Sunshine lie to the southwest, and Peaks 13,832′ and 13,811′ lie to the northeast. Roughly 1.7 miles up the trail, you can turn south on the trail up the south fork of Silver Creek, which will lead you to a cairn-marked route on the west side of Redcloud Peak.

Grizzly Gulch

From the same point on the road for Silver Creek Trail, a trail heads in the opposite direction (southwest) up Grizzly Gulch Creek. After 2 miles, you will reach tree line at approximately 12,000′. The summit of Handies is 4 miles from the trailhead.

Cooper Creek Trail

Cooper Creek Trailhead is 0.8 mile northwest of the Silver Creek/Grizzly Gulch Trailhead on the north side of Cinnamon Pass Road and provides access from the southeast to "C.T. Peak", "Gudy Peak," "Every Mountain," and "Cooper Creek Peak."

Alpine Gulch Trail

Alpine Gulch Trail provides access from the north for Peaks 13,180′, 13,811′, and 13,832′; "Cooper Creek Peak"; and "Every Mountain." From downtown Lake City at the junction of Second Street and Gunnison Avenue (CO 149), find a sign for Engineer Pass. From here, leave CO 149 and go two blocks west on Second Avenue to a T-junction at Bluff Street. Turn south (left) onto the gravel road that heads west up Henson Creek. After 2 miles, Alpine Gulch Trailhead is on the left.

Williams Creek Trail

Williams Creek Trail provides access to Peaks 13,832′ and 13,811′ and alternative access to Redcloud and Sunshine. From Lake City, drive 2.2 miles south on CO 149 and turn right on Lake San Cristobal Road. Continue around the west side of the lake for 8.9 miles to the signed trailhead and small parking lot on the north side of the road at 9,160′.

Burns Gulch

Burns Gulch is the best means of access for Jones Mountain, Niagara Peak, and Crown Mountain. In addition, it is possible to climb American Peak (13,806′) from Burns Gulch. Drive east from Silverton past Howardsville and Eureka. The turnoff for Burns Gulch is 11 miles from Silverton on an old mining road on the east side of the Animas River. There is a river crossing here, and the road ascends to the southeast. From the Animas, it is 2.5 miles and 2,500 vertical feet to the 13,220′ saddle between Jones Mountain and Niagara Peak.

Grouse Gulch

The abandoned mining road up Grouse Gulch is 0.2 mile north of the Burns Gulch turnoff. When climbing Jones, Niagara, and American from the Animas River, Grouse Gulch can be used as an alternate ascent or descent route to Burns Gulch. You climb 2,200 vertical feet over 2 miles to reach the 13,020′ saddle that connects you with American Basin.

Cinnamon Pass

Cinnamon Pass is a 12,620′ 4WD pass, 15 miles northeast of Silverton. To reach it, drive past Howardsville and Eureka. After 11 miles, the road crosses to the east side of the Animas. At mile 12.6, arrive at a sharp switchback to the right, which you take toward the pass. Cinnamon Pass (and the road that leads to it) provides excellent access for Cinnamon Mountain, Wood Mountain, Peak 13,708′, Peak 13,688′, "Animas Forks Mountain," Peak 13,427′, Peak 13,540′, "C.T. Peak," and "Gudy Peak." In addition, it provides access to Cooper Creek Trail, Grizzly Gulch, Silver Creek Trail, and American Basin from the Silverton side.

American Basin Trailhead

American Basin is located 3.5 miles southeast of Cinnamon Pass or 18.5 miles from Silverton. It is 24 miles from Lake City and 5 miles past Silver Creek Trailhead. Four-wheel-drive is essential to get up into the upper portion of the basin, where the road ends and the trail begins. The basin provides excellent access for Handies Peak and American Peak, as well as reasonable access to Jones Mountain and Niagara Peak. For those not interested in climbing peaks, the hike to Sloan Lake at 12,900′ is worthwhile.

Cataract Gulch/Cuba Gulch

These are the best points of access for Half Peak, which is one of the most isolated mountains in the San Juans. From Lake City, go 2 miles south on Colorado Highway 149 and turn right (southwest) onto Lake San Cristobal Road. Pass Williams Creek Trailhead after 8.9 miles and reach the junction of the Sherman and Cinnamon Pass roads at mile 14.3. Head left (west) on the Sherman Road (Hinsdale CR 35) and pass the old Sherman townsite. At mile 15.5, reach Cataract Gulch Trailhead at 9,600′. Four-wheel-drive vehicles can continue west on the road an additional 3.4 miles to reach Cuba Gulch Trailhead at 10,700′.

Pole Creek Trail

Pole Creek Trail provides access to Pole Creek Mountain, "Northwest Pole," and Half Peak from the south. Pole Creek Trailhead is located off the same road for Stony Pass (see the Silverton East Group section, p. 140) and Ute Creek Trail (see the Rio Grande Pyramid–Mount Oso Group section, p. 239). If coming from Stony Pass, continue 6.2 miles, and just after you cross the Rio Grande River, the trailhead is on your left (north). From Creede and Ute Creek Trail near Rio Grande Reservoir, continue 9.1 miles west to the same location. This road is difficult 4WD from both directions.

Lost Trail

Lost Trail provides a long-mileage access point from the southeast for many peaks in the "Off the Beaten Path" section, including Carson Peak, Bent Peak, "Coney Benchmark," Peak 13,581', Peak 13,580', and Peak 13,540'. From Ute Creek Trailhead (see the Rio Grande Pyramid–Mount Oso Group section, p. 239) on the northwest end of Rio Grande Reservoir, continue an additional 1.1 miles and turn right (north) to find Lost Trail Trailhead.

Carson Ghost Town Road—Carson Pass

This rugged 4WD road provides an access point for those interested in "ridge running," starting from the far east section of the group at Coney Benchmark along the Continental Divide heading west in order to bag peaks listed in the "Off the Beaten Path" section, including Bent Peak and Carson Peak. It can also be used for a backpacking start for several 13er summits, including Pole Creek Mountain, Northwest Pole, and Half Peak. Follow the road instructions for Silver Creek/Grizzly Gulch trails on Hinsdale CR 30 from Lake City. Reach Williams Creek Trailhead and continue 2.25 miles and turn left (south) onto CR 36 (Carson Ghost Town Road). The road climbs 4.9 miles to the summit of Carson Pass, an excellent starting point with ample parking.

CLIMBING ROUTES

Redcloud Peak

14,034' **RANK 46**

Redcloud Peak and Sunshine Peak, often climbed together, are two of the easiest 14ers in Colorado. Redcloud is 2 miles east of Silver Creek Trailhead and identifiable from afar by the bright red rock that adorns the summit. A fun loop can be done from Silver Creek Trailhead for both Redcloud and Sunshine in either direction.

Redcloud and Sunshine, as seen from near Peak 13,832′.

Northeast Ridge

From Silver Creek TH at 10,420′: 4.6 miles, 3,780′

Combined with Sunshine Peak: 6 miles, 4,300′

From Silver Creek Trailhead, climb northeast for 1.7 miles to a trail junction. If combining Sunshine with Redcloud, take note of this junction, as the route to and from Sunshine begins here. To head up Redcloud first, stay straight (east) on the trail as it wraps around Redcloud's north face and switchbacks up to a 13,020′ saddle between Redcloud and point 13,561′. From this saddle on the northeast shoulder of Redcloud, the northeast ridge is an easy Class 2 climb over loose, small scree. Note: You can also access Peaks 13,832′ and 13,811′ from the 13,020′ saddle.

Sunshine Peak

14,001′ RANK 53

Located 1.3 miles south of Redcloud Peak, Sunshine Peak is one of the friendliest mountains in the San Juans (and one of the most popular).

North Ridge

From Silver Creek TH at 10,420′ via Redcloud Peak: 6 miles, 4,300′

Most people climb Redcloud Peak and Sunshine together, and the preferred route is to climb Redcloud and then traverse south along the ridge to reach the summit of

Sunshine. When climbed as such, Sunshine is a walk-up. Rather than hiking back over Redcloud, it is better to return via the northwest face route as described below back to Silver Creek Trailhead.

Northwest Face

From Silver Creek TH at 10,420′: 4 miles, 3,730′

From Silver Creek Trailhead, climb northeast for 1.7 miles to a cairned trail junction at 11,350′ near the stream on your right. Turn right (south) and cross the stream. Follow a small trail to gain the northwest face on Class 2+ terrain.

East Ridge

From Mill Creek Campground at 9,510′: 3.5 miles, 4,600′

This is a popular winter or spring route for Sunshine when the road is not open all the way up to Silver Creek Trail. From Williams Creek Trailhead, drive 3.9 miles to the Mill Creek Campground. Locate the start of the trail at a green utility box, 150′ up the road and on the north side. The trail ascends the southeast slope of Sunshine on gentle but steep Class 2 terrain.

Peak 13,832′

RANK 90

Peak 13,832′ is 1.3 miles northeast of Redcloud Peak and shares a saddle with its sister, Peak 13,811′, to the northwest. These two peaks are gentle giants and make for excellent easy climbs for beginners. They can be accessed from either Williams Creek Trail or Silver Creek Trail.

Northwest Ridge

From Silver Creek TH at 10,420′: 4.9 miles, 3,600′

Combined with Peak 13,811′: 6.3 miles, 4,270′

This standard route for Peak 13,832′ shares the same route as Redcloud on Class 2 terrain. Follow the northeast ridge route for Redcloud to the 13,020′ saddle northeast of Redcloud. From here, ascend northeast on a broad ridge before traversing the north side of point 13,561′ on steep terrain. After the traverse, gain the northwest ridge where moderate chiprock leads you to the summit. If you want to combine Peak 13,832′ with Peak 13,811′, it is a 1.3-mile gentle walk on grassy slopes from peak to peak. The only disadvantage of this route is that you must reclimb Peak 13,832′ to get back to your car at the Silver Creek Trailhead. Note that the mileage listed above is one-way.

Left: On the downclimb from Peak 13,832', with Handies and Whitecross in the distance. **Right:** Peak 13,811', as seen from Peak 13,832'.

South Slopes

From Williams Creek TH at 9,160′ via Peak 13,811′: 7.1 miles, 5,370′

This route is a great way to combine Peak 13,832′ and Peak 13,811′ when the road is not yet open to Silver Creek Trailhead, although it is longer and involves more elevation gain. This Class 1 route, which winds its way through beautiful alpine terrain, does not see much traffic, and will test your routefinding skills. From the trailhead, hike west for 0.7 mile, crossing the creek twice. You will leave the trail here by hiking west for 1 mile up a drainage to reach a saddle at 10,000′ where you will encounter an old road. Follow the road for 1.9 miles as it climbs to 11,500′ to a ridge. Climb the ridge for 0.5 mile to tree line near point 12,195′, where you can see the remainder of the route before you. Continue on the road for 0.5 mile, leaving the road at 11,800′ and ascending northwest to a ridge at 12,600′. From here, continue up to the summit of Peak 13,811′ and over to Peak 13,832′.

Peak 13,811′

RANK 99

Peak 13,811′ is located 1.2 miles northeast of Peak 13,832′.

Southwest Ridge

From Silver Creek TH at 10,420′ via Peak 13,832′: 6.3 miles, 4,270′

From Williams Creek TH at 9,160′: 6 miles, 4,740′

This route can be done either by first climbing Peak 13,832′ from Silver Creek Trailhead or by coming up from Williams Creek Trailhead per the route guidance for the south slopes route of Peak 13,832′ (above).

Handies Peak

14,048′ RANK 91

Handies Peak is one of the easiest 14ers in Colorado and a fantastic first choice for anyone looking for an introduction to the San Juans. The summit offers stunning views of the entire range—a truly awe-inspiring experience.

South Slopes

From American Basin TH at 11,660′: 2.65 miles, 2,430′

This Class 2 route is the easiest and the standard for Handies. From American Basin Trailhead, follow the well-established trail south to the shores of Sloan Lake at 12,940′ where the trail ascends and switchbacks east and north up the gentle slopes of Handies.

North Ridge

From Grizzly Gulch TH at 11,660′: 3.8 miles, 3,670′

This is the best route on Handies when approached by Grizzly Gulch Trail. From Grizzly Gulch, the Class 2 trail winds up and switches back, finally reaching the low point between Handies Peak and Peak 13,577′ just north of Handies. Avoid the cliffs on the east face of Handies and then follow the ridge directly to the summit.

The epic view looking north from Handies, with the Grenadiers and Needles on display.

Whitecross Mountain

13,542′ **RANK 222**

Whitecross Mountain is 1.4 miles northeast of Handies Peak and usually climbed with Handies, but it can be done by itself by bushwhacking up the return route described below.

Southwest Ridge

From American Basin TH at 11,660′ via Handies Peak: 4.2 miles, 3,020′

From the summit of Handies, traverse north along the long ridge to point 13,577′, which is marked on the USGS topo map. From here, drop down to the northeast to the 12,950′ saddle and begin your ascent up Whitecross on solid Class 2 rock. Once at the summit, enjoy views of Uncompahgre and Wetterhorn to the north. Assuming you began your ascent of Handies from American Basin, you can return by going back to the 12,950′ saddle and then down a steep, grassy drainage to the north that eventually enters the trees. This involves some unenjoyable bushwhacking on steep, wooded terrain but is the most direct route down. You'll eventually find the road that connects with Cinnamon Pass and upper American Basin at approximately 11,000′ from this arduous route.

Whitecross as seen from the traverse from Handies.

Niagara Peak

13,807′ RANK 101

Niagara Peak is a wonderful Class 2 climb that can be accessed from many directions. Located 0.65 mile southwest of Jones Mountain and 2.3 miles southwest of Handies Peak, Niagara is a perfect target for those looking for a peaceful day of solitude at high elevation.

Northwest Ridge

From Grouse Gulch–Burns Gulch TH at 10,770′: 3.2 miles, 3,030′

From Burns Gulch 4WD parking at 11,600′: 1.75 miles, 2,150′

The most direct and easiest route up Niagara, the northwest ridge starts at the 13,220′ saddle between Jones and Niagara, which is best gained from Burns Gulch. Burns Gulch Road is a 4WD road, and at about 11,600′, it becomes treacherous for most vehicles. Follow the 4WD road by foot to 12,200′, where a faint climbers' trail ascends in zigzag fashion southwest toward the saddle between Jones and Niagara. From the saddle, follow a well-established Class 2 trail up steep rock to gain the summit and enjoy enticing views of Crown Mountain and North Crown Mountain to your south.

Crown Mountain

13,569′ UNRANKED

Crown Mountain is an unranked 13er located 0.67 mile south of Niagara Peak and combines well with Niagara.

North Ridge via Niagara Peak

From Grouse Gulch–Burns Gulch TH at 10,770′: 3.9 miles, 3,300′

From Burns Gulch 4WD parking at 11,600′: 2.5 miles, 2,420′

From Niagara, follow a faint trail directly off the south face on Class 2+ terrain consisting of loose rock and dirt. The trail gets easier and gently climbs down to the ridge between Crown and Niagara. From the saddle, follow a faint trail up and stay left (east) to avoid loose boulders on the north face of Crown Mountain. From Crown's summit, it's a quick jaunt over to North Crown Mountain.

North Crown Mountain

13,599′ UNRANKED

North Crown Mountain is slightly higher than Crown Mountain and 0.23 mile directly northwest of it.

Southeast Ridge via Crown Mountain

From Grouse Gulch–Burns Gulch TH at 10,770′: 4.1 miles, 3,340′

From Burns Gulch 4WD parking at 11,600′: 2.7 miles, 2,460′

From Crown Mountain, follow a climbers' trail along the ridge for a quick ridge walk to the summit. Enjoy wonderful views of a high mountain lake just southwest of the summit.

Left: Niagara from the summit of Jones. **Right:** Niagara from the Crown-Niagara saddle.

Crown (middle) and North Crown (right), from Niagara.

Jones Mountain

13,860′ RANK 78

Jones Mountain is located 1.6 miles southwest of Handies Peak and can be equally accessed from American Basin, Grouse Gulch, or Burns Gulch.

Northeast Ridge

From American Basin TH at 11,660′: 2.2 miles, 2,230′

This marvelous Class 2 approach affords fantastic views and begins quite high. From American Basin, hike 1 mile and 900 vertical feet to 12,480′, where you leave the trail and ascend southwest while picking your way up tundra and grass, aiming for the 13,290′ saddle between American Peak to the east and Peak 13,444′ to the northwest. From the saddle, continue southeast and south, aiming for the Jones-American saddle at 13,360′. Once here, continue up a trail to Jones's summit to the southwest. You can combine either American or Niagara from here with a clear weather window for a long day.

South Ridge

From Grouse Gulch–Burns Gulch TH at 10,770′: 3.4 miles, 3,080′

From Burns Gulch 4WD parking at 11,600′: 2 miles, 2,180′

Follow the Northwest Ridge route for Niagara and instead of turning right (west) to ascend Niagara, turn left (northeast) and ascend a solid trail to Jones's summit.

Peak 13,806′—“American Peak”

RANK 102

American Peak is located 1 mile southwest of Handies Peak and 0.8 mile east of Jones Mountain.

West Ridge

From American Basin TH at 11,660′: 2.3 miles, 2,330′

This Class 2 route is the easiest way to approach American Peak. You can reach the west ridge from American Basin, Grouse Gulch, or Burns Gulch, and it makes for a great combination with Jones Mountain. Gain the 13,340′ saddle between Jones and American. From the saddle, follow a trail 0.1 mile north then northeast to approximately 13,400′, where you will continue heading east just below point 13,744′ west of American on some nasty talus. You will be tempted to gain point 13,744′; however, stay on the faint trail to avoid even worse talus. From the 13,580′ saddle between point 13,744′ and American, stay south (right) and continue 0.15 mile to the summit of American for a great view of Handies Peak, Jones Mountain, and Niagara Peak.

On the way to Jones from American Basin with Niagara at back right.

American Peak from American Basin.

Wood Mountain

13,660′ **RANK 169**

Wood Mountain is located just 1 mile north of the summit of Cinnamon Pass.

South Face—West Ridge

From Cinnamon Pass at 12,643′: 1.36 miles, 1,100′

From the top of Cinnamon Pass, contour up the south face on an old mining road to reach the saddle to the left (west) of the peak. From the saddle, follow the easy west ridge to the summit. Wood is an excellent starting peak for a combination of 13ers from Cinnamon Pass that includes Peak 13,427′, Peak 13,540′, C.T. Peak, and Gudy Peak from west to east with a finish at Cooper Creek Trailhead.

Peak 13,708′

SOFT RANKED

Peak 13,708′ is located 0.75 mile west-northwest of Wood Mountain.

Southeast Ridge

From Cinnamon Pass at 12,643′ via Wood Mountain: 2 miles, 1,400′

Peak 13,708′ is a few feet shy of the 300 vertical feet requirement used by many to define a peak. Nevertheless, it combines well with Wood Mountain and "Animas Forks Mountain" and for that reason is described here. From Wood Mountain, it is a simple ridge walk over to the summit.

Peak 13,722′—"Animas Forks Mountain" RANK 136

Animas Forks Mountain is located 1 mile southwest of Wood Mountain on a connecting ridge with Northwest Wood Mountain.

Northeast Ridge

From Cinnamon Pass at 12,643′ via Wood Mountain and Peak 13,708′: 2.4 miles, 1,800′

From the summit of Peak 13,708′, use the ridge between the two peaks to climb Animas Forks Mountain via a Class 2 catwalk that looks impossibly narrow at first but is quite stable.

Southeast Face

From Cinnamon Pass Road at 12,200′: 0.7 mile, 1,520′

From a flat area around 12,200′ on Cinnamon Pass Road, pick your route up the grassy slopes of the southeast face on Class 2 terrain.

Half Peak 13,841′ RANK 86

Half Peak is one of the most recognizable mountains in the San Juans due to its gentle south slopes, which terminate at a precipice on the north face. Located 4 miles southeast of Handies Peak, Half Peak towers alone, disconnected from any other major summit.

South Slopes

From Cataract Gulch TH at 9,600′: 6.3 miles, 4,240′
From Cuba Gulch TH at 10,700′: 5.3 miles, 3,140′

Gain the south slopes of Half Peak either from Cataract Gulch Trailhead or Cuba Gulch Trailhead. Both are Class 2 and about the same, difficulty-wise, but the Cuba Gulch route is shorter (if you have 4WD), and the Cataract Gulch route offers a pleasant backpack to Cataract Lake.

From Cataract Gulch Trailhead, follow the trail for 4.7 miles to Cataract Lake. Continue on the trail for 0.4 mile to reach the Colorado Trail junction at 12,230′ and turn right (west) on the Colorado Trail for 1 mile to 12,480′. Turn right (north) to ascend the gentle south slopes of Half Peak. The slopes narrow at 13,500′ at a choke point 0.2 mile shy of the summit. The terrain here may surprise you, but with careful routefinding on this stable rock, you can keep it at Class 2 with some moderate exposure—a rousing end to an otherwise easy climb.

Left: On the way up Half Peak; the large south ramp makes Half Peak stand out from most directions. **Right:** Half Peak's final approach where it narrows to fun climbing.

The route from Cuba Gulch Trailhead is more complicated but rewarding. To start, cross Cottonwood Creek, which can be challenging in June due to snowmelt but easy in August. After crossing the creek, continue 0.4 mile south and cross Cuba Creek on a bridge. Continue 1.2 miles south, crossing three streams on the way. After crossing the third stream at 11,400′, continue 0.2 mile and turn left (east) onto a prominent unsigned trail that climbs southeast. Continue on this trail to 12,300′. Note that it becomes harder to follow at 11,800′, when it enters willows. From here, enjoy excellent views of Half Peak. Leave the trail and head east (left) for 1 mile following a series of game trails below the north face of point 13,164′. At this point, you will find yourself on the Colorado Trail, which continues east where you can begin your ascent of Half Peak's south slopes per the Cataract Gulch route above.

Pole Creek Mountain

13,716′ RANK 138

Pole Creek Mountain is a lonely giant on the southern flank of the group, located 5.1 miles southeast of Half Peak. Due to its isolated location, it is rarely climbed, but often combined with its more challenging neighbor to the northwest, the aptly named Northwest Pole.

North Slopes

From Pole Creek TH at 10,550′: 4.9 miles, 3,160′

From Cataract Gulch TH at 9,600′ via Northwest Pole: 9.5 miles, 5,520′

From Pole Creek Trailhead, hike 2.5 miles north and leave the trail at 11,220′ to your right (northeast) into the drainage between Pole Creek Mountain and Northwest Pole. Aim for the 12,860′ saddle between Pole Creek Mountain and Northwest Pole and turn right (south) up grassy Class 2 slopes. This same approach can be done from Cataract Gulch Trailhead by ascending the easy Class 2 grassy slopes north-northwest of Pole Creek from Cataract Trail–Colorado Trail junction at 12,220′. In this case, it is likely you'll want to climb Northwest Pole first and continue southeast to the connecting saddle with Pole Creek Mountain.

"Northwest Pole"

13,660′ RANK 167

This challenging peak sits far from other notable peaks except for its large neighbor to the southeast, Pole Creek Mountain, located 1.5 miles away. What makes this mountain a challenge is the Class 3 summit block, which seems quite out of place in this part of the San Juans.

South Slopes

From Pole Creek TH at 10,550′: 4.2 miles, 3,110′

From the trailhead, hike 2.5 miles north and leave the trail at 11,220′ to your right (north) up the south slopes of Northwest Pole. After 4 miles of climbing on grassy slopes, reach the summit block, composed of solid rock and talus. Circumvent the summit block to the north and attack from that side on a short Class 3 scramble to the top.

North Ridge

From Cataract Gulch TH at 9,600′: 7.6 miles, 4,540′

From Cataract Lake, find the cairned intersection of the Colorado Trail, the West Lost Trail, and Pole Creek Trail at 12,480′ and continue south-southwest up the north slopes of Northwest Pole on tundra that becomes rockier as you continue south to reach the Class 3 summit block.

OFF THE BEATEN PATH

Cinnamon Mountain

13,328′ RANK 370

0.5 mile southwest of Cinnamon Pass

From Cinnamon Pass at 12,640′: 0.65 mile, 700′

East Slopes: A Class 2 walk-up from the summit of Cinnamon Pass. Often combined with Peak 13,535′.

Peak 13,535′

RANK 232

1.1 mile southeast of Cinnamon Mountain

From Cinnamon Pass at 12,640′: 1.8 miles, 1,390′

Northwest Ridge: A Class 2 walk-up from the shared saddle with Cinnamon Mountain.

Peak 13,688′

RANK 154

0.46 mile north-northwest of Wood Mountain

From Cinnamon Pass at 12,640′ via Wood Mountain: 2.2 miles, 1,730′

West Face Gully: After dropping into the basin northwest of Wood, this route is a Class 3 scramble up a gully. You can also climb the west-face gully from Hurricane Basin via the same route. Avoid the rotten Class 4 or 5 on the ridge between Peak 13,688′ and Wood.

Seigal Mountain

13,274′ RANK 422

1.6 mile northwest of Wood Mountain

From Cinnamon Pass at 12,640′ via Wood Mountain: 2.8 miles, 1,720′

South Slopes: This is a Class 2 traverse on talus from Peak 13,708′ and is typically combined with Wood Mountain and Animas Forks Mountain.

Peak 13,427′

RANK 303

1.3 miles northeast of Wood Mountain

From Cinnamon Pass at 12,640′ via Wood Mountain: 2.6 miles, 1,500′

South Slopes: Scramble down rugged Class 3 terrain from Wood Mountain from the west and up Class 2 scree to the summit from Cinnamon Pass.

Peak 13,540′

RANK 225

2.3 miles east-northeast of Wood Mountain

From Cinnamon Pass at 12,640′ via Wood Mountain and Peak 13,427′: 3.6 miles, 1,990′

Southwest Ridge: A simple Class 2 walk-up from Peak 13,427′.

"C.T. Peak"

13,312′ **RANK 382**

3.9 miles east-northeast of Wood Mountain and 0.77 mile southwest of Gudy Peak

From Cinnamon Pass at 12,640′ via Wood Mountain, Peaks 13,427′, and Peak 13,540′: 3.6 miles, 1,990′

Southwest Slopes: From Peak 13,540′, follow loose talus down and scramble down Class 2+ rock to the saddle between Peak 13,540′ and C.T. Peak and finish with an easy Class 2 walk-up.

"Gudy Peak"

13,566′ **RANK 211**

0.77 mile northeast of C.T. Peak and 1.9 miles west-southwest of Every Mountain

From Cinnamon Pass at 12,640′ via Wood Mountain, Peaks 13,427′, and Peak 13,540′: 4.5 miles, 2,680′

Southwest Slopes: A straightforward traverse on Class 2 terrain from C.T. Peak. If looping from Cinnamon Pass to Cooper Creek Trailhead, head back to the saddle between C.T. Peak and Gudy Peak and left (south) down scree and grass to find Cooper Creek Trail.

"Every Mountain"

13,691′ **RANK 151**

1 mile northwest of Cooper Creek Peak and 2.6 mile north of Redcloud Peak

From Cooper Creek TH at 10,630′: 5 miles, 3,390′

South Slopes: Ascend Cooper Creek Trail, aiming for the Every Mountain–Cooper Creek Peak saddle and continue left (northwest) up Class 2 grassy slopes and talus to the summit. Often combined with Cooper Creek Peak and Peak 13,180′.

"Cooper Creek Peak"

13,688′ **RANK 153**

1.6 miles north of Redcloud Peak

From Cooper Creek TH at 10,630′: 5.3 miles, 3,390′

North Slopes: Ascend Cooper Creek Trail, aiming for the Every Mountain—Cooper Creek Peak saddle and continue right (southeast) up Class 2 talus to the summit. Often combined with Every Mountain and Peak 13,180′. If coming from Every Mountain, beware of cliffs below Every Mountain that can be circumnavigated.

Peak 13,180′

RANK 500

2.5 miles northeast of Cooper Creek Peak

From Alpine Gulch Trailhead at 8,970′: 6.3 miles, 4,490′

Northeast Slopes: From Alpine Gulch Trailhead, hike southwest off-trail starting with point 10,698′ and then through a gap to higher ground above to the northeast slopes, all on Class 2 terrain.

"Sundog"

13,432′ RANK 300

1 mile northwest of Sunshine Peak

From Silver Creek TH at 10,420′: 3 miles, 3,090′

North Slopes: A Class 2 off-trail climb from the trail junction at 11,350′ for the northwest face route of Sunshine Peak.

"Campbell Creek Peak"

13,454′ RANK 287

2.3 miles southwest of Sunshine Peak

From 1 mile southeast of Silver Creek TH on the road at 10,300′: 1.8 miles, 3,170′

Northwest Slopes: Often climbed in conjunction with Peak 13,795′ starting from the road 1 mile southeast of Silver Creek Trailhead at the Campbell Creek drainage. Bushwhack up steep Class 2+ terrain.

Peak 13,795′

RANK 109

1.3 miles east-southeast of Handies Peak; 1 mile west of Campbell Creek Peak

From Grizzly Gulch TH at 11,660′: 3.2 miles, 3,430′

Northwest Couloir: Hike Grizzly Gulch Trail to 11,790′, turn left (south), and aim for the lake at 12,323′. Continue up talus toward the southwest and locate a couloir on Class 2+ terrain that brings you up to the ridge. Turn left (southeast) to gain the summit. If you are continuing to climb Campbell Creek Peak, note there is Class 3 and upper Class 4 terrain to be negotiated on the traverse.

Peak 13,069′

RANK 597

4.2 miles southwest of Half Peak

From Cuba Gulch TH at 10,700′: 15.4 miles, 5,210′

Southeast Slopes: Follow the Cuba Gulch Trail south-southwest for 14.7 miles just past the Middle Pole Trail turnoff to the summit of point 13,038′, turn right (northwest), and follow the ridge on Class 2 talus to the summit.

"Quarter Peak"

13,674′ RANK 161

1.2 miles northeast of Half Peak

From Cuba Gulch TH at 10,700′: 1.4 miles, 2,950′

North Ridge: The ascent begins 0.7 mile northwest of Cuba Gulch Trailhead from the road at Square Gulch at 10,630′. Climb southeast up steep grassy slopes then talus in Square Gulch to gain the north ridge and then the summit.

Peak 13,164′

RANK 511

1.3 miles southeast of Half Peak

From Cataract Gulch TH at 9,600′ with Half Peak: 6.9 miles, 4,700′

From Cuba Gulch TH at 10,700′ with Half Peak: 5.8 miles, 3,500′

East Slopes: Often climbed in tandem with Half Peak on Class 2 terrain by ascending from the Half Peak–Peak 13,164′ saddle.

Bent Peak

13,393′ RANK 322

4.7 miles east of Half Peak and 0.8 mile west-northwest of Carson Pass

From Carson Pass at 12,430′: 0.8 mile, 930′

East Slopes: It is possible to climb six 13ers in a day in a loop, starting from Carson Pass, from Bent Peak to Peak 13,581′ (described last in this section). Add two more by combining Coney Benchmark and Peak 13,260′ to the east of the pass. From Carson Pass, the summit of Bent Peak is a simple Class 2 walk-up to the west.

Carson Peak

13,657′ RANK 245

1.9 miles west of Carson Pass

From Carson Pass at 12,430′: 2.2 miles, 1,620′

East Slopes: A short Class 2 walk-up from Bent Peak.

"Tundra Top"

13,450′ RANK 290

2.3 miles east of Half Peak and 3.1 miles west of Carson Pass

From Carson Pass at 12,430′: 3.5 miles, 2,000′

South Slopes: A short class 2 walk-up from Carson Peak.

"Cataract Peak"

13,524′ RANK 240

0.6 mile north of Tundra Top

From Carson Pass at 12,430′: 4.1 miles, 2,430′

West Ridge: From Tundra Top, continue north on talus slopes, aiming for the west ridge, where you'll encounter more Class 2 talus to the summit.

Peak 13,580′

RANK 202

1.5 miles south-southeast of Tundra Top

From Carson Pass at 12,430′: 6.3 miles, 3,620′

Northeast Slopes: Follow a trail up the northeast slopes from the Colorado Trail south of Tundra Top up the Class 2 grassy slope.

Peak 13,581′

RANK 196

1.2 miles east of Peak 13,580′ and 2 miles southwest of Carson Pass

From Carson Pass at 12,430′: 7.9 miles, 4,200′

West Slopes: This is the crux of your loop from Carson Pass. From Peak 13,580′, continue to point 13,568′ on Class 2 scree then east to the saddle between point 13,568′ and Peak 13,581′ and drop to your left (north), losing approximately 150′ in elevation to avoid unstable rock on the ridge. Regain the ridge up grassy slopes and climb north to the summit block, where you will encounter Class 3 climbing on large broken rock to the summit.

"Coney Benchmark"

13,334′ **RANK 366**

1.2 miles east-northeast of Carson Pass

From Carson Pass at 12,430′: 2 miles, 1,040′

South Slopes: An easy Class 1 walk-up on the Colorado Trail.

Peak 13,260′

RANK 434

2.2 miles northeast of Carson Pass

From Carson Pass at 12,430′ via Coney Benchmark: 3.5 miles, 1,340′

Southeast Slopes: An easy Class 1 walk-up from the Colorado Trail via Coney Benchmark.

UNCOMPAHGRE GROUP

13

Wetterhorn and Uncompahgre are unmistakable giants from most vantage points in the San Juans; here seen from Jones with Sunshine Mountain right of center.

Contrasts typify the Uncompahgre Group, with difficult climbs located adjacent to walk-ups. The area's two 14ers are a case in point. While Uncompahgre Peak is one of the easier 14ers to climb, nearby Wetterhorn is one of the more difficult. The Coxcomb and Redcliff pair is another example. Coxcomb is by anyone's standards a difficult climb. Redcliff, located immediately north, is a walk-up. Many difficult climbs are interspersed throughout the area, and technical routes have been established on the north faces of Wetterhorn, Coxcomb, and Wildhorse and the south face of Chimney Rock. Heisshorn and El Punto are challenging even by their easiest routes. On the other hand, Matterhorn, Wildhorse, Courthouse, and Fortress are easy to moderate climbs.

The group is best approached from two entirely different directions. Wetterhorn, Matterhorn, and Wildhorse are best approached from the south and east (Lake City). The northeast peaks are more accessible when approached from the north or west (Montrose or Ridgway). Virtually all the peaks in the area are day hikes. Another aspect of the area that deserves note are the wild rock formations in the northern areas. Rotten pinnacles near Dunsinane and Precipice and the nearby ridges give you a feeling that you are in another world.

CLIMBING HISTORY

Uncompahgre Peak was probably climbed by Native Americans before the arrival of the surveyors. The San Juan Mountaineers reported in the *San Juan Mountaineers Climber's Guide to Southwestern Colorado* that there was "direct evidence" that Native Americans had "carried their hunting expeditions at least to an elevation of 13,000 feet on the peak."

Uncompahgre Peak is one of several peaks in the San Juans on which the Wheeler and Hayden Surveys overlapped territory. The Hayden team climbed Uncompahgre on August 8, 1874. Although they anticipated a difficult climb, the team reportedly found it quite easy. But while the Hayden team did not encounter technical difficulties, surveyor Franklin Rhoda reported in *Summits to Reach* that they were "terribly taken aback, when, at an elevation of over 13,000 feet, a she grizzly, with her two cubs, came rushing past them from the top of the peak." William L. Marshall of the Wheeler Survey noted an even closer bear encounter with "a

The core of the Uncompahgre Group in panoramic glory, left to right: Sheep Mountain C, Uncompahgre, Wetterhorn, Fortress, Precipice, and Dunsinane.

large cinnamon bear and her cub" when his team climbed Uncompahgre that same year. As described in Marshall's 1875 report, one of the packers from the Wheeler team was raising his head above a ledge when "the bear happened to be about to look down over the same place." Although both bear and packer "tumbled off the cliff together," the packer escaped with only "a good fright and a few bruises."

Wetterhorn Peak was climbed in 1906 by George C. Barnard, David Utter, Will P. Smedley, and Clyde Smedley, who set out with plans to climb Uncompahgre Peak. According to *Trail and Timberline* (August 1929), as the team passed the base of Wetterhorn, it was "evident to everyone that we were passing a peak that was worthy of our metal [sic], both in difficulty and in height." They climbed the peak by what is now the standard route of the south ridge, remarking as to a feeling of "half exhilaration and half fear, which was created by the 600-foot exposure of the last pitch."

Uncompahgre was the last peak in the San Juans climbed by William S. Cooper and John Hubbard during their 1908 excursion. Cooper wrote in *Mountains* that "Uncompahgre is a magnificent mountain, but disappointingly easy. A friend of mine, approaching it from a different direction from ours, climbed to within 700 feet of its summit on his motorcycle."

Several first ascents were made in the area during the 1929 summer outing of the Colorado Mountain Club. Two of the peaks climbed during the outing are unnamed on topographical maps: Heisshorn, which lies 1 mile north of Wetterhorn Peak at 13,411', and El Punto, which lies a little under 2 miles north of Matterhorn Peak at 13,300'. Both peaks were climbed by Dwight Lavender and Forrest Greenfield, who reported in *Trail and Timberline* (October 1929) that although El Punto "looked like an unconquerable pillar of stone," actually the Heisshorn was the more difficult climb of the two and probably the most difficult of the outing, "second only to Coxcomb."

During the outing, Lavender and Greenfield set out to reconnoiter a route on Coxcomb, finding a way up its summit block via a chimney on the southwest side. However, they were stopped just short of the summit by a 32' vertical gap in the summit block. Having no rope, they were forced to give up the climb. Two days later, a party of seven led by Henry Buchtel made the first complete ascent of Coxcomb. The first-ascent party learned of the gap in the summit block from Lavender and Greenfield and came prepared with a rope.

Chimney Rock was first climbed on September 15, 1934, by Mel Griffiths and Robert Ormes, who described their route as "via a chimney and crack which splits the south face of the rock." New routes were not reported in the area until the 1960s, when the north face of Coxcomb and the northeast face of Wildhorse Peak were climbed. Coxcomb's north face was climbed in August 1965 during a CMC

Left: 1874 Hayden Survey photo of Uncompahgre Peak. W. H. Jackson, courtesy of USGS
Right: Robert Ormes and Mel Griffiths on the summit of Chimney Rock during the first ascent on September 15, 1934. Photo by Mel Griffiths

outing by Dick Yeatts, Mike Stults, Dick Guadagno, and Martin Etter. Wildhorse's northeast face was climbed in August 1968 by Etter, John McDermott, Henry Barker, and Greg Simmons.

The 800′ vertical north face of Wetterhorn that gives the peak its striking profile had been the subject of speculation for several decades. The face's first ascent was finally made in September 1973 by Jeff Lowe and Paul Hogan, with Lowe reporting in *American Alpine Journal* (1975) that they finished this difficult climb "in a snowstorm that added an alpine quality to the climb."

Some of the first winter climbing in the San Juans took place in the area in 1934. Gordon Williams and Mel Griffiths skied from the San Juan Mountaineers shelter cabin in Blaine Basin to Ouray. From Ouray, they skied to Engineer Pass and climbed Engineer Mountain. After climbing Engineer Mountain, they skied across American Flats and climbed Wildhorse Peak. Later they established camp on the north fork of Henson Creek, aiming to make an ascent of Wetterhorn. After weathering a furious storm, Griffiths and Williams climbed Dolly Varden Mountain instead and then skied into Silverton to conclude their journey.

ACCESS AND HIKING

Nellie Creek

From downtown Lake City, take the gravel road that heads west up Henson Creek. The turnoff from Lake City is marked by a sign directing you toward Engineer Pass. Travel through Henson, at 4 miles, reaching the Nellie Creek turnoff at 5.5 miles. At

UNCOMPAHGRE (NORTH)

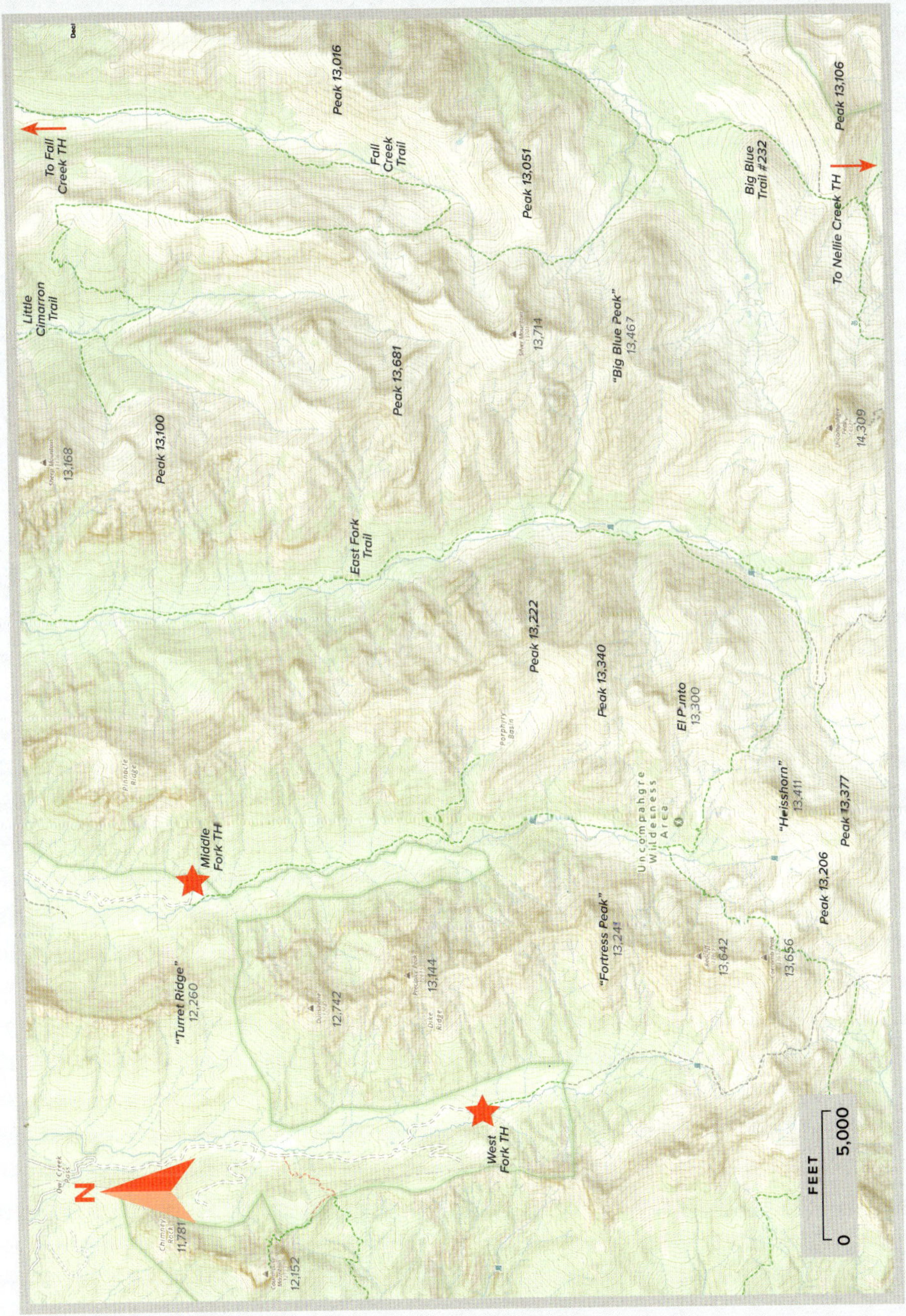

UNCOMPAHGRE (CENTRAL)

UNCOMPAHGRE (SOUTHWEST)

the junction of Nellie and Henson Creeks, turn right on a jeep trail (#877) that heads north up the Nellie Creek drainage. If you have 4WD, it is possible to drive 4 miles to a trailhead at 11,700′. Keep a close lookout for a sharp switchback to the left, which you take at 2.5 miles. From the trailhead, a trail heads west toward Uncompahgre, while another trail heads north over a 12,360′ pass to Big Blue Creek. The Nellie Creek jeep trail is the best approach for climbing Uncompahgre only.

Matterhorn Creek

To reach Matterhorn Creek, take the same gravel road up Henson Creek that leads you past the Nellie Creek turnoff to the North Henson Road, located 9.5 miles west of Lake City. Turn right and continue 2.1 miles up the drainage of the north fork of Henson Creek to Ridge Stock Driveway Trail. It is possible to continue almost a mile up Matterhorn Creek drainage on this jeep trail until you are blocked by a metal gate at the boundary of the Uncompahgre Wilderness. From the trailhead, you can hike up an old jeep trail to reach tree line in the basin southeast of Wetterhorn Peak and south of Matterhorn Creek. Matterhorn Creek is the best means of access for climbing Matterhorn and Wetterhorn. It is also the best approach if you wish to climb Wetterhorn and Uncompahgre in a long day.

The heart of the Cimarrons, left to right: Coxcomb, Redcliff, Chimney Rock, Precipice, and Turret Ridge.

Engineer Pass—American Flats

Uncompahgre and Wetterhorn are most frequently approached from Lake City. It is possible, however, to approach from Silverton or Ouray by the 4WD road over Engineer Pass. From Silverton, follow the road up the Animas River past Howardsville, Eureka, and Animas Forks to reach Engineer Pass. From Ouray, the turnoff to Engineer Pass is just over 3 miles south of Ouray. From Engineer Pass, the road takes you east to American Flats with Wildhorse Peak to the north. From American Flats, drop down into Henson Creek and travel through Capital City and Henson before reaching Lake City.

Bear Creek Trail

Bear Creek Trail, located 1.75 miles south of Ouray on US Highway 550, provides access from the west for Wildhorse Peak and surrounding 13ers.

West Fork of the Cimarron Road

The turnoff for this long, well-maintained gravel road is 2.7 miles west of the town of Cimarron (Cimarron is 20 miles east of Montrose) on US Highway 50. From the US 50 turnoff, drive past the turnoff to the Silver Jack Reservoir before reaching

the roads to the east fork of the Cimarron at 20.3 miles and the middle fork at 20.5 miles. Bear right at both road junctions and continue past the turnoff to Owl Creek Pass on FSR 860 at 27.1 miles until you cross the stream at 30 miles and reach the trailhead at 30.6 miles. To negotiate the last few miles and to cross the stream, a 4WD or high-clearance vehicle helps. From the trailhead, it is 2.5 miles and 1,800 vertical feet to the 12,500′ pass, connecting you with Wetterhorn Basin. The approaches for Coxcomb Peak, Redcliff, and Fortress all start on the West Fork Trail (#226). Precipice, Dunsinane, Courthouse, and Chimney can be climbed from various points on the road north of the trailhead.

Owl Creek Pass Road

This road provides access to the west, middle, and east forks of the Cimarron from US Highway 550 and starts by turning right (east) 1.8 miles north of Ridgway. From US 550, it is approximately 14 miles east to Owl Creek Pass and the intersection with the west fork of the Cimarron Road (FSR 860). Another 4 miles on the 4WD road north on FSR 860 takes you to the West Fork Trailhead (#226), which provides access to Coxcomb and Redcliff.

Uncompahgre at sunrise from the summit of Wetterhorn.

Fall Creek Trail

Fall Creek Trail (#231) offers the best access for Peak 13,016′, Peak 13,051′, Silver Mountain, as well as Peak 13,681′, Peak 13,100′ A, and Sheep Mountain C, which are typically climbed in that order for a huge 23-mile loop on a long day that connects with the Little Cimarron/Alpine Trail (described next). From Montrose, drive east on US 50 for 22 miles and look for Little Cimarron Road on the left (south) shortly after Cimarron Road. Continue south for 16 miles to the Little Cimarron/Alpine Trailhead, then continue an additional 4.5 miles to reach the Fall Creek Trailhead.

Little Cimarron/Alpine Trail

This trail is a great access point for Sheep Mountain C and Peak 13,100′ A if you are looking to climb just those two peaks. From Montrose, drive east on US 50 for 22 miles and look for Little Cimarron Road on the left (south) shortly after Cimarron Road. Continue south for 16 miles to the trailhead.

Middle Fork Cimarron Trail

This trail is a great way to access El Punto, Heisshorn, Peak 13,222′, Peak 13,340′, Peak 13,377′, Peak 13,206′, Coxcomb, and Redcliff from the north. The road begins

Sunrise from the summit of Uncompahgre, showcasing the entire group in one magical scene.

at a junction between Owl Creek Pass and Silver Jack Reservoir on the south end of a bridge crossing the east fork of the Cimarron River. If coming from the north and Silver Jack Reservoir, drive 0.67 mile southeast, taking a right at the junction for Owl Creek Pass. Cross the bridge and take a left at the fork toward the Middle Fork Cimarron River. Going right will take you to Owl Creek Pass. If coming from Owl Creek Pass, turn right after heading north and east for 6.7 miles toward Silver Jack Reservoir. The trailhead and a parking lot are at the end of the easy 4WD road 4.6 miles from the Owl Creek Road junction south of the bridge.

CLIMBING ROUTES

Uncompahgre Peak

14,309′ RANK 6

Uncompahgre Peak is a giant—the highest of the San Juans. Located 13 miles west-northwest of Lake City, it is recognizable from all angles due to its prominent pyramid shape.

South Ridge

From Nellie Creek TH at 9,300′: 8 miles, 5,010′

From Nellie Creek 4WD TH at 11,460′: 4.1 miles, 2,850′

The south ridge of Uncompahgre Peak is the standard route. When Uncompahgre is approached from Nellie Creek, you can either follow the trail that contours around the basin southeast of Uncompahgre or head due west to gain the ridge at 13,800′, just north of the prominent notch. At 13,800′, the trail skirts the ridge to the west and requires a scramble in a few spots before you reach the broad summit plateau. On the summit, note several stone windbreaks that have been constructed by overnight campers. Views to the north and west are nothing short of magnificent.

Southeast Face

From Nellie Creek TH at 9,300′: 8 miles, 5,010′

From Nellie Creek 4WD TH at 11,460′: 4.1 miles, 2,850′

A prominent band of cliffs runs along the southeast face at approximately 13,800′. It is possible to climb this band of cliffs by several routes, which vary in difficulty, but all involve problems with loose rock. While at least one of the routes toward the western end of the cliff can be climbed as Class 3; as a general rule, you will want a rope, helmet, and protection.

Wetterhorn Peak

14,015′ RANK 49

Wetterhorn Peak is one of most fun, rewarding climbs in the San Juans thanks to incredible views of Uncompahgre and surrounding peaks as well as the excellent Class 3 route that provides a good introduction to this type of climbing for newer climbers when conditions are favorable.

Southeast Ridge and Southwest Face

From Matterhorn Creek TH at 10,400′: 4.25 miles, 3,620′

From Matterhorn Creek 4WD TH at 10,720′: 3.65 miles, 3,300′

From the summit of Wetterhorn, a view down to all the lesser peaks to the west in American Flats, right to left: Wildhorse, Dragon's Back, Darley, and more.

This route, the standard, contours up the eastern side of the southeast ridge until near the summit, where you reach a keyhole separating the summit from a southern pinnacle. The last 150′ of the southwest face, which is reached by passing through the keyhole, is what you will remember about this climb. It is made up of small ledges that are sprinkled by a covering of loose gravel. What makes the section exciting is the 600′ of exposure. Early in the year when there is a chance of encountering snow and ice or in poor weather conditions a rope is comforting on this last section.

Matterhorn Peak

13,590′ RANK 193

Matterhorn Peak is located 0.9 mile east of Wetterhorn via a connecting ridge.

South Face

From Matterhorn Creek TH at 10,400′: 4.25 miles, 3,200′

From Matterhorn Creek 4WD TH at 10,720′: 3.65 miles, 2,880′

The lower portion of the south face consists of a grassy slope that you hike up directly toward the summit. As you near the summit, you will encounter easy Class 2+ scrambling.

Silver Mountain

13,714′ RANK 139

This seldom-climbed high 13er offers incredible views of Uncompahgre and Coxcomb Peaks. There are numerous ways to reach the summit, but all require significant mileage and elevation gain.

East Ridge

From Little Cimarron TH at 9,730′: 11.1 miles, 5,180′

From Fall Creek TH at 11,000′: 7.4 miles, 3,480′

From Nellie Creek TH at 9,300′: 9.5 miles, 5,550′

From Nellie Creek 4WD TH at 11,460′: 5.5 miles, 3,340′

From Fall Creek TH at 11,000′ via Peaks 13,016′ and 13,051′: 7.7 miles, 4,370′

Huge Loop: From Fall Creek TH at 11,000′ via Peaks 13,016′ and 13,051′ to Peak 13,681′, 13,100′ A, and Sheep Mountain C to the Little Cimarron TH and then the Fall Creek TH: 23.5 miles, 7,940′

From the north either via Fall Creek Trail or Little Cimarron Trail, make your way to the gentle saddle at 12,720′ between Silver Mountain and Peak 13,051′. From here, it is mostly a gentle climb on grassy slopes to a brown cliff band at 13,430′. Stay north (right) of the band to decrease the difficulty, which requires minor scrambling

Matterhorn and Uncompahgre, as seen below Wetterhorn.

on Class 2+ rock. After the brown cliff band, you will encounter a white cliff band, which is steep and loose but can be kept at Class 2+. The summit is yours.

If you're looking to complete the loop that finishes on Sheep Mountain C, continue north down the grassy slopes of Silver Mountain to Peak 13,681′ on Class 2 terrain, then up and over the unranked Peak 13,503′ en route to Peak 13,100′ in the distance. Finishing on Sheep Mountain C is easy on Class 2 slopes, and your descent from there should be from the Sheep Mountain C–Peak 13,100′ saddle down a steep grassy slope to Little Cimarron Trail. From the trail, you can hike north to the trailhead and then hike the road east to your car at Fall Creek Trailhead.

There is a route up the east ridge of Silver from the south via Nellie Creek, but you will need to regain 1,000′ to return. From the south via Nellie Creek, ascend the trail as you would for the south ridge route of Uncompahgre 0.9 mile from the 4WD trailhead, where you will find a trail junction for Big Blue Creek Trail #232. Turn right (northeast) and climb this trail for 0.6 mile to a saddle at 12,400′ between Peak 13,106′ and point 12,780′ to another junction. Stay left (north) and descend to 11,400′, reaching a junction with Fall Creek Trail. Turn left (west) and ascend to the 12,720′ saddle between Silver Mountain and Peak 13,051′, finishing the same way as from the north route described earlier.

North Ridge

From Little Cimarron TH at 9,730′ via Sheep Mountain C, Peak 13,100′ A, and Peak 13,681′: 8.2 miles, 5,930′

This route follows the loop route instructions for the east ridge except in reverse order. It is a good way to avoid the Class 2+ cliffs if that is desired.

Wildhorse Peak

13,266′ RANK 425

Wildhorse Peak is a prominent point located 2.6 miles north of Engineer Pass and is often accessed from there.

Southwest Face

From the summit of Engineer Pass at 12,240′: 3 miles, 1,020′

From Bear Creek TH at 8,480′: 7.6 miles, 6,000′

Hike north from the summit of Engineer Pass on Horsethief Trail up Class 2 grassy slopes.

Northeast Face

The October 1969 *Trail and Timberline* reports a climb on the left side of the face consisting of three-plus leads on the prominent corner of the face. The route was rated 5.6.

A snowy San Juan scene from Wetterhorn, with Dragon's Back and Wildhorse on prominent display at center.

Peak 12,968′—"Dragon's Back"

RANK 656

Dragon's Back is a Class 4 climb located 0.9 mile east-northeast of Wildhorse Peak and is recognizable from many vantage points due to its aptly named spine, which seemingly erupts from the earth.

South Face

From the summit of Engineer Pass at 12,240′: 3 miles, 1,020′

From Bear Creek TH at 8,480′: 7.6 miles, 6,000′

From American Flats north of Engineer Pass, approach the south face of Dragon's Back just east of the summit and climb up a talus slope to a Class 4 unexposed cliff band. From the top of the cliff band, negotiate Class 4 terrain to a chimney on the west side and up a Class 4 gully to the summit. You will want protection and a rope.

Coxcomb Peak

13,656′ RANK 171

Coxcomb Peak is one of the most recognizable peaks in this area due to its "hammerhead" summit block that appears flat, long, and rectangular from the north and south, and as a steep pinnacle from the east and west. Located 1.8 miles northwest of Wetterhorn Peak, Coxcomb is often considered the most challenging mountain of the second-highest two hundred (otherwise known as the Bicentennials) in Colorado.

Southwest Chimney

From West Fork Cimarron TH at 10,780′: 3.5 miles, 3,740′

From Middle Fork Cimarron TH at 10,050′: 6.1 miles, 3,860′

The approach to this route, rated Class 5.3, is roundabout at best. From the end of the road up the west fork of the Cimarron, hike up the trail to reach the 12,500′ pass 0.5 mile west of Coxcomb. From the pass, you have a choice between a high, rotten traverse or dropping down the trail to 12,100′ and climbing up the basin southwest of Coxcomb. It saves time to avoid the traverse. Alternatively, you can gain this same section southwest of Coxcomb by climbing from the Middle Fork Cimarron Trail to the northeast. Once at the base of the summit block on the southwest end, you will find a 12′ vertical chimney by which you gain the easier middle section of the summit block. The last 80′ consist of a sloping chimney. Most climbers will want a belay on the first and last portions of the chimney. The middle section is an easy scramble. Once on the top of the summit block, head northwest toward the summit until you are stopped by a 30′ gap. Negotiating the gap is the most difficult portion of this climb and requires a rope belay. The best way to negotiate the gap is for one climber

Coxcomb, Redcliff, and Chimney Rock, from Wetterhorn.

at a time to be belayed down the gap and then back up after scrambling out to the true summit and signing the register. On the downclimb, most climbers rappel the very top portion of the chimney and downclimb the rest. The chimney is unusual in that, with the exception of the very top, it seems easier to climb down than to ascend.

Redcliff

13,642′ RANK 175

Redcliff is just 0.5 mile north of Coxcomb, and its east face shares the same sheer characteristics as its southern neighbor.

South Face

From West Fork Cimarron TH at 10,780′: 3.6 miles, 2,880′

From Middle Fork Cimarron TH at 10,050′: 5.8 miles, 3,830′

The 13,642′ saddle between Redcliff and Coxcomb can be reached from either the west or middle fork of Cimarron. Once at the saddle, the south face is an easy walk-up over stable Class 2 talus.

Precipice Peak

13,144′ **RANK 530**

This impressive-looking beast of a mountain is easily spotted even from the town of Montrose on a clear day. The south face ramps up into the sky in a pose of royal stature. Located 2.7 miles north of Coxcomb Peak along the same ridgeline, Precipice is iconic.

South Ridge

From West Fork Cimarron TH at 10,780′: 3.6 miles, 2,880′

From the West Fork Cimarron Trailhead, head east and slightly north to gain the south ridge, which you then follow to the top on Class 2+ solid, yet peculiar volcanic rock. The climb is of particular interest because of the unusual rock formations north and east of the summit area.

Dunsinane Mountain

12,742′ **RANK 824**

Located 0.75 mile north-northwest of Precipice along a ridge and 1.1 miles south of the infamous Turret Ridge along the same ridgeline, Dunsinane got its name from the United States Board on Geographic Names in 1966 due to its resemblance of the castle Dunsinane of Shakespeare's *Macbeth*.

Precipice and Dunsinane, from Silver Jack Reservoir.

A view looking down Middle Cimarron River, left to right: Coxcomb, Precipice, and Dunsinane.

West Face—North Ridge

From West Fork Cimarron TH at 10,780′: 3.6 miles, 2,880′

From the West Fork Cimarron Road at 10,200′, your goal is the saddle between Dunsinane and Turret Ridge. The route first crosses the river off-trail and continues up through thick, challenging timbered terrain. You will reach rocky pinnacles through which you will ascend. Above the pinnacles, the ridge becomes narrow and steep. It appears almost unclimbable, but with care, you will find a weakness. The rock is stable at steeper sections, where you will find the Class 4 crux on exposed rock. A rope may be of value here. Above the steep cliff, bypass another set of cliffs by staying on the western side of the peak and find another weakness on Class 2+ terrain to the summit.

Peak 12,260′—"Turret Ridge"

RANK 1,165

Turret Ridge is a southwest Colorado icon among climbers and photographers, but because it does not rise above 13,000′, it is less heavily traveled than higher peaks in the area. Affectionately known as "the hardest 12er" in Colorado due to the rotten nature of the rock, it is considered by many to be the hardest ranked point above 12,000′ to reach in the state.

West Gully

From West Fork Cimarron Road at 10,220′: 1.8 miles, 2,040′

This Class 5.9 route is complex, dangerous, and includes over 300′ of sustained technical climbing on rotten rock. From the turnoff from Owl Creek Pass onto the West Fork Cimarron Road, drive 1 mile and park. Gain the Dunsinane–Turret Ridge saddle and continue north on game trails. Pass the first gully system. The second gully is where the route begins up a system of Class 5 chimneys, gullies, and small ledges where bolts are available to be used as belay stations.

Courthouse Mountain

12,152′ RANK 1,221

Courthouse Mountain and its neighbor to the north, Chimney Rock, are iconic, easy-to-recognize summits. From US Highway 550 near Ridgway, the two giants, while failing to rise above 13,000′, are hard to miss. Courthouse is the blocky, tent-like summit along a short ridge connected to the more famous Chimney Rock, located just 0.8 mile north.

Turret Ridge with Dunsinane and Precipice behind at center. From the horizon, right to left at center: Coxcomb, Heisshorn, and Wetterhorn.

East Ridge

From West Fork Cimarron Road at 10,380′: 1.75 miles, 1,890′

The trail to begin a climb of Courthouse is 1.6 miles south of the Owl Creek turnoff on the West Fork Cimarron Road. From the road, the east ridge is steep, short, and direct on Class 2+ terrain. The forest gives way to steep bands of grass and rock near the summit. The summit offers excellent views of Chimney Peak to the north and Dunsinane and Precipice to the east.

Chimney Rock

11,781′ RANK 1,418

Chimney Rock, which was the backdrop for the shootout scene in the 1969 film *True Grit*, is a source of affection for many landscape photographers, especially in autumn due its tendency to glow red at sunset. This Chimney Rock is not to be confused with Chimney Rock National Monument near Pagosa Springs.

South Face

From West Fork Cimarron Road at 10,360′: 1.3 miles, 1,420′

The Class 5 climbing starts on Chimney Rock before you even reach the base of the chimney for which the peak is named. The approach requires a runout, unprotectable lead in a lower fifth-class amphitheater composed of brecciated tuff with embedded pebbles, fist-size rocks, and small boulders. Above the amphitheater, the

Chimney Rock and Courthouse in autumn.

From left to right: Dunsinane, Precipice, Chimney Rock, Courthouse.

prominent, near-vertical chimney splits the south face of Chimney Rock. The first of three 5.6 pitches starts awkwardly and then eases up before reaching the huge chockstone that Robert Ormes made famous when, on the first ascent, he and Mel Griffiths climbed up different sides of the chockstone leaving the rope between them draped under the chockstone. "Must have been excited," said Ormes. It's easy to see why; there are hundreds of holds in the near vertical chimney with high exposure and little protection. The chimney above the chockstone leads to broken ground on the summit with an assortment of surreal rock features. An exposed traverse gains the true summit, which is east of the point where the chimney tops out.

Peak 13,300′—"El Punto"

RANK 402

This chossy peak is capped by a thin 80′ band of steep rubble resembling Coxcomb on a smaller scale and on much looser rock. Located 1.8 miles east of Redcliff in the Middle Fork Cimarron basin, El Punto is no easy task and is often combined with Heisshorn.

The dark spire right of center is El Punto; behind it is the sweeping north ridge of Sheep C.

North Ridge

From Middle Fork Cimarron TH at 10,050′: 6.2 miles, 3,250′

From the pass between Heisshorn and El Punto, hike up El Punto's north ridge toward the steep, broken, loose summit cone. As you gain elevation, grass slopes give way to a steeper slope of broken, black scree, and you have to fight backsliding with each step as you near the summit. The exposure and unstable nature of the summit cone warrant a Class 4 rating for the route. Don't be shy about breaking out a rope on the summit. Anchors are scarce or nonexistent, but it makes sense here for the strongest climber in the group to give a belay to other members of the party. Most climbers hand-tag the tiny, tottering summit rather than striking a hero's pose.

Peak 13,411′—"Heisshorn"

RANK 311

Located 1.2 miles north of Wetterhorn at the head of the Middle Fork of the Cimarron River, Heisshorn's sheer northwest face juts upward like a rotten tooth from the earth.

Northeast Ridge

From Middle Fork Cimarron TH at 10,050′: 5.9 miles, 3,360′

From the saddle between Heisshorn and El Punto, hike up Class 2 tundra and talus to reach the ridge, 400 vertical feet below the summit. The final 400′ of this Class 4 route is exposed, complex, and loose. Continue up the exposed ridge testing every hold on the chossy summit block. The crux is a 50′ loose wall on the final 200′ of the

Heisshorn, as seen from Wetterhorn, with Turret Ridge at far left.

ridge, where solid anchors are hard to find. Stay on the ridge crest for the entire ridge minus two small sections where you'll want to veer left (southeast) to avoid difficult terrain just before the summit proper.

Peak 13,222′

RANK 460

Nestled in the high reaches of Porphyry Basin, Peak 13,222′ is rarely climbed due to its Class 4 ridge on rotten rock. When it is attempted, it is often climbed with El Punto and Heisshorn and is located 2.8 miles northwest of Uncompahgre Peak on the west side of the east fork of the Cimarron River and 2.7 miles east-southeast of Precipice Peak on the east side of the middle fork of the Cimarron River.

Northwest Ridge

From Middle Fork Cimarron TH at 10,050′: 5.9 miles, 3,360′

From Porphyry Basin, gain the saddle between Peak 13,222′ and point 13,195′ and climb to the base of the steep northwest ridge and then traverse around to exposed Class 3 rock on the right (south) edge. Ascend to a cairned bench and up a short Class 4 section on solid rock. The terrain eases to Class 3 for the final section to the summit.

OFF THE BEATEN PATH

Peak 13,241′—"Fortress Peak"

RANK 446

0.75 mile north of Redcliff

From West Fork Cimarron TH at 10,780′: 2.1 miles, 2,420′

South Ridge: Turn left (east) off the trail at the wilderness boundary and aim for the prominent buttress on the ridge, which is skirted to the right. A Class 2 scramble leads to the ridge above the buttress.

Peak 13,206′

RANK 480

0.6 mile southeast of Coxcomb Peak

From West Fork Cimarron TH at 10,780′: 4.2 miles, 4,190′

Northwest Ridge: Typically climbed after summiting Coxcomb via an easy Class 2 traverse to the Coxcomb–Peak 13,206′ saddle and up.

Peak 13,377′

RANK 338

1.1 miles southeast of Coxcomb Peak and 0.8 mile north-northwest of Wetterhorn

From West Fork Cimarron TH at 10,780′: 4.9 miles, 4,730′

Southwest Ridge: Typically climbed with Coxcomb and Peak 13,206′ via an easy Class 2 traverse from Peak 13,206′.

Peak 13,340′

RANK 360

0.6 mile north-northeast of El Punto

From Middle Fork Cimarron TH at 10,050′: 4.9 miles, 3,290′

East Ridge: A Class 2 climb up loose scree from Porphyry Basin.

Blackwell Mountain

13,073′ RANK 593

0.7 mile north of Dragon's Back

From the summit of Engineer Pass at 12,240′: 4.4 miles, 1,450′

South Slopes: A Class 2 hike up grass and scree to the summit.

Peak 13,132′

RANK 544

1.7 miles southwest of Wildhorse Peak

From the summit of Engineer Pass at 12,240′: 2.2 miles, 890′

East Ridge: A short Class 2 hike up jumbled rock on a pointed ridge; often combined with Darley and Engineer.

Darley Mountain

13,260′ RANK 432

0.5 mile north-northwest of the summit of Engineer Pass

From the summit of Engineer Pass at 12,240′: 0.7 mile, 1,020′

Southwest Ridge: A short, enjoyable Class 2 ridge walk on varied terrain; often climbed with Peak 13,132′ and Engineer Mountain.

Engineer Mountain

13,218′ RANK 469

0.4 mile southwest of the summit of Engineer Pass

From the summit of Engineer Pass at 12,240′: 0.3 mile, 980′

Northwest Slopes: A quick Class 1 saunter on easy terrain.

Cow Benchmark

13,111′ RANK 559

2.4 miles west of Wildhorse Peak and 2.5 miles east of Ouray

From the summit of Engineer Pass at 12,240′: 4.7 miles, 1,440′

Southeast Slopes: Often climbed in conjunction with Peak 13,132′ and Darley Mountain up Class 2 tundra and rock.

Dolly Varden Mountain

12,932′ RANK 694

2.4 miles southwest of Wildhorse Peak

From the summit of Engineer Pass at 12,240′: 4.4 miles, 940′

Northeast Slopes: Often climbed in conjunction with Wildhorse, Peak 13,093′, and Sunshine Mountain; an easy Class 1 walk-up.

Peak 13,093′

RANK 574

0.5 mile east of Dolly Varden Mountain

From the summit of Engineer Pass at 12,240′ via Dolly Varden: 4.9 miles, 1,330′

West Slopes: From Dolly Varden Mountain, a steep Class 2 hike on talus.

Sunshine Mountain

13,321′ RANK 375

1.4 miles east of Peak 13,093′

From the summit of Engineer Pass at 12,240′ via Dolly Varden and Peak 13,093′: 6.7 miles, 2,120′

Northwest Ridge: Class 2 climbing on a gentle grass slope.

Broken Hill

13,256′ RANK 436

2.5 miles east-southeast of Wetterhorn Peak

From Matterhorn Creek TH at 10,400′: 4.9 miles, 3,070′

From Matterhorn Creek 4WD TH at 10,720′: 4.3 miles, 2,660′

Northwest Ridge: Easy climbing on Class 2 terrain from Wetterhorn Basin below Matterhorn Peak.

Peak 13,300′

RANK 400

0.7 mile west-southwest of Wetterhorn Peak

From Matterhorn Creek TH at 10,400′: 4.2 miles, 2,900′

From Matterhorn Creek 4WD TH at 10,720′: 3.6 miles, 2,500′

South Slopes: An easy Class 2 climb from the Peak 13,201′–Peak 13,300′ saddle.

Peak 13,201′

RANK 490

0.8 mile southwest of Wetterhorn Peak

From Matterhorn Creek TH at 10,400′: 5.6 miles, 2,800′

From Matterhorn Creek 4WD TH at 10,720′: 5 miles, 2,400′

West Ridge: From the saddle between point 13,129′ and Peak 13,201′, negotiate below a cliff band and up Class 2 terrain to the summit.

Peak 13,158′

RANK 516

1.8 miles southeast of Uncompahgre Peak

From Nellie Creek TH at 9,300′: 6.2 miles, 3,920′

From Nellie Creek 4WD TH at 11,460′: 2.2 miles, 1,700′

Northwest Ridge: A steep Class 2 ascent from the saddle between point 12,932′ and Peak 13,158′ around the southwest side of the steep ridge; often climbed with Peaks 13,106′ and 13,091′.

Peak 13,106′

RANK 564

2.2 miles east of Uncompahgre Peak

From Nellie Creek TH at 9,300′: 6.2 miles, 3,920′

From Nellie Creek 4WD TH at 11,460′: 2.2 miles, 1,700′

West Slopes: From Nellie Creek 4WD TH, hike northwest for 0.9 mile to the Big Blue Trail junction at 11,900′ to gain the saddle between Peak 13,106′ and point 12,780′. From here, it is a direct Class 2 ascent from the saddle between Peak 13,106′ and point 12,780′ on steep, solid terrain. Peak 13,091′ can then be gained via a hike east by bypassing a cliff band and up the long ridge.

"Big Blue Peak"

13,467′ SOFT RANKED

0.8 mile south of Silver Mountain

From Nellie Creek TH at 9,300′: 8.9 miles, 5,160′

From Nellie Creek 4WD TH at 11,460′: 4.9 miles, 2,940′

South Ridge: From Nellie Creek TH, follow the trail north and east similar to Peak 13,106′ to the Big Blue Trail and follow it north to Big Blue Creek. Turn left (west) and gain the south slopes of Big Blue Peak for a Class 2 walk-up.

Peak 13,091′

RANK 575

1.8 miles east of Peak 13,106′ and 4.1 miles east of Uncompahgre Peak

From Nellie Creek TH at 9,300′: 8.3 miles, 4,700′

From Nellie Creek 4WD TH at 11,460′: 4.3 miles, 2,480′

West Ridge: From Peak 13,106′, descend east and bypass a cliff band and follow a Class 2 ridge to the summit.

Peak 13,681′

RANK 159

1 mile northwest of Silver Mountain

From Fall Creek TH at 11,000′: 7.4 miles, 3,480′

Southeast Slopes: From Silver Mountain, a quick jaunt up Class 2 slopes; could be combined as part of many possible loops described in the Silver Mountain entry (p. 286).

Peak 13,016′

RANK 629

2.3 miles northeast of Silver Mountain

From Fall Creek TH at 11,000′: 4.9 miles, 2,480′

South Ridge: Often the first leg of the huge loop described in the Silver Mountain east ridge route from Fall Creek TH. From Fall Creek Trail at 11,800′, hike east up a steep Class 2 grassy slope to the south ridge and the summit.

Peak 13,051′

RANK 608

1.1 miles east of Silver Mountain

From Fall Creek TH at 11,000′: 6.5 miles, 3,350′

South Ridge: Often the second leg of the huge loop described in the Silver Mountain east ridge route from Fall Creek TH. From Peak 13,016′, continue south on a long but gentle, grassy ridge to the summit.

Peak 13,100′ A

RANK 569

2.9 miles northwest of Silver Mountain

From Fall Creek TH at 11,000′ via Peaks 13,016′ and 13,051′, Silver Mountain, and Peak 13,681′: 11.1 miles, 5,880′

From Little Cimarron TH at 9,730′: 6 miles, 3,580′

South Slopes/North Slopes: The south ridge route is often the fourth peak of five on a huge loop involving Silver Mountain. From Peak 13,681′, climb north ver Peak 13,503′

and across a grassy slope to the summit, all on Class 2 terrain. From the north, climb up Class 2 terrain from the Sheep Mountain C–Peak 13,100′ A saddle.

Sheep Mountain C

13,168′ RANK 507

6.1 miles north of Uncompahgre Peak; 3.7 miles north-northwest of Silver Mountain

From Fall Creek TH at 11,000′ via Peaks 13,016′ and 13,051′, Silver Mountain, Peak 13,681′, and Peak 13,100′ A: 12 miles, 6,450′

From Little Cimarron TH at 9,730′: 6 miles, 3,660′

South Slopes: Climbed as the first leg on the way to Silver Mountain from Little Cimarron TH or the last leg of a loop from Fall Creek TH (or on its own from Fall Creek TH). Climb 4.5 miles south on Fall Creek Trail to a junction on the right (west) up a grassy slope to the Sheep Mountain C–Peak 13,100′ A saddle and head north (right) up Class 2 terrain to the summit.

Top: Sheep Mountain C, Peak 13,100′ A, Peak 13,681′, and Uncompahgre, from the north at sunset. **Bottom:** Coxcomb, Wetterhorn, and Uncompahgre, from Tower.

SAN LUIS GROUP

14

Left to right: Column Ridge, Stewart, and Baldy Alto, from San Luis.

High, rounded summits with grassy slopes and long hiking approaches typify the San Luis group. The main group of peaks, of which San Luis Peak at 14,014′ is the highest, is located north of Creede. In addition to San Luis, Stewart Peak (just 17′ shy of being a 14er), Balto Alto, Organ Mountain, and Blady Chato comprise the main group. There is no short way to approach these climbs. The quickest trips can be made from the east via trails in the Nutras, Stewart, and Cochetopa Creek drainages, but each involves several miles of hiking before reaching the base of the peaks. Longer approaches are available via West Willow Creek to the south and Bondholder Trail to the northwest. A somewhat separate group of peaks lies northwest of Creede in the La Garita Wilderness Area. Phoenix Peak (13,895′) and La Garita Benchmark (13,718′) are the highest peaks in this group, which can be approached from Creede by the Middle Fork Trail, the Inspiration Point Trail, or East Willow Creek and the La Garita Stock Driveway.

SAN LUIS (WEST)

SAN LUIS (EAST)

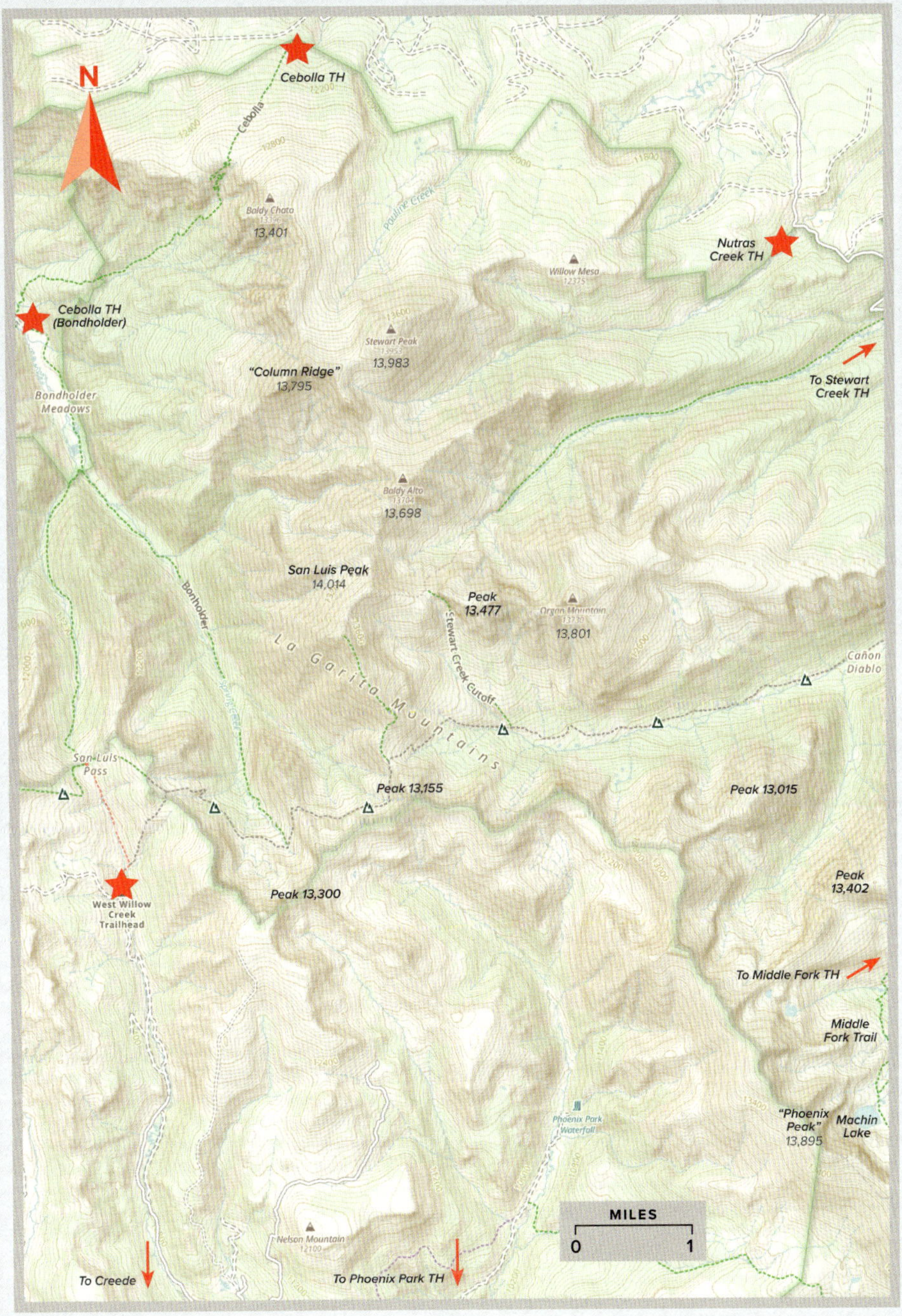

ACCESS AND HIKING

Stewart Creek

A long drive over a maze of dirt roads is a prerequisite to reach Stewart Creek Trailhead. The initial turnoff is on Colorado Highway 112, 20 miles south of US Highway 50 and 43 miles northwest of Saguache. The road is marked as "Road NN 14." Follow this road for 7.2 miles to a junction, where you turn right on Cochetopa Road/"Road 15 GG." Turn right at 11.3 miles (Cochetopa Road) and at 11.6 miles (Road 15 GG), and turn left at an unmarked junction at 15.4 miles and the junction with Big Meadows Road at mile 24. Cross Chavez Creek at mile 25, Nutras Creek at mile 26.4, and reach Stewart Creek Trailhead at mile 28.6. The Stewart Creek drainage is filled with beaver ponds and hence the well-maintained trail stays on the right (north) side of the drainage on the wooded slope. From the trailhead, it is 4 miles and 1,500 vertical feet to tree line at 12,000′. Stewart Creek Trail provides excellent access for Organ Mountain, San Luis Peak, and Baldy Alto.

Nutras Creek

Reach Nutras Creek at mile 26.4 on the dirt road approach to Stewart Creek. Either drive (4WD) or hike up the jeep road on the right (north) side of the drainage until the road gives out, and then make your way via an assortment of sketchy trails. From the main dirt road, it is 4 miles and 1,600′ to the basin between Stewart Peak and Baldy Alto. Nutras Creek is the best approach for Stewart Peak and Peak 13,795′, as well as a good approach for Baldy Alto. Although roundabout, Baldy Chato can also be climbed from Nutras Creek.

The views of the Uncompahgre Group from the traverse between San Luis Peak and Baldy Alto.

The Stewart Creek drainage is popular for those seeking to climb the group's sole 14er, San Luis Peak.

Spring Creek—Bondholder Trail

Bondholder Trail in the Spring Creek drainage approaches San Luis from the northwest. The trail is too long for a one-day climb of San Luis but makes for a nice backpack. To reach the trailhead, turn off Colorado Highway 149, 10 miles southeast of Lake City, and head northeast on dirt roads. Take the right fork at junctions at miles 15.7 and 16.8 to reach the trailhead. It is necessary to cross private property before reaching the national forest boundary. From the trailhead, it is 6 miles and 1,300 vertical feet to Bondholder Meadows at 10,400', where campsites are available.

West Willow Creek Trail

West Willow Creek Trail is the best way to access San Luis Peak, Baldy Alto, Stewart Peak, and Baldy Chato from the Creede area. Follow West Willow Creek Road north out of Creede to the Equity Mine. Those with 4WD can shave off 1.6 miles of hiking by continuing on a spur road just before and west of Equity Mine to West Willow Creek Trailhead. From here, follow the trail north to San Luis Pass to the Colorado Trail junction. Access the southeast ridge route of San Luis from here or continue north on the seldom-traveled Spring Creek Trail to Bondholder Meadows as described above. This access point makes for an excellent multiday backpacking loop if you are looking to summit all the aforementioned peaks in one go.

Cebolla Trail

The east end of the Cebolla Trail, described here, can be used as a northern approach for Baldy Chato or a southern approach via Bondholder Meadows. Although the approach by road to the trailhead is accurately depicted on the Gunnison Forest

Service map, the USGS quad (Stewart Peak), which was last revised in 1965, is inaccurate. The trailhead is located where the road crosses East Los Pinos Creek and can be reached from the east or west. From the west, it is 29 miles from the Colorado Highway 149 turnoff, 10 miles southeast of Lake City. From the east, it is 32 miles from the Colorado Highway 112 turnoff, 20 miles south of US Highway 50. From the trailhead at 11,400′, the trail climbs to 12,500′ in 2 miles to the northwestern flank of Baldy Chato before following the Sheep Creek drainage down to Spring Creek.

Inspiration Point Trail

Inspiration Point Trail offers access for Phoenix Peak and La Garita Peak. Although long, it is a pleasant climb on easy terrain. The trailhead is located on the east side of Creede behind some buildings at 8,800′. Initially you hike the steep trail north, then northeast through aspens to Inspiration Point. Continue northeast across large aspen meadows to the base of La Garita Peak. It is 7 miles and 3,600 vertical feet to the base of the mountain.

East Willow Creek—Phoenix Park Trail

Phoenix Park Trail is an excellent access point for La Garita Peak and Phoenix Peak from the west. From Creede, drive north for 0.6 mile on FSR 503.4 and turn right at the junction for FSR 502.2. Continue north for 3.1 miles to the Phoenix Park Trailhead.

Middle Fork Trail

This is the best way to access Phoenix Peak, but getting to the trailhead, at 10,160′, is an adventure. While 4WD is not a requirement, travelers will want to have high clearance and traction. Note that there is a stream crossing, which early in the season or in high snow run-off years may be impassable by vehicle. Access to the trailhead begins by traveling south on Colorado Highway 114 east of Gunnison or west on CO 114 west of Saguache. Once on CO 114, turn south on Saguache County Road 17GG, which is 25.9 miles south from the US 50–CO 114 intersection if coming from Gunnison or 35.7 miles west from Saguache on CO 114. Once on 17GG, travel 14 miles south to County Road NN14 and turn left. Travel 1.1 miles east on NN14 and turn right (south) on County Road 17FF (BLM 3088). This junction also has a sign for Stone Cellar, which is a good indication that you are in the right place. The drive from here is beautiful and scenic. You will reach the Continental Divide in the Cochetopa Hills at mile 8.4. As you pass into Gunnison National Forest, the road becomes FSR 787. Continue south, pass through Saguache Park, and turn right (west) onto FSR 744 at mile 13.3. Continue west on FSR 744, pass the Stone Cellar guard station on the south side of the road at mile 13.7, the Lake Fork Trail at mile 15.3, and ford the middle fork of Saguache Creek at mile 15.4, which may be difficult, especially in June or early July. Continue west on the dirt road and climb a steep hill that is not advised in a low-clearance vehicle. At mile 18.8, reach the top of the hill and the end of the road to find the trailhead. Ample parking is available at the trailhead.

Spring Creek Pass

Spring Creek Pass is on Colorado Highway 149 between Creede and Lake City and provides access to the La Garitas from the west, notably Baldy Cinco. It is also the start of segment 22 and the end of segment 21 of the Colorado Trail. Hiking east from the pass is a great way to complete segment 21 in reverse while accessing the western section of the La Garitas. It offers excellent backpacking opportunities, and the views from Snow Mesa, just east of the pass, are stunning. From Creede, take CO 149 west for 32.4 miles to the parking lot at Spring Creek Pass, where the trailhead begins on the east side of the highway.

CLIMBING ROUTES

San Luis Peak

14,014′ RANK 50

Located 9 miles north of Creede, San Luis Peak is the sole 14er in this group, towering above surrounding peaks. San Luis is a gentle giant and the "sun" within the La Garita Mountains "solar system."

Northeast Ridge

From Stewart Creek TH at 10,490′: 6 miles, 3,500′

This is the standard and easiest route up San Luis. From Stewart Creek, the large face you see at the head of the drainage is not the summit of San Luis. It is the northeastern flank. The fastest way to go is to aim for the 13,175′ saddle left (east) of the northeastern flank. Climb straight up the eastern ridge of the flank to the top and then follow the northeast ridge to the summit. There is a trail of sorts that you can follow to bypass one of the ridge points to the left (east). This climb, like many in this area, is a Class 2 walk-up.

Southeast Ridge

From West Willow Creek TH at 11,520′: 6.5 miles, 3,210′

From San Luis Pass to the west, follow the Colorado Trail 3.8 miles to a branch in the trail (the Colorado Trail continues east here) and continue north up a gentle trail to the summit on Class 2 terrain.

Left: San Luis Peak from Baldy Alto. **Right:** The Needles and Grenadiers above Snow Mesa, as seen from San Luis during the 416 Fire that burned near Durango in 2018.

Organ Mountain

13,799′ RANK 106

Organ Mountain, just 2 miles east of San Luis Peak, features prominent rugged rock cliffs near the summit.

Northwest Ridge

From Stewart Creek TH at 10,490′: 5.5 miles, 3,310′

After reaching tree line in the Stewart Creek drainage, continue upstream for about 0.3 mile before contouring to the northwest ridge. Initially, follow the ridge directly until you can begin traversing to the right (south) toward the saddle just north of the summit. The last 200′ are on Class 2 talus. The rest of the climb is on grassy slopes.

Organ from the summit of San Luis.

Stewart and Baldy Alto, from near San Luis.

Baldy Alto

13,698′ RANK 147

Located 1.4 miles north northeast of San Luis Peak, this chossy summit ridge is worth climbing for its fantastic views of the surrounding peaks from its summit.

Southwest Ridge

From the summit of San Luis Peak, follow the standard northeast ridge route down to a point where following the trail any farther would cause you to lose elevation en route to Baldy Alto. Viewing Baldy Alto directly to the north, you'll notice the peak's steep southwest ridge, which appears much more difficult from afar than it really is. Scramble down easy talus to a gentle ridge between San Luis and Baldy Alto and make your way up a steep but technically easy conglomerate of rock and dirt to the summit.

Southeast Ridge

From tree line in Stewart Creek, the best route for Baldy Alto alone is to climb directly up the ridge and drop down to the southwest from the summit.

Stewart Peak

13,983′ RANK 55

Stewart Peak was one of the first recorded ascents in the San Juans, climbed in 1873 by the Hayden Survey team. As late as 1965, Stewart Peak was considered to be a 14er. The current USGS quad map lists Stewart at 13,983′. A huge herd of two to three hundred elk often graze on Stewart's north slopes, which can be an amazing scene to witness.

Southeast Face

From Nutras Creek TH at 11,030′: 4 miles, 2,960′

From the Nutras Creek drainage, you can't go wrong as long as you are headed up. The entire southeast face is a gentle, grassy slope on Class 2 terrain.

Southwest Ridge

From Stewart Creek TH at 10,490′: 8.5 miles, 4,820′

From Cebolla TH at 11,580′ via Baldy Chato and Column Ridge: 4.4 miles, 2,870′

From West Willow Creek TH at 11,520′ via San Luis, Baldy Alto, and Column Ridge: 8.7 miles, 4,870′

Baldy Chato's rugged southwest face.

A wonderful adventure awaits if you choose to ascend via San Luis Peak and Baldy Alto or from the north via the Cebolla TH or Bondholder Meadows via Baldy Chato and Column Ridge. Following the southwest ridge route of Baldy Alto (above, p. 311), make your way directly northwest toward Peak 13,795′, "Column Ridge," which is a bonus to ascend. From here, climb the gentle southwest ridge to the summit.

Baldy Chato

13,401′ **UNRANKED**

"Chato" means flat-nosed in Spanish, and because of this peak's steep southwest face, it makes for an apt description when viewed from the lower Cebolla Trail via Bondholder Meadows. Baldy Chato is located 1.5 miles northwest of Stewart Peak.

South Ridge

From Nutras Creek TH at 11,030′: 5.4 miles, 2,810′

From Stewart Creek TH at 10,490′ via San Luis Peak, Baldy Alto, and Column Ridge: 10.2 miles, 5,150′

From West Willow Creek TH at 11,520′ via San Luis, Baldy Alto, and Column Ridge: 9.7 miles, 4,800′

Although a long, somewhat roundabout approach, Baldy Chato can be climbed from Nutras Creek, Stewart Creek, or West Willow Creek by the gentle south ridge. From the saddle between Stewart and Peak 13,795′, you lose more elevation than you gain to reach the summit, dropping about 350′ to the level ridge and only regaining 200′ of it on the climb to the summit.

Northwest Face

From Cebolla TH at 11,560′: 2.2 miles, 1,820′

The best route for Baldy Chato alone is to leave Cebolla Trail as it begins to drop down into Sheep Creek and climb up the northwest face on Class 2 terrain.

Northwest Face Alternative

From Bondholder Meadows and Cebolla TH at 10,110′: 3.9 miles, 3,330′

Head north from Boldholder Meadows to make a long trip to Baldy Chato via the seldom-traveled Cebolla Trail. Cebolla Trail ascends north and east from Spring Creek, loosely following Sheep Creek and gains the gentle saddle between Baldy Chato and Peak 12,751′. From here, leave the Cebolla Trail and climb the northwest face on Class 2 terrain.

Beautiful Machin Lake en route to Phoenix Peak.

Peak 13,895′—"Phoenix Peak" RANK 73

Phoenix Peak, otherwise known as "Creede Crest," is 7 miles north-northeast of the town of Creede, 2 miles northwest of La Garita Peak, and 1 mile northwest of Machin Lake.

East Ridge

From Middle Fork TH at 10,160′: 9.8 miles, 4,240′

From Middle Fork TH, the trail winds down a hill to a meadow and several creek crossings. Shortly after crossing the creek, the trail splits to the right and left. Either route is fine, but the upper (right) trail is more straightforward. The trail meanders for several miles up through grassy land used primarily for cattle grazing and eventually enters a dense forest of aspen trees. Beaver ponds, which can be fished, appear throughout the hike. At about mile 4, there are several well-established campsites near Saguache Falls. Once past Saguache Falls, the trail steepens and climbs several switchbacks in a field strewn with beautiful fireweed flowers. After several switchbacks, reach a trail junction for Lake Fork Cochetopa Creek. Continue west (left) toward Machin Lake. From here, the trail winds up through wooded forest. Eventually, views of the surrounding area open up considerably. Above tree line, the trail climbs gently through high alpine tundra, boulders, grass, and wildflowers. Once at the lake, the area flattens considerably. The lake sits at the base of several high peaks and makes for a quiet, idyllic, high-alpine experience.

Phoenix Peak from the east; challenging Class 2+ terrain awaits.

Phoenix Peak sits just above Machin Lake to the northwest and offers challenging scrambling opportunities on Class 2+ boulders. There is no trail up Phoenix Peak. Follow the east ridge up, over, or around loose boulders and continue up the ridge to the summit where a giant cairn awaits.

Southeast Ridge

From Phoenix Park TH at 9,920′: 7 miles, 4,840′

This is the shortest and easiest route up Phoenix Peak. Hike northeast then west on the Phoenix Park Trail and shoot to gain the ridge between Phoenix Peak and La Garita Peak at the 13,580′ saddle just southeast of the summit on Class 2 terrain.

Baldy Cinco

13,383′ RANK 328

Baldy Cinco sits at the far eastern edge of the La Garita Wilderness just 3.2 miles northeast of Spring Creek Pass.

South Slopes

From Spring Creek Pass TH at 10,920′: 4.5 miles, 2,460′

From Spring Creek Pass TH, climb east up the Colorado Trail to Snow Mesa. After 3 miles and 1,500′ of elevation gain, leave the trail and ascend north up a grassy slope to the summit.

OFF THE BEATEN PATH

Many of the San Luis Group's "Off the Beaten Path" peaks are located along a west-east ridge north of Snow Mesa (upper left).

Peak 13,313′—"Baldy No Es Cinco"

RANK 379

0.7 mile west of Baldy Cinco

From Spring Creek Pass TH at 10,920′: 4 miles, 2,420′

South Slopes: Follow Spring Creek Pass Trail to the gentle south slopes and up Class 2 terrain. Often climbed with Baldy Cinco and Peak 13,162′.

Peak 13,162′

RANK 512

1.3 mile east of Baldy Cinco

From Spring Creek Pass TH at 10,920′ via "Baldy No Es Cinco" and Baldy Cinco: 6.4 miles, 3,380′

West Slopes: Follow the ridge from Baldy Cinco on Class 2 slopes.

Peak 13,510′

RANK 248

1.9 miles northeast of Baldy Cinco

From Spring Creek Pass TH at 10,920′ via Baldy No Es Cinco, Baldy Cinco, and Peak 13,162′: 7.8 miles, 4,390′

South Slopes: From Spring Creek Pass, follow the ridge from Peak 13,162′ east then north up Class 2 slopes.

Peak 13,111′

RANK 558

3.3 miles west-southwest of San Luis Peak

From West Willow Creek TH at 11,520′: 2.8 miles, 1,590′

North Slopes: From the Colorado Trail west of San Luis Peak, it is a short Class 2 walk-up to the summit. Often combined with Baldy Lejos and Peaks 13,111′ and 13,034′.

Peak 13,100′—"Baldy Lejos"

RANK 570

3.8 miles west of San Luis Peak

From West Willow Creek TH at 11,520′: 4.6 miles, 2,220′

South Slopes: From San Luis Pass, hike west on the Colorado Trail then north up Class 2 grassy slopes to the summit. Often combined with Peaks 13,111′ and 13,034′.

Peak 13,034'

RANK 618

5 miles southwest of San Luis Peak

From West Willow Creek TH at 11,520′: 3.6 miles, 2,000′

Northeast Ridge: Follow steep 4WD roads (suitable for OHVs or extreme vehicles) to a ridge north of the summit and climb Class 3 terrain to the summit. Alternatively, approach the peak from the west on easier terrain if coming from Baldy Lejos and the saddle between Peak 12,952′ and Peak 13,034′.

Peak 13,300′

RANK 395

2.4 miles south-southwest of San Luis Peak

From West Willow Creek TH at 11,520′: 2.5 miles, 1,960′

Northwest Ridge: Marked as Peak 13,285′ on the USGS topo, the summit is actually on the eastern side and is a solid 15′ higher. A steep Class 2 climb on talus and scree.

Peak 13,155′

RANK 519

1.5 miles south-southeast of San Luis Peak

From West Willow Creek TH at 11,520′: 2.5 miles, 1,960′

North Ridge: From the Colorado Trail–San Luis Peak junction at 12,620′, it is a short 0.4 mile climb up grass slopes to a short section of Class 3 climbing near the summit.

Peak 13,795′—"Column Ridge"

UNRANKED

1 mile southwest of Stewart Peak

From Stewart Creek TH at 10,490′: 7.9 miles, 4,620′

From Cebolla TH at 11,580′ via Baldy Chato and Column Ridge: 3.8 miles, 2,670′

From West Willow Creek TH at 11,520′ via San Luis and Baldy Alto: 8.1 miles, 4,670′

East Slopes: Column Ridge is the twin-summit peak. Both summits can be climbed from the saddle between Column Ridge and Stewart on Class 2 terrain. There is only about 250 vertical feet of elevation gain from the saddle to the western summit.

Peak 13,477′

UNRANKED

0.65 mile west of Organ Mountain

From Stewart Creek TH at 10,490′: 5.8 miles, 3,100′

West Ridge: From the saddle between San Luis and point 13,477′, traverse left (north) to avoid the cliffs on Class 3 terrain to the point just west of Peak 13,477′ before gaining the ridge higher up and following it to the summit.

From Stewart Creek TH at 10,490′: 6.3 miles, 3,510′

East Ridge: There is a large, prominent gap that prevents a ridge walk between Organ and Peak 13,477′. From Organ, it is necessary to drop to the left (south) about 250 vertical feet on a rotten Class 3 downclimb before climbing back up the ridge once the gap is passed.

Peak 13,015′

RANK 630

2.2 miles north of Phoenix Peak

From Phoenix Park TH at 9,920′: 1 mile, 5,840′

West Slopes: From Phoenix Peak, traverse the ridge northwest across unranked Peaks 13,628′, 13,495′, and 13,346′ to gain the west slopes on Class 2 terrain. Often climbed with Peak 13,402′.

Peak 13,402′

RANK 318

1.7 miles northeast of Phoenix Peak

From Phoenix Park TH at 9,920′: 9.2 miles, 5,530′

Southwest Slopes: From Phoenix Peak, traverse the ridge connecting Peak 13,402′ with unranked Peak 13,628′ on Class 2 terrain.

La Garita Peak

13,710′ **UNRANKED**

1.9 miles southwest of Phoenix Peak

From Phoenix Park TH at 9,920′: 7 miles, 4,840′

Southwest Face: Follow the ridge southeast from Phoenix Peak on Class 2 terrain.

La Garita Peak with the moon above.

Beautiful wildflowers in American Basin below American Peak.

ACKNOWLEDGMENTS

During the first edition of this guide, many people contributed information on climbing routes, access, and climbing history, including Tim Duffy, Rich Riefenberg, Art Tauchen, Michael Covington, Jon Lawyer, Haskell Rosebrough, Erine Stromeyer, Mike Butyn, Larry Coats, Tom Norton, Bill Henry, Jim Gehres, Kenneth Heil, Cy Dickson, Hal Brown, George Bell Sr., George Bell Jr., Bob Beverly, Kent Beverly, Steven Matous, Ted Kerasote, Joe Kramarsic, Bill Bueler, Mike Foster, Robert M. Ormes, John Nelson, Joe Stettner, Jack Fralick, R. J. Campbell, Bob Bliss, George Polorny, Dick Guadagno, Paul Mahoney, Henry Buchtel, David Belknap, Earle R. Whipple, Sally Ross, David Carter, and John Flisinger.

A special thanks to Tim and Carrie Cooney of climb13ers.com for sharing with us many of their route descriptions for this project! A huge thank you, also, to John Kirk for creating and maintaining his website, Lists of John (listsofjohn.com); it contains a massive database of peaks, maps, trip reports, and interesting lists of mountains that every mountaineer should be aware of. We highly recommend you donate to both of these amazing sites.

A large part of any climbing history or guide are the photographs that bring the people, mountains, and routes to life. Again, a large number of people contributed, including Mel Griffiths, Kiefer Thomas, Regina Thomas, Tom Sawyer, Tim Duffy, Ernie Stromeyer, Joe Merhar, Bob Beverly, David Kozak, Melina Marinaro, George Bell Sr., Werner Schnackenberg, Joe Stettner, Pat Armstrong, Bob Bliss, R. J. Campbell, Michael Covington, John Nelson, Louise Roloff, Antonine Savelli, Haskell Rosebrough, David Cooper, Carl Blaurock, Bill Bueler, Walt Borneman, Spencer Swanger, Stuart Krebs, John Filsinger, Doug Ward, and Mason Cummings.

Climbing is always more enjoyable when shared with good friends. While good climbing partners are sometimes hard to come by, we have been blessed with some of the best in Ernie Stromeyer, Ike Weaver, Hal Brown, Craig Pirlot, David Nordstrom, and Peter Tempest, who have been regular climbing partners with Bob, and in Silas Musick and Regina Thomas, as well as many other amazing people who have climbed with Matt.

BIBLIOGRAPHY

BOOKS

Borneman, Walter R., and Lyndon J. Lampert. *A Climbing Guide to Colorado's Fourteeners*. Boulder: Pruett Publishing, 1978.

Bueler, William M. *Roof of the Rockies: A History of Colorado Mountaineering*, 3rd ed. Golden, CO: The Colorado Mountain Club Press, 2000. First published by Pruett Publishing, 1974.

Chapin, Frederick H. "The San Juan Mountains." *Appalachia* 6 (December 1890).

Cooper, William Skinner. *Mountains*. Tapiola Press, 2022.

Ellingwood, Albert L. "First to Climb Lizard Head." *Outing* LXXIX, no. 2 (November 1921).

Griffiths, Thomas M. *San Juan Country*. Boulder: Pruett Publishing, 1984.

Hart, John L. Jerome. *Fourteen Thousand Feet: A History of the Naming and Early Ascents of the High Colorado Peaks*. 2nd ed. Denver: The Colorado Mountain Club, 1931.

Lavender, Dwight, T. Garrigues, Melvin Griffiths, and Carleton Curtis Long. *The San Juan Mountaineers Climber's Guide to Southwestern Colorado*. Unpublished manuscript, 1932.

Marshall, Lieutenant William L. "Executive and Descriptive Report of Lieutenant William L. Marshall, Corps of Engineers, on the Operations of Party No.1, Colorado Section, Field Season of 1875." *Annual Report Upon the Geographical Surveys West of the One Hundredth Meridian, in California, Nevada, Utah, Colorado, Wyoming, New Mexico, Arizona, and Montana*. Washington, DC: Government Printing Office, 1876.

Rhoda, Franklin. *Summits to Reach: An Annotated Edition of Franklin Rhoda's "Report on the Topography of the San Juan Country."* Edited by Mike Foster. Boulder: Pruett Publishing, 1984.

Ruffner, E. H. *Report of a Reconnaissance in the Ute Country: Made in the Year 1873*. Washington, DC: Government Printing Office, 1974.

Thomas, Percy W. "Mountaineering in Southern Colorado." *Alpine Journal* XV (August 1891).

Woolsey, Elizabeth D. *Off the Beaten Track*. Wilson, WY: Wilson Bench Press, 1984.

MAGAZINES AND MOUNTAINEERING JOURNALS

The American Alpine Journal. The American Alpine Club, 710 10th Street, Suite 100, Golden, Colorado 80401.

Appalachia. Appalachian Mountain Club, Five Joy Street, Boston, Massachusetts 02108.

The Chicago Mountaineer. The Chicago Mountaineering Club, P.O. Box 1025, Chicago, Illinois 60609.

Climbing. P.O. Box E, Aspen, Colorado 81612.

Summit, A Mountaineering Magazine. P.O. Box 1889, Big Bear Lake, California 92315.

Trail and Timberline. The Colorado Mountain Club, 710 10th Street, Suite 200, Golden, Colorado 80401.

INDEX

Note: Page numbers in **boldface** designate primary descriptions. Page numbers followed by the letter *p* indicate photos; those followed by the letter *m* indicate maps.

ABOUT THE AUTHORS

Bob Rosebrough is an avid outdoorsman, mountaineer, lawyer, and author of multiple books, including two prior editions of *Climbing Colorado's San Juans*. Bob lives in Gallup, New Mexico, which he feels blessed to call home. Bob has climbed in the San Juans for over fifty years.

Matt Payne is a mountaineer and nature/landscape photographer living in Durango, Colorado, and is the host of the popular photography podcast, *F-Stop Collaborate and Listen*. Matt has climbed the highest one hundred mountains in Colorado and all of Colorado's 14ers and has been climbing mountains for over thirty years. Matt's photography can be purchased on his website at mattpaynephotography.com.

Recreate with RIMS

Give back to the land you love with the CMC RIMS (Recreation Impact Monitoring System) mobile app: If you spot a downed tree, trail erosion, trash, or poor signage while you're exploring the places in this book, open the app and submit a quick report so that land managers can address the issue. Learn more and get started at cmc.org/RIMS.

COLORADO MOUNTAIN CLUB

cmc.org/RIMS